MONEY

~ FROM ~

NOTHING

OR, WHY WE SHOULD LEARN
TO STOP WORRYING ABOUT DEBT
AND LOVE THE FEDERAL RESERVE

ROBERT HOCKETT
AND AARON JAMES

MELVILLE HOUSE
BROOKLYN · LONDON

MONEY FROM NOTHING

First published in September 2020 by Melville House
Copyright © Robert Hockett and Aaron James, 2020
All rights reserved
First Melville House Printing: September 2020

Melville House Publishing
46 John Street
Brooklyn, NY 11201
and
Melville House UK
Suite 2000
16/18 Woodford Road
London E7 0HA

mhpbooks.com
@melvillehouse

ISBN: 978-1-61219-856-9
ISBN: 978-1-61219-857-6 (eBook)

Library of Congress Control Number: 2020940412

Designed by Betty Lew

Printed in the United States of America
1 3 5 7 9 10 8 6 4 2

A catalog record for this book is available
from the Library of Congress

Dedicated to the memory of

ALEXANDER HAMILTON

AND HIS CONTINUING LEGACY

I refer to the debt—the new red menace, this time consisting of ink.

—Mitch Daniels (former Republican governor of Indiana), said without irony

I think there is an element of truth . . . in the superstition that the budget must be balanced at all times. [O]nce debunked [that] takes away one of the bulwarks that every society must have against expenditure out of control.

—Paul Samuelson, Nobel laureate in Economics

Now look at them yo-yos
that's the way you do it
You play the guitar on the MTV
That ain't workin'
that's the way you do it
Money for nothin' and chicks for free

—Dire Straits, "Money for Nothing"

CONTENTS

PREFACE

"You've always had the power, my dear, you just had to learn it for yourself."

—Glinda, the Good Witch of the North,
The Wizard of Oz (1939)

You probably saw the movie version of *The Wizard of Oz* as a kid, as so many of us did. You might even recall the crucial line just quoted, which comes in the story's culminating scene. Glinda, the Good Witch, is explaining to Dorothy what her long ordeal (being swept away by a great storm from her home in Kansas) could possibly mean.

The big lesson is: You've had the power to go back to Kansas all along—by tapping your shoes together. You merely didn't realize it. So you had to learn it for yourself. *But you can empower yourself, now, by understanding what you're capable of.*

That sounds like a message of female empowerment, and it may well have been. But today we often forget that the film, based on a children's book by L. Frank Baum, is ultimately a parable about *money*. Baum was not only a one-time actor and the author of numerous tales about the land of Oz, an imagined American utopia, he was also a political activist who once owned a newspaper. The story we think we know so well was responding to the economic crises of his day.[1]

This book is not a parable, but if it has a big thesis, it's that we still haven't taken Glinda's (and Baum's) lesson to heart, even a hundred years later. The lesson is: Although we Americans have suffered through financial crises, we've had the power to take control of our money all along. But we haven't fully realized how it can help heal our society. Now the time has come to empower ourselves by understanding what we're capable of.

Really? *The Wizard of Oz*—a neglected tract of political philosophy, the key to future prosperity and maybe to saving the republic? Yup. Just think back to that famous scene when Dorothy and Co., having followed the yellow brick road, finally arrive at the Emerald City. The great wizard is putting on an awesome spectacle. Suddenly, Toto the dog pulls back the curtain, revealing a coy, bumbling man conjuring with smoke and mirrors. We now use "pulling back the curtain" as a cliché for *unveiling* or *unmasking*. We've largely forgotten what the original parable was pulling back the curtain on.

When Baum's book was published in 1900, it was meant to expose the "gold standard" as an illusion. There was no "yellow brick road," paved in golden rocks, to a green Emerald City of shared prosperity. That was always mythology, so much propaganda.

Just recall the main characters. Who was the bumbling "Wizard of Oz" behind the curtain ("oz." meaning "ounce," which is of course the unit of measure for precious metals)? Government officials of the day.

Who were the Wicked Witches of the East and West? The bankers of the East and West Coast cities, who propagated the gold myth for private profit—profit that came at the expense of the great hinterland.

And the Cowardly Lion? The political class and intellectuals that let the bankers have their way.

What about the Tin Man without a heart? The industrial workers in the cities, who never aligned with the farmers.

Who, then, was Dorothy? A daughter of the Midwestern farm families, who suffered under a recession and wave of home foreclosures in the 1890s. The recession was the great cyclone that swept Dorothy from her home in Kansas.

If this isn't obvious, consider the crises of Baum's day, the ones he lived through. By 1900, the American economy had been starved of money decade after decade. That was the *whole point* of the "gold standard," after all—to limit the supply of money to the scarce supply of certain specific yellow rocks dug up from the ground. So when the gold diggers out west or in Australia or South Africa had a bad year, well, there just wasn't going to be enough money for a growing economy. That brought what economists call "deflation," or "too little money chasing too many goods," and thus economic contraction in the Midwest. Farmers outside of the big cities, in Kansas for example, were hit hardest.

The early American colonies were short on precious metals, so they used book credit, paper called "scrip," and even tobacco or shell beads as moneys. Then the founders of the post-Revolutionary republic took over and declared a new unit of account, "the dollar," officially tying it to both gold and silver. But in practice it was often the one or the other, depending on what metal was available. During the Civil War, paper money "greenbacks" were issued with no strict connection to either gold or silver, as Treasury bonds were now deemed to be "good as gold." To a degree that seems strange to us now, by the mid- to late-nineteenth-century major political movements—the "Greenbackers" and then the "free silver men"—feverishly organized around monetary policy decisions. It was a coinage act later called the "crime of 1873," which gave us what we now call "the gold standard," that would eventually draw particular ire. Word had it that London and New York bankers such as the Rothschilds and the Morgans had duped gullible congressmen to "demonetize" silver in last-minute, dead-of-night legislation. And so, during the cycle of depressions that followed, distrust and suspicion only heightened. By 1896, William Jennings Bryan, the loudmouthed "populist" US representative from Nebraska, condemned the exclusive tie to gold in what some regard as the most famous speech in American history. "You shall not press down upon the brow of labor this crown of thorns. You shall not crucify mankind upon a cross of gold," he thundered.

Bryan was an unsubtle man with a serious proposal, in line

with what Americans had done in the past when they turned to shells, scrip, and other forms of currency: if there aren't enough dollars out there, *just issue more of them*, now backed by silver alongside gold. Baum, a progressive former journalist and early feminist, well aware of the politics of his era, seemed to agree. In his original story, Dorothy wore a *silver* slipper, alluding to "bi-metallism," the use of two metals as a monetary standard. How do you "click the shoes together" and "go back to Kansas"? Officials need only call off the exclusive commitment to gold, in a public announcement. More money in circulation would "re-inflate" the economy for the benefit of farm workers, at that time still a major economic constituency.

President Franklin Delano Roosevelt finally made just such an announcement in 1933, when he declared that neither gold—nor any other rock, for that matter—would stand behind domestic conversions from that point forward. The great British economist J. M. Keynes called the decision "splendidly right." "Bi-metallism" sounds looney to us now. Idea: we need *more rocks*, this time *silver* rocks. But that's only because of how radically our understanding of money has evolved, and how looney, in retrospect, the gold standard itself was.

By "pulling back the curtain" on money, Baum's parable invited a deeper question: Why fixate on *rocks* at all, any more than on shells on the beach or stars in the galaxy, for that matter? They aren't where the money is. Money *never was* gold, silver, paper, or any tangible stuff, which there was never quite the right amount of. While Baum's book didn't have immediate political influence, that philosophical point is one we still benefit from today. Who knows, when the United States began to take the lesson, issuing money by fiat about thirty years later, perhaps the children, by then full grown, remembered Glinda's good lesson from their bedtime reading.

William Jennings Bryan was himself a critical player in the establishment of the US central bank, the Federal Reserve, in 1913, which set the stage for the establishment of unambiguously fiat money twenty years later with FDR's 1933 announcement. The dollar was finally "socialized" in full, meaning issued and managed by a public bank. After some initial growing pains, the new central bank paid for heavy wartime spending by issuing new money, while offsetting the potential inflationary impact with Treasury-issued "Liberty Bonds." America was poised to make good on its promise of shared prosperity. Which it then did, better than ever before, in the 1950s and '60s, the postwar "golden era" of American capitalism that so many celebrate today.

Somehow the remarkable success of our central, public bank and "socialized" dollar as the backbone of capitalism never did clear up all the confusion caused by America's sixty or so years on the official gold standard. Perhaps that shouldn't be so surprising; this is America, after all. When historian Richard Hofstadter famously identified what he called the "paranoid style in American politics," his lead example of "the sense of heated exaggeration, suspiciousness, and conspiratorial fantasy," along with the McCarthyism of the 1950s, was that of "populist" leaders in 1895 fretting about "the secret cabals of the international gold ring." No surprise many Americans resisted the establishment of the Fed for fear of "socialism." No wonder FDR's 1933 abandonment of the gold promise was seen as a government takeover. Louis Douglas, FDR's own budget director, resigned, calling it "the end of Western civilization."

The paranoid style comes and goes with the times, as the fringes gain a greater or lesser influence over otherwise sane people. But as Hofstadter explained, it has always been especially influential on the political right:

> [T]he modern right wing, as Daniel Bell has put it, feels dispossessed: America has been largely taken away from them and their kind, though they are determined to try to repossess it and to prevent the final destructive act of subversion. The old American virtues have already been eaten away by cosmopolitans and intellectuals; the old competitive

xvi Preface

capitalism has been gradually undermined by socialistic and communistic schemers; the old national security and independence have been destroyed by treasonous plots, having as their most powerful agents not merely outsiders and foreigners as of old but major statesmen who are at the very centers of American power.

This certainly resonates today. And yet it was written, mind you, in 1964.[2]

In that same year Stanley Kubrick's dark-comedy master-piece, *Dr. Strangelove or: How I Learned to Stop Worrying and Love the Bomb,* first graced American movie screens. Paranoia was one of its major themes. Runaway Air Force Gen. Jack D. Ripper launches a nuclear strike on the Soviet Union in retaliation for an imagined stealth attack on the American water supply. A sneak attack, that is, by fluoride: "I can no longer sit back and allow Communist infiltration, Communist indoctrination, Communist subversion—and the international Communist conspiracy—to sap and impurify all of our precious bodily fluids." Bizarre as that sounds, viewers at the time would immediately recognize Kubrick's spoof of the John Birch Society's then prominent opposition to public water fluoridation as "mass medicine," yet another threat of communism.

In this book we argue that the "green menace" of runaway debt and inflation isn't that different from the "red menace" hysteria Hofstadter and Kubrick understood and spoofed so well. Indeed, irrational fears have always stood in the way of a sound understanding of money. They drive the popular appeal of films such as *Goldfinger* (Special Agent James Bond foils a plot to steal gold from Fort Knox), as well as suspicions about whether there still is gold in Fort Knox, and, if not, where it all went. They also drive more consequential developments such as fiscal austerity after the 2008 crash, and the re-emergence of goldbugs like former congressman Ron Paul, who over decades called for investigation into "the Fort Knox issue," a return to a gold standard, and even the Fed's outright abolition ("End the Fed"). The paranoid style of politics explains why money cranks, hucksters, and zealots have always emerged from the shadows after a financial crisis, and why in the wake of the 2008 crisis, Senator Ted Cruz would call for a gold standard yet again, imagining he'd score points for sounding serious to his supporters. To be sure, paranoia is not just a malady of the political right. In part due to the Fed's mismanagement of the pre-2008 boom years, and in part for the inequities of its first efforts at relaxing the money supply ("quantitative easing"), some Occupy Wall Street protesters joined Ron Paul's call for the Fed's abolition.[3]

Alas, things today are not so different from a hundred years ago, when the Federal Reserve was just getting started, as we ask ourselves how to ensure capitalism works for most everyone, or whether it's even up to the task. The bargain that emerged last time gave us American capitalism's "golden years" and the once seemingly ineluctable rise of liberal democracy with a "mixed economy" of relatively free markets and social insurance. Today, established democracies the world over are "backsliding" into authoritarianism, rule by the richest or least competent, and crony capitalism. The viability of the very idea of a democratic republic is in question.

So we really should wonder: Have we taken the full measure of Glinda's (and Baum's) lesson? Do we really understand the power of money, and what we are capable of as a society? Might *understanding money better* usher in a *new* "golden" age?

It happened once. It could happen again.

Our hope is that reading this book will help you appreciate how crucial money is to our shared political project. You'll see how the Federal Reserve can better work in your favor. You'll even become savvier about the money in your pocket and bank account. Some investors rake in serious money for having that kind of advanced knowledge. But shouldn't we *all* understand our money, which, after all, is one of our major public institutions? Surely that's essential to a working democracy.

If you really want to understand money, though, you probably shouldn't ask a conventional academic economist. You wouldn't know it from all the coins and dollar signs featured on the covers of economics textbooks, but mainstream economists in the major US universities pay very little attention to money and banking. Better to ask a central banker, a market trader, or a financial law expert—the people who tend to know how our institutions actually work (their livelihoods, after all, depend on it).

Fortunately, one of us—Bob—happens to be an expert in financial regulation and to have firsthand experience working at the New York Federal Reserve, the International Monetary Fund, and a boutique investment bank in Midtown Manhattan.

But the question of what money is, ultimately, isn't just a legal or technical matter; it's a philosophical one as well. And fortunately the other of us—Aaron—happens to be a professional philosopher who works at the intersection of economics and political philosophy.

Bob has training in both finance and philosophy. Economists and financiers will be impressed to hear of his tutelage at Yale with Nobel laureate Robert Shiller. Philosophers will be impressed to hear that, while a Rhodes Scholar at Oxford University, he studied mathematical logic and philosophy with the great Michael Dummett. Aaron wrote a book about fairness in the global economy—the idea of it, anyway—and became well acquainted with economists who do philosophy and call it "social science." He also studied with the renowned T. M. Scanlon as a graduate student at Harvard University, which has paid dividends (if you'll pardon the pun) in our thinking of money as part of the social contract by which we give what we owe to each other. (Scanlon wrote a famous book of moral philosophy called *What We Owe to Each Other*.)

Probably it was inevitable that we'd at some point meet each other and join forces. And so we did. Indeed we became fast, dear friends. As we discovered in our late-into-the night conversations—which occasionally last as long as eight hours—

much of money's philosophical and political importance has fallen through cracks in academic hyperspecialization. That's a golden research opportunity. Yet we believe the topic of money is far too important to become buried under scholarly quibbling, and far too urgent to wait for the peer-review publication process. Given the state of public confusion about money and public finance, we decided to do our bit to pull back the curtain again, for the twenty-first century.

Our idea is to pull the strands of law, economics, history, and philosophy all together in one place, in a book the general reader can understand and follow, hopefully without the eyes glazing over. The polemical style of many books and writings about money makes for breezy reading and vague feelings of comprehension. But, too often, beneath the vague slogans and worldly posturing, big mistakes travel under the guise of wisdom. What's assumed to be obvious really *shouldn't* be. We want to demystify money, really understand it, get to the bottom of things. So we've eschewed many of the usual rhetorical devices. At the risk of making readers sleepy, we've tried to explain even the basics slowly and clearly, in plain English, in hopes of helping the befuddled citizen get his or her head around ideas often shrouded in obscure or technical language. If we're lucky, the sophisticated reader accustomed to polemics will thank us for clearing the fog of commentary.

And once we are all clearer in our thinking, if only about our good options, maybe, just maybe, we'll start making better choices together about our society's future.

INTRODUCTION

Dollars, dollars, dollars—we have no choice but to get dollars, one way or another, as long as we live on US soil or remain citizens. Whatever it takes: work a job we hate for dollars, try to save in dollars, try not to go broke in dollars, borrow from a friend or grandparent or "payday" lender in dollars, organize our lives, loves, and leisure around dollars, generally chasing dollars, dollars, dollars. Here in the land of liberty, we celebrate our freedom to make money. Truth be told, we're forced to "buy" our freedom, in dollars, year after year after year (until death frees us).

Death and taxes—as they say, there's no avoiding taxes. Not to mention all those irritating fees, fines, and traffic citations. If you crashed your bicycle or shopping cart into a parked car's fender, maybe it was just an accident. Even so, you could be held liable to pay damages, perhaps by a court order. It could cost you serious money. And for any such legally mandatory payments, officials at the appropriate government offices absolutely will not accept euros, bitcoins, or Facebook shares. They will only accept dollars.

Unless you pony up the dollars, whether in cash or bank credits, you'll at some point have your wages garnished or be carted off to prison. In colonial America, poorer folk were sometimes allowed to pay taxes in grain, or whatever they could grow themselves. Money was difficult to get ahold of. These days, it is dollars or nothing, which is to say, dollars keep you out of the slammer.

Freedom comes easy for those already rich (in dollars), whether they got them by work, luck, or inheritance. To the majority of Americans, buying freedom is expensive, not to mention exhausting. In a recent survey, over 60 percent of respondents said they'd have to borrow in order to pay $500 in car repairs, for lack of savings.[1]

We hear nostalgic tales of those "golden" decades after the war, when America more or less delivered on the promise of a "rising tide lifting all boats," yacht and dinghy alike. A large middle class flourished. Jobs were much better than they'd been. Wages were higher, for less time at work. Everyone enjoyed the new forty-hour workweek, which afforded more time for leisurely evenings, weekends, and vacations with friends and family on golden days at the lake or the beach. It sounds like a social bargain that could make this whole system of coercion seem acceptable. But that was fifty years ago. Which, by the way, is *half of a century*. By now the halcyon dreams are fading, as the promise of shared prosperity recedes into history's rearview mirror.

One could easily feel hopeless. If America is failing its promise of shared prosperity, what could possibly restore faith? Fortunately, there is a way forward. We need only understand the power of money.

While discussing the nature of time, Saint Augustine offered a confession: if no one asks me what time is, I know. But if I'm asked to explain, I have no idea.

Money can feel about as elusive. We spend a lot of our lives chasing it, trying to get more of it. But as for what it is we hope to get our hands on, few of us have a clear idea.

Few things have a more profound influence on human dealings. We work long hours for it, worry about having too little or too much of it, quarrel about it, and maybe sour a marriage, friendship, or business partnership over it. It's a good question, given all its troubles, whether one shouldn't steer clear of the stuff, or at least find more worthy preoccupations. Even so, all but the most ascetic among us probably would like a bit more of it ourselves.

And what is this odd thing that so commands our attention? Few of us, when asked what money is, could answer. Like time, and the Cheshire Cat, it disappears when you try to gaze at it. As Lewis Carroll put it in *Alice in Wonderland*, it's "a grin without a cat."

Money, which rules the world more than ever, is ever less understood by even the well educated. Many appreciate that, nowadays, "money isn't based on anything"—not gold bullion, not piles of coins or paper currency, stored in a bank vault somewhere. Money is now "fiat money," which governments issue into existence, by simply deciding to, as though by a king's decree. It somehow exists in our banking system, flowing between our bank accounts as electronic credits and debits. We easily get the hang of new payment technologies. One can get by in a major city with only a debit or credit card, or buy a car or house with an electronic bank transfer. In developing countries, payments are now often made by text message—*phones* now hold money, in a very real sense. Perhaps we'll never have a completely cash-free future. But we can now easily imagine it, and that itself tells us something. Cash itself isn't money, but rather its symbol, representative, or embodiment.

And yet, many of us still find the "virtual" reality of money bewildering or even untrustworthy in comparison to gold or paper or coinage—you know, stuff you could hold in your hand, lock in a safe, or put under the mattress. After all, there is real cause for philosophical puzzlement about the airy nature of "fiat money" and whether it is somehow different from what money has always been.

Money is definitely still *something*—one of the more important forces in human affairs. But then, what is it? Certainly we need some better understanding of this thing, this metaphysical peculiarity, which has such power to improve or to warp our lives.

While the nature of time may not be the most pressing of problems, the nature of money matters enormously for each of our lives, our society, and its future.

So it's a natural philosophical and practical question: What is money? For the start of an answer, look again at a dollar bill. Across the top, you'll see the words "Federal Reserve Note." Most of us have no idea what that means. But a lawyer will tell you that "note" here abbreviates a legal term of art, "promissory note." It's a technical term for an IOU. A dollar bill is an IOU issued by the US central bank, the Federal Reserve—a.k.a "the Fed"—which stands for some sort of promise. And so assuming the Fed, which has issued our money for over a century, isn't completely wrong about what money is, money *itself* is . . . a promise.

What sort of promise? Well, in short, it is a tax credit. And more, of course, because you can spend it on all manner of things. But aside from its commercial use, a dollar is a promise by the government not to put you in jail if you present that very dollar (or enough of them) in payment of your tax bill. A dollar is a "get-out-of-jail-free card," your yearly "ticket to freedom."

But if dollars are a kind of promise, they can be issued in the way any promise can, just by deciding to make a promise. How does one promise to meet a friend for coffee? Just decide to say the magic words, "See you there, then; I promise!" If we are going to restore a sense of shared prosperity to our republic, the way forward is beautiful in its simplicity. Just make new and better dollar promises. Specifically, the central bank can give each and every one of us money, directly. Or *Congress* can decide to give us money through either the fiscal *or* the monetary authority—in the United States, that's the Treasury and the Fed—as Congress has done during the coronavirus pandemic.

Does that sound naïve, or just too easy? If so, you might need a better sense of how money already works in practice. The banking system creates and gives us money *already*, it just does it in an indirect and inefficient manner. The central bank could do its current job far more effectively if it simply put money in our bank accounts directly. (It must also manage inflation, of course—and we'll explain how it can do that reliably.) Most people won't find that obvious. But that only shows we need a deeper grasp of what money is and what banks do already.

Optimism came easily during the boom years before 2008. We'd had three or four decades of stagnant wages and increasingly divisive politics. But, you know, this is America! We are a can-do country! And then, suddenly, the American haze of confident normality and ineluctable prosperity had lifted. The big investment houses were bailed out by the taxpayer. Millions more of those taxpayers lost their jobs, homes, and hopeful futures. The financial system was laid bare as dysfunctional and corrupt. Trust collapsed before an uncertain future.

Officials in the Bush and Obama administrations did what they had to in order to restore the banking system. They prevented an even worse catastrophe. The Troubled Asset Relief Program (or "TARP"), designed to clean up balance sheets, even turned a profit for the public. But, politically, it was no matter. The griping began almost immediately. The Dodd-Frank Act passed and instituted stricter regulations of the private banks, but it seemed rather modest in the face of the meltdown we had all just witnessed. Few if any of the main perpetrators suffered for their sins. The financiers briefly lost stature, but quickly went back to hand-over-fist moneymaking.

And there were *so many* perpetrators to blame. Was it mainly the greedy, shortsighted bankers? Or the economists who had given them cover? Or, a favorite target on both far right and far left, "the Fed," the central bank? Was it Alan Greenspan, the boom-years chairman of the Federal Reserve, who chose not to "pull away the punch bowl" as the party got hopping? Greenspan deliberately allowed the real estate bubble to grow and burst, presuming we could maybe, hopefully, clean up the mess afterwards. (He later admitted this was a mistake—that he'd misjudged investor prudence.) Or was it really Fannie Mae and Freddie Mac, which made the American Dream of home ownership too easy? Or, for that matter, the thousands upon thousands who'd stretched their credit and bought extra homes assuming they could only appreciate in value? Because, you know, the neighbors were buying up houses on "stated income" loans and, seemingly, getting rich quick.

Left and right favored different diagnoses, but found a basic point of agreement: something was very wrong. And after all the self-dealing, the self-serving rationalizations, and the plain lack of understanding of what the hell was going on, who could now be trusted to fix things? The bankers themselves barely understood the complex financial markets, beyond their niche for grinding out profits. Regulators had often deferred to the banker's perspective, following a mindless "trust the markets" mantra. And the economics profession had been the biggest cheerleader of all for deregulation, with no sense at all of the looming crisis, and a certain forgetfulness about or indifference to the history of busts and crashes. So, one wondered, who were the "experts"? Or were there genuine experts any longer?

Eventually, America would find an unlikely hero—a modest, soft-spoken Princeton professor and student of the Great Depression named Ben Bernanke.

Surprising as it may sound, economists in the major academic departments in the United States do not really know the "plumbing" of central banking, money, and credit. They mostly aren't trained in such practicalities and learn them only in side gigs or by independent study. "Macroeconomics" is taught at a basic level, and there are still specialists, but it has long been out of favor as a serious research project. For most "serious" economists, it's "micro" or "macro that's micro" or nothing.

Bernanke was an older style of economist. He studied history carefully, relied less on the models that so mesmerized recent economists, and found the courage to imagine unorthodox actions. Once appointed as chairman of the Federal Reserve, his leadership would finally draw the economy into recovery.

The economy saw a long run of gradual but steady improve-ment—at least until the coronavirus pandemic broke out. (As of our last chance to edit this book, the stock market has crashed and the Fed has injected $1.5 trillion into the economy—doing just what we'd recommend. As for what toll the pandemic takes, we're now waiting nervously.) Yet despite the "good economy" we enjoyed for a time, America remains adrift. It's distrustful, searching for people to blame, and its promises are more uncer-tain than ever. We are forgetful, or eager to put the past behind us, and now blindsided by a public health emergency that will likely bring grave economic, social, and medical consequences. There's plenty in life one needn't fully comprehend; one can live or work in a building without understanding its plumbing system. It's when there's an emergency and the plumbers are called in that one can really learn a thing or two about what's ordinarily taken for granted. If the coronavirus outbreak is like living through a bad horror movie we've seen already, the 2008 emergency can feel long gone and forgotten. But in the decade or so since, we never have learned what the great financial crisis has to teach us about money—including what Bernanke showed us about how we can restore our democracy.

What was Bernanke's masterstroke as Fed chairman? He revived measures once practiced by the Bank of England. The Fed would engage in expanded "open market operations," mean-ing that it would buy up lots and lots of housing-related financial assets, instead of confining itself to more traditional US Treasury securities. A third phase of "quantitative easing" (called "QEIII"), this would effectively put a "floor" under housing prices. That's where most Americans have their livelihoods and fortunes, so buoyed prices would create a ripple effect throughout the econ-omy. Unorthodox as it was at the time, it worked splendidly. (The Fed has announced similar if more dramatic measures in response to the coronavirus pandemic.)

In a 2009 interview for *60 Minutes*, journalist Scott Pelley asked Bernanke what appeared to be a very sound question: how exactly the Fed was paying for all this. Millions of homes, and hence mortgage assets, are expensive, right? Here's how the interview went:

> **Journalist Scott Pelley:** Is that tax money that the Fed is spending?
>
> **Fed Chairman Bernanke:** It's not tax money. The banks have accounts with the Fed, much the same way that you have an account in a commercial bank. So, to lend to a bank, *we simply use the computer to mark up the size of the account* that they have with the Fed. [Italics added.]

Bernanke's answer still sounds surprising: "We simply use the computer."

Meaning—by pushing buttons? That sounds incredible, so let's go through this slowly. Officials at the Fed sit down at a computer. They then add numbers to bank accounts and snap up millions in mortgage securities. They indirectly buy houses—and a fix to the housing crisis—by making money "from nothing." They do that by so many keystrokes on a computer, hitting the zero button over and over.

But if *that's* how money gets created, if it's as easy as pushing computer buttons, one might wonder: Why can't *I* have more of it? Can't the Fed just add zeroes to my personal bank account?

The answer is: yes, it can.

Should it? This book explains why it should—and how. Done properly, what works in an emergency—whether the financial crisis of 2008 or the coronavirus pandemic of 2020—can help repair and renew our fraying social contract over the long run. Monetary policy can help bring a much more prosperous future for all of us.

Money, we explain, is a kind of promise—a spendable promissory claim or IOU. And since that's *all* money is, we actually can all have more of it. We can make money by simply making more

promises—creating new claims, which then make a real difference to people's lives.

To many this will stoke fears of runaway inflation. We'll have
a lot to say about what central banks can and should do to manage the supply of money in circulation. For now, note that monetary policy is all about making sure we neither overpromise nor
underpromise—and that we promise in the most fruitful ways.
Lately we've been *underpromising*—there is not enough money
in the right places. So what we actually need are new promises,
which we can make simply because we decide to.

If the Fed now "uses the computer" to give money to the private banks, those same keystrokes can be used to generate new
money in the ordinary bank accounts of each citizen. The central
bank's basic mission, after all, is to increase the purchasing power
of citizens. The question is only how best to do that. The Fed now
gives money to private banks, and just *hopes* they'll lend more
to citizens. But we don't have to do things in this indirect, inefficient manner. We can simply cut out the middleman. The Fed can
keystroke newly created money directly to us when needed and
"apply the brakes" later, when the economy is at risk of becoming
"overheated."

This book is about how and why to do that.

When Bernanke explained his unorthodox approach, he
pointed to our mistaken assumptions about what was possible.
The problem with so-called quantitative easing, he quipped, "is
that it works in practice but it doesn't work in theory."[2] The real
problem was bad theory—bad ideas mistaken for worldly wisdom.
But then, we really should fix our theory: our ideas about money
should better align with what money in practice actually is.

If professional economists are supposed to be the "plumbers"
for our economy, we should probably worry. Most orthodox economists in the major US universities ignore money almost entirely.
(You may be surprised to hear that money and banks are simply
ignored in the main economic models, or if included, they make
no difference.) Little wonder mainstream economists were caught

unawares by the 2008 financial crisis, which started in our banking system. If our democracy remains in a state of emergency, orthodox economists cannot be called upon to address our urgent problems. We need a deeper diagnosis and fix. And maybe, as befits a democracy, we should learn a thing or two about money ourselves.

There is one prominent exception, a relatively new school in economics called modern monetary theory ("MMT"). The school has revived and built upon certain older traditions of thought that were somehow forgotten—"chartalist" or "state" theories of money, "credit" theories of money, "post-Keynesianism," the theory of "functional finance," and other traditions we'll get to. MMT is mostly a *description* of how monetary systems already operate—at least when, as in the United States, England, Japan, or Switzerland, a government issues its own money and borrows mainly in that money, without a fixed exchange rate. It is less a "theory," at bottom, than a simple observation: if you borrow and repay obligations in your own money, you cannot go bankrupt, for you can always issue more money to pay off your debt.[3] The challenge, in that case, is less about solvency than about managing possible inflation. And once we inspect the financial "plumbing," the idea goes, we can correct certain mistakes in conventional economic thinking, and see our way clear to much better policies.

MMT caught quite the buzz in the blogosphere and in the financial media for a while. It looked new and fresh at a time when "austerity" grew old and stale. Yet many of its key insights are still not well appreciated. That's in part because it is often caricatured as the view that we can "print money" without limit, with no worries about deficits or inflation. The idea of a "free lunch" is then pummeled with straw man arguments and wild-eyed predictions of hyperinflation (*Weimar Germany! Zimbabwe! Venezuela!*), by ordinarily intelligent people who really should know better. If you listen very carefully, you can hear Strangelovian echoes "precious bodily fluids" and "red menace" behind such hysterical warnings. The sober task of plausible risk assessment gives way to fearmongering.

We are fellow travelers with MMT economists, but working from a different point of departure, in law and philosophy. We also have some key differences, which could help MMT answer its critics. MMTers often call upon legislators to manage trends in deflation and inflation. To many, this immediately prompts fears of shortsighted politicians "spending like drunken sailors" in their bids for reelection. We agree with MMT on the need for far more public spending in productive places. But we think the central bank can and should have a much more fine-grained role in managing inflation, using new tools we'll describe later. (See Chapter 12 especially.) So what's really needed is a better understanding of public money *and* central banking—including its history, plumbing, and crucial role in our democracy. That, ultimately, is what this book is about.

Once we're clearer about money, we'll know what we spend so much of our lives chasing. We'll see what exactly money is, how we can all have more of it, and how more sophisticated monetary policy can help mend our social contract. We can worry less about our society invariably coming apart at the seams. And we can stop what Hofstadter called "the paranoid style" of money politics from eating our brains, warping our discourse, and hobbling our choices. With a better understanding of our social contract itself, we'll see how to renew it, with promises of greater prosperity and a healthier society and politics to us all.[4]

PART I

MODERN MONEY

It shouldn't be surprising that most of us are confused about money. The dark arts of obfuscation go way back in American history—from the early colonial debates about money, to the South's view that a metallic standard was as "natural" and as necessary for civilization as slavery, to the secret backroom deals of J. P. Morgan in the early twentieth century, to today's bad habit of calling money issuance "printing money" (which, as we explain later, is *impossible*). Today those confusions skew our thinking and political philosophies—even among sophisticated intellectuals.

What we've lost sight of, first and foremost, is money's foundation in our social contract. The promise in money is part and parcel of our government's rule over our lives. Now more than ever, we need new money-promises, in a renewed social compact, in order to keep our democracy from slipping further into authoritarianism.

CHAPTER 1

WHAT MONEY IS BASED ON—VIZ., "NOTHING"

In the spring of 2018, the legendary boxer Manny Pacquiao announced his own new cryptocurrency. This surely led many to wonder: A *boxer*, somehow creating what some might regard as real money? Can that even be a thing?

It isn't so incredible, actually. As the great heterodox economist Hyman Minsky memorably said, "Everyone can create money; the problem lies in getting it accepted."

Pacquiao is one of the most successful and best paid athletes of all time, so what he's calling a "PAC Token" will at least enjoy some name recognition. On the other hand, the great boxer has twice now been semiretired and is pursuing a new vocation as a senator of the Philippines. He's never had trouble raising funds for his bouts, and is not short of money himself. So it wasn't obvious what Pacquiao was promising or why he was promising it. His explanation—"it can be a way to be in touch with the fan base and [there are] a lot of things we can do with this cryptocurrency"—didn't exactly clear things up.

And while Pacquiao's promises weren't exactly clear, another coin recently offered on the market promised even less. It was even called a "Useless Ethereum Token"—and dubbed by some the "NothingCoin." Its founding documents stated explicitly that the coin "transparently offers investors no value." And yet what may have started as a clever hoax promptly raised nearly $200,000. A subsequent offering, the "Do Nothing for You Coin," might have done just as well—except that, in this case, its webpage dutifully informed would-be investors that the offering was simply a ruse.

All this comes amidst recent fervor about bitcoin, ether, CryptoKitties, and a slew of other crypto-offerings. According to news reports in November 2017, people were going so far as to borrow against their homes for crypto-speculation. To those of us who are just beginning to forget the Great Recession, it all suddenly sounded scarily familiar—too much like the "bubble" of overexuberant mortgage speculation that exploded in 2008 and caused the political and cultural upheaval we find ourselves in today. To many, the bitcoin craze and new financial technology also raised deeper puzzlement about what money is. Is bitcoin money? If not, what is money anyway?

We dropped a clue in the Introduction. Look again at a dollar bill—or at any US currency note you happen to have in your pocket. It can be a $1, a $5, a $10 . . . an *any*-dollar bill. If you look across the top, you'll see the words "Federal Reserve Note," which, again, is a legal term for a promissory note. It's a technical term for an IOU. But if "IOU" means "I owe you," what does the Fed owe to us? How could it be in debt to us, with "obligations" to us?

We saw the answer already: a dollar is a promise by the government not to put you in jail if you present that very dollar (or enough of them) in payment of your tax bill. It's a kind of tax voucher. Our government spends it into existence, and vouches for its value by promising to recognize it as payment for any of your debt obligations (for "all debts, public and private"). You can stand firm on that promise and claim your freedom. Just hand over the bills, shouting about the inscription—"'Note'—as in 'promissory note'—so now let me go!"

Do we then chase dollars because the "almighty dollar" inspires market confidence as a "store of value," as economists like to say? Is it that the dollar travels well on vacations we rarely take? Is it that investors aren't, at the moment, fleeing US government bonds?

Not really. It has more to do with paying your debts and thereby avoiding prison. Call it "love of liberty," if you mean not sitting in jail. Because all those legally mandatory taxes, fees, and fines can only be paid in dollars.

And that is why private "crypto-coins" like bitcoin will never rival the dollar or the euro or the peso. They aren't and probably won't ever be accepted in payment of taxes or other government liabilities.

MONEY IS THEREFORE NOT GOLD

During the gold standard era, the Fed did expressly promise to produce some amount of gold for each dollar if you went to the trouble to ask for it. Federal Reserve notes, in effect, were a "warehouse warrant," in J. M. Keynes's phrase. Much as the coat-check worker at the museum takes your umbrella and gives you an IOU, promising to return the umbrella when you present the "claim check," a dollar bill in hand allowed you to reclaim your gold from the central bank. Instead of lugging your stuff around, the bank would hold it for (literal) safekeeping.

Nowadays there's no physical thing to reclaim—no gold bullion, not even gold certificates. If you show up at the various Federal Reserve System buildings around the country flashing a $100 bill, you'll be lucky to get change back in twenties—which would only be *further* bills marked up as "Federal Reserve notes" anyway, and so just more promises. To paraphrase the old folktale about the earth's being grounded on mythological turtles, Fed notes are promises "all the way down."

President Richard Nixon cut any remaining tie between the dollar and gold in 1971. Even by that time only a foreign central bank was entitled to a dollar-for-gold exchange, as FDR had ended the right of individuals to claim gold thirty-eight years earlier. Yet the various "gold standards" were always misleading. They encouraged the notion that gold itself was money, when in reality gold was just the symbol of a promise for payment—and that promise is the real money. If a promise can be "golden," that's only to say it is *credible*.

The presence of gold in vaults like those at Fort Knox and the Federal Reserve Bank of New York did once assure people of the promise of money. And now the fact that there *used* to be gold in certain vaults encourages the misguided notion that something is suspiciously airy and untrustworthy in the fact that gold is no longer held. But you'll be glad to know that the "fiat money" dollars in your hand or in your bank account really are bona fide dollars. As long as the Fed's promises are golden—which is to say, credible—they're what money has been all along.

THE FEAR OF PRISON

The story of modern money begins way back at the 1648 Treaty of Westphalia, when the state system was first established. Ravaged by the Thirty Years War, the kings and princes of Europe struck a bargain: they'd divide authority over different lands, each acknowledging the right of the others to rule over their separate domains. The deal was kept, pacifying Europe.

A few hundred years later (after a long, dark spell of worldwide colonial subjugation, which really only ended in the years after the Second World War), the nation-state system encircled the globe. This is the legal system that now separates the United States, Canada, and Mexico as different "sovereign" nations. It pre-dates every existing government, and now defines when states lawfully exercise jurisdiction within their respective borders. It's what gives any government a right to establish a monetary authority and issue a money—whether dollars, pesos, pounds, euros, yuan, or something else.

The fact that a government may issue its own official money doesn't necessarily guarantee that anyone will use that money in the local marketplace. Even once a new unit is declared, people might go on as before by local custom. Yet sovereign governments were also granted the right to collect fees and taxes, if need be at gunpoint, *in their chosen unit of account*. Wrong unit, no tax payments—whereupon the tax man cometh, with the police to follow.

Money, in other words, is a "creature of the state." This was explained in 1797 by none other than Immanuel Kant, one of the greatest philosophers of all time. He asked, "But how is it possible that what were at first only goods finally became money?" His answer:

> This would happen if a powerful, opulent *ruler* who at first used a material for the adornment and splendor of his attendants (his court) came to levy taxes on his subjects in this material (as goods) (e.g., gold, silver, copper, or a kind of beautiful seashell, *cowries;* or as in the Congo a kind of matting called *makutes,* in Senegal iron ingots, or on the Coast of Guinea even black slaves), and in turn paid with this same material those his demand moved to industry in procuring it, in accordance with exchange regulations with them and among them (on a market or exchange).[1]

Note the plethora of items—beautiful seashells, iron ingots, even slaves—that can become money, all because of a sovereign's tax demands.

Here Kant anticipated another German, the economist G. F. Knapp, who is usually credited with explaining the state's role in constituting money in 1905—Kant being forgotten on this point. "Money is a creature of law," was how Knapp put it.[2] That idea had a big influence on J. M. Keynes, who would become the pre-eminent economist of much of the twentieth century. As Keynes put things, money is "anything which the State undertakes to accept at its pay-offices, whether or not it is declared legal-tender between citizens."[3]

To see why a state-issued money would get noticed, imagine a sunny country called Eudamia. The government has just declared a new unit of account, called "happies." Serious about the country becoming a vacation destination, it designates the unit with this symbol: :) The government also then declares that it will henceforth accept payment for taxes only in happies. Officials dutifully wheel into action, refusing anything else as payment. Happies will quickly gain "currency"—not just for tax payments, but for payments all over Eudamia.

Why? Because, faced with arrest and jail time, everyone will go to great trouble, happily or unhappily, to get their hands on enough happies to meet their tax obligations, through work or borrowing or currency exchange or whatever. It's inconvenient to work entirely in a different money in one's business, only to convert that money into happies around tax time. So happies will soon become accepted in normal business. Maybe competing moneys are still in circulation. Or maybe no money was established beforehand. You'd still have every reason to get ahold of the new unit. And so happies will quickly gain predominance—all because people reliably wish to avoid prison.

That was why, by 2002, the euro had been quickly adopted in all of the eurozone states. Was there any need for confidence in the euro as a "store of value"? The Greeks already trusted the drachma, the Italians the lira, the Spanish the peseta—and what money could be more reliable than the deutschmark! But officials didn't have to wait for the euro to gradually catch on, gaining traction as though through market competition with other currencies. The European Union wasn't about to topple, so people just assumed they'd need to get hold of euros in order to pay any fines, fees, and taxes. They could feel confident others would jump on the euro bandwagon, as they, too, would be faced with a chance of arrest or garnished wages. But even that confidence in others wasn't necessary. People started trading in euros just to stay out of prison themselves.

The influential twentieth-century libertarian economist Ludwig von Mises would say that the euro's adoption couldn't have gone as it in fact did. In reply to G. F. Knapp's idea that taxes drive money, Mises writes, "It is not the State, but the common practice of all those who have dealings in the market, that creates money."[4] He's right that common practice is *part* of it. But the state isn't just another player in the marketplace, even one with unusual influence; it determines *what* means of payment becomes "common practice." It establishes the conditions in which people recognize a particular money amongst themselves, using it to settle debts and make payments. History may be littered with weak governments or peculiar complications. But contemporary governments have ample devices—especially their taxing authority—by which to establish a society's chosen money.[5]

For Mises, a "credit currency" that the state creates out of thin air—including a fiat money such as the euro—would have to tie itself to something that's *already* money in common practice. Otherwise, he warns us, menacingly, "commerce would always protect itself against any other method."[6] What is he imagining, exactly? Violent insurrection—with weapons most consumers and business types don't have, can't get, and won't use against riot police? When police officers appear at the front door, brandishing an IRS letter, go ahead and call the police, on the police. Better still, call a lawyer—your only real option, since our state has a legal monopoly on the use of force.

One can of course buy gold bars and bury them in the back yard for safekeeping, or plow money into bitcoin. It is easier than ever to buy or sell things online without using government money. But one still has to live somewhere, in some physical location, where you pay for stuff. Everyone living around you will need at least some of the ruling government's money at some point, short of tax evasion. And that, along with the sheer inconvenience of running one's affairs in a lot of different moneys, will be quite enough for most everyone to accept government money for payments in daily business. The state will have established its money no matter what came before, even if there was no money before.

"THAT WHICH PAYS"

But can't money exist without government? Yes, it can. In ancient and premodern times, a village or community would have a money—in clay tablets, tally sticks, chickens, pigs, or llamas—with no encouragement from what we'd now call a "government." In modern times, cigarettes circulated as money in POW camps during the Second World War and in Germany in the years following. And they've since been used for payment and savings in certain prisons without approval from prison authorities.

So modern governments aren't part of money's very essence. What then is *money*, as such, in any place or era?

In Voltaire's famous satire *Candide*, our hero Candide and his valet Cacambo happen upon the remarkable country of El Dorado, where the "useful and agreeable are equally blended." Children in tattered garments play games in the streets with lustrous stones of yellow, red, and green, which the little ragamuffins leave behind, with their other playthings, when they scurry off to school. The wayward travelers soon discover that the stones are gold, emeralds, rubies, and diamonds, of quality fit for kings. They gather the gems in amazement, noting the children's excellent education in "being taught to show such a contempt for gold and precious stones."[7]

Later, after attending a nice party, the two guests think they should pay their hosts handsomely for the entertainment. When they present the gems, the hosts "burst into a fit of laughing and held their sides for some time." One host finally explains: "Pardon us . . . for laughing when you offered us the common pebbles of our highways for payment of your reckoning. To be sure, you have none of the coin of this kingdom; but there is no necessity of having any money at all to dine in this house."

Good of the hosts to be so gracious. Candide and Cacambo had the gems, but not the money. Why? Because the colorful stones were not "recognized" as a way of paying or settling whatever debt they may have incurred to their host. Where *was* the money in El Dorado? The tale doesn't say. But if one wanted to find it, the proper moral of the story—if we may ad-lib a bit—is: Don't look for gems, or indeed any other tangible stuff, per se. Look for *what settles debts* (in this case to the party's host). The village's money is its understood means of payment, which is to say, debt settlement.

Adam Smith missed this crucial point in his celebrated *Wealth of Nations*. Suppose a baker would like to procure meat, being willing to trade bread for it. But, alas, the butcher, who has meat, has all the bread he needs already. What then? Smith famously worried they'd "have nothing to offer in exchange. . . . No change can in this case be made between them. He cannot offer to be their merchant nor they his customers."[8] They'd have to exchange something *else* they both wanted, in some commodity such as gold or silver, Smith reasoned.

Smith evidently wasn't a historian. This was rarely a problem in trusting communities. The baker would just take the meat *on credit*, owing a debt of repayment, in something of comparable value later.

The baker would be credible; he had a trade and a solid reputation. And the community would enforce any debt obligation he undertook, providing extra assurance he'd settle up eventually. As the diplomat and economist A. Mitchell Innes explained in 1913: "There is absolutely no reason for assuming the existence of so clumsy a device as a medium of exchange when so simple a system would do all that was required." What was needed was not "a strange general agreement to accept gold and silver, but a general sense of the sanctity of an obligation . . . based on the antiquity of the law of debt."[9]

With promises trusted, the butcher could then borrow as well. Suppose he wanted candlesticks, but the candlestick maker was a vegetarian. He, too, could just borrow from her on credit, on the strength of his promise to pay her back later. By promising, he creates a debt—an IOU—to her. And the clever butcher would realize that he wouldn't himself have to make the payment—not if she'd accept the bread that the *baker* owed to him. The debt in candlesticks could be settled, fair and square, by just transferring the baker's IOU to him over to her. With a simple bread delivery, the debts are then settled all around! (We explain how this works in a favor economy in Chapter 7.)

So an IOU can be money—as "that which pays." Money, if you will, is just a circulating, spendable promise, of the sort that pays or settles debts or other obligations (such as taxes).

What our butcher, baker, and candlestick maker accomplished isn't so different from what we do in ordinary commercial exchange when we pay for stuff. That's also about debt settlement. You'd like to buy an apple from a vendor. Grasping the apple, you ask, "What do I owe ya?" You're asking about your debt to the vendor for the apple, and what it would take to *settle* that debt, to tender payment, in order for the apple to become yours. ("Tender" is archaic legalese for "payment." "Tendering" is a particular kind of "rendering"—rendering what is owed.)

Every relationship, whether in work, marriage, or friendship, in a village or a large society, comes with debts and obligations. We owe things to others, they owe things to us. Think of how often you say "I owe you one," "This one's on me," "You get it next time," and so on. One good turn deserves another, we say. And if a wrong was done we "make things right," "make it up to you," and "even things out." What we're doing is keeping track of the always shifting balance of what we owe and are owed, which is to say, of our liabilities and our assets, deficits and surpluses.

We humans seem to be natural accountants. We hold each other and ourselves "accountable," keeping track of where things stand between us by our best bookkeeping. But keeping track of where things stand isn't easy. When we presume "things will work out" eventually, it's a courageous assumption: We all know things often don't go swimmingly. Memories fade or fail. Time is short, and the messy details require concentration. Even just to "stay on the same page" about where things stand can be complicated and tiresome, the cause of dispute, quarrel, distrust, and strain.

We easily fall into confusion or disagreement, never reaching any final resolution, even if everyone shows good faith.

So whether in a village in the ancient Near East, a city in Renaissance Italy, or one of today's modern states, people have long found a handy way to smooth out the bookkeeping. Just agree that some item, which should be relatively easy to keep track of, *counts as paying what's due or owed.* Once enough people adopt the convenient arrangement, settling a wide range of debts and obligations in their daily business, they've got money.

This is why almost anything can be money—tokens, scrip, coins, paper, checks, or, these days, bank credits. What a community is doing is *representing* its IOUs—whether in clay tablets, scrawled-on napkins marked "IOU," or electronic marks on bank computers. The device has always varied with time and place, depending on technology and politics. What's true across the continents and the ages is that money is "that which pays"—that which is counted as paying or setting debts, so to facilitate a community's bookkeeping.

What is money, then? That thing, whatever it happens to be, that a community agrees to count as settling accounts between them. Whatever that is, that's their money. That's their "common currency."

To nail that idea down, let's define "basic money" as follows, first stated as a mouthful:

> A transferable promissory claim or IOU that a large portion of a community will accept as settling accounts in fulfillment of a large share of market obligations, debts, or other liabilities.

A money thus has these four features:

1. It's a promissory claim (e.g., an IOU; a promissory note— or what the note stands for).
2. It's transferable (e.g., as with an endorsed bank check; a

dollar or euro bill or other unit of currency; or what lawyers call a "negotiable promissory note").

3. It's widely accepted in the community for settling accounts.
4. It fulfills a large share of market obligations, debts, or other liabilities.[10]

"ALL DEBTS PUBLIC AND PRIVATE"

Money, in short, is a promise you can pay for stuff with. What stands for the promise has always varied with technology and culture. Why then does money now take the *same* form the world over, more or less? What happened? The answer is: modernity happened.

The modern era is ruled by sovereign governments, many of which are established and authorized by sovereign peoples who make collective decisions democratically. These governments acting in the names of their peoples can decide what *becomes* "basic money" within their jurisdictions, in the way we explained earlier. They just announce a unit of account, impose a tax debt in that unit, and it's more or less ensured of wide currency. What pays our legal debt to the government in taxes then gets used to make payments and settle debts amongst ourselves in the marketplace—for "all debts public *and* private." Money today—with few exceptions—is thus what we might call *modern money*: basic money issued by modern states, which is to say by governments, with a demand that taxes be paid in it, under threat of prison or other sanction.[11]

After an hour spent in a bike shop, you wheel a bicycle up to the counter for purchase. You ask what you owe, what your debt to the seller is. You're not stealing the bicycle ; you hope to acquire legal title over it, and for that you have a "market obligation." Much as with the apple vendor earlier, you're *liable* to the seller to make payment before the bike is yours.

The shopkeeper has obligations as well. She won't be obliged to accept just anything you offer up as "payment." She'll refuse foreign coins from your last vacation—"No dollars, no bicycle, I'm afraid," she might say. When you do put dollars on the counter—enough of them, at the posted or agreed-upon price—you're laying *claim* to have now paid what you owe, to have settled your debt. Then she can't simply refuse you. You have a *right* to have your currency (or check or debit card) accepted as tendering payment. Which is to say, she has a corresponding *obligation* to accept it, write out a receipt, and refrain from calling the police as you wheel the bicycle out the door. The state-issued money you've tendered is after all *legal* tender.[12]

And what goes for bicycles also goes for all manner of goods and services, as well as for loans, stocks, or other financial assets—including the ones that make people boatloads of money. When we "settle up," in paying off a loan, buying a good or a service, and so on, we're presenting claims and settling debts. Economists and worldly commentators often talk as though "the market" is all about morality-free deals and prices. But as we are all buyers and sellers at one time or another, we all traffic in what sounds a lot like morality—what we owe each other.

Modern societies don't leave these matters to custom or convention. Governments regulate buyers and sellers, imposing "vertical" payment obligations upon each of them, in two main ways. First, they tend to legally regulate "contracts," which are just explicit exchanges of promises and their reciprocal obligations that meet certain formal requirements. Here private obligations are "socially recognized" and enforceable in courts in the event of a dispute. Second, most states adopt special laws that define what counts as "legal tender," and hence as "money," for the express purpose of *fulfilling* these contractual obligations.[13] "This," we have in effect decided as a society, "shall be our legal tender; this is our money."

If you look at the dollar bill, it calls itself legal tender for "all debts public and private." The "private" obligations are the ones just noted, the obligations we have to each other in the market-place, as "horizontally" related buyers and sellers. The "public" obligations go to the heart of modern money.

When the US Federal Reserve issues dollars, they represent an *obligation*, a *debt*, a *liability* of the Fed. That liability is cor-respondingly a *claim*, a *credit*, or an *asset*, for those of us with dollar bills in our pockets or dollar units in our bank accounts. Each dollar in our pocket or bank account is at once our personal asset *and* the government's liability—a *public debt*. If you happen to like money, then you like public debt.

That means the Fed and our federal government are obligated to us in some way. What is our government obligated to do? The answer, again, is: to credit any dollar you present at tax time as good for one dollar off of your tax bill. A dollar is that promise, which the government owes to us on pain of arbitrary tyranny.

The taxpayer may feel a light sense of obligation. Many people feel like the man who heard a sermon on Psalm 52:3-4, on the topic of lies and deceit, who then wrote the Internal Revenue Ser-vice: "I can't sleep knowing that I have cheated on my income tax filing. Enclosed is a check for $150. If I still can't sleep, I'll send the rest." We *are* legally obliged to pony up, and we'll do it if we're at all smart—in order to avoid prison.

This obligation pales in importance compared to the govern-ment's obligation to us. When our check arrives in the IRS offices, the officials had better not refuse our dollars—not in the way they *will* refuse yuan, euros, Microsoft shares, bitcoins, or PAC Tokens. Whatever their mood, whims, or preferences, they are duly *obliged* to accept dollar payments and credit us for having paid our due. For just consider what might happen if, feeling lazy or sour in the stomach, officials were to refuse our check, or sud-denly demand payment in gold bullion or fine watches. Then per-haps a judge, noting that the IRS record does not show payment, feels compelled by duty to meet out "justice" and garnish your wages or post a warrant for your arrest. That isn't just accountant misconduct. It's a gross injustice—of the very sort that led the

American revolutionaries to revolt. As we'll see later, the promise in money is the very foundation of our republic, and in that way sacrosanct.

CRYPTOCURRENCY

Bitcoin certainly seems a lot *like* money. It inspires dreams of getting rich quick, and "bitcoin billionaires" certainly feel wealthy. After Mark Zuckerberg allegedly stole Facebook from the Winklevoss twins, one can understand why the twins might feel vindicated by the bitcoin billions they have since amassed. But they shouldn't count their chickens. Bitcoin isn't friendly enough or trusted enough for wide use, not in any current society. So it isn't quite bona fide money and may not ever be.[14]

Better to think of bitcoins as akin to coupons down at the local grocery store, or gift cards issued by bookstores and other retail outlets during holiday seasons, which can be redeemed only at particular stores and then buy only watermelons, laundry detergent, or certain books or gift items. They aren't widely spendable—they won't pay for dental work and fuel at most gas stations—so they aren't money. Crypto-coins can certainly be worth something, as stocks and bonds are. They can have value and be sold for real money. But when was the last time you found yourself able to buy things with stocks and bonds directly? Rarely or never, is the likely answer.

Crypto-coin offerings are still in very early stages of regulation. The US Securities & Exchange Commission has announced its view that new crypto-coin issuances should be called "initial coin offerings" ("ICOs"), by analogy to stocks issued by firms in "initial public offerings" ("IPOs"). Once they're thoroughly regulated, as they should be, they'll seem less like money and more like what they are: either a vehicle to launder funds from such illicit activities as terrorism, oil plunder, or sex trafficking, or just another device for speculation—just one more commodity or financial instrument available for purchase or sale in units of real money. Since bitcoin "mining" also has a *huge* carbon footprint, it really should be regulated if only to encourage use of greener power sources.

A crypto-"coin" such as bitcoin or ether shouldn't be confused with its underlying "blockchain" technology. For all the blathering about "game-changing" innovation, just remember one thing: what people call "fintech" is just *payment* tech. (Pity it wasn't named "paytech" in the first place; we'd all feel less in the dark.) The new technology is just an *accounting and payments* technology. What "blockchain" does is allow a public ledger to be kept on so many computers—as a "distributed ledger"—without having to trust any one central manager to keep accounts.

As we'll see later, sovereign governments can benefit from that distributed ledger technology as well. Today, most governments rely heavily on private banks to keep accounts and make payments. With the new technology, a government could run its money on a single ledger across so many different computers and depend less on the banks. Singapore, Denmark, China, India, and Brazil are planning to do this already. In February 2020, Sweden launched its first pilot. In Chapters 10 and 11, we suggest that the Fed should and will likewise run a digital currency or "crypto-dollar" in the United States. Digital technology really does seem to be the future of public money, and the coronavirus pandemic of 2020 seems to be drawing that future quite quickly into the present.[15]

But wouldn't that defeat the whole point of crypto-money? Bitcoin originally got hot amid the fever dreams of anarchist libertarians who hoped to free money from government management entirely, and eventually make government unnecessary. But can money be separated from government? The answer is occasionally, yes, but mainly, no. And they won't be fully separable, ever.

One now rarely has a choice between a dollar and an ether payment. With Wall Street and even Facebook now getting in on the crypto-action, however, we probably should expect to see an easy crypto-payment system in the near future. (Though Facebook's

"Libra" is already facing serious regulatory trouble.[16]) Even so, private crypto-offerings will *never* pose serious competition to government money—not unless governments *themselves* begin issuing it or allowing people to pay their taxes in it. Government money will *always* predominate. Because, again, prison. US officials will not accept euros or Microsoft shares or bitcoins or CryptoKitties. Only dollars keep you out of prison.

Apparently, a libertarian water-world utopia off of Tahiti is now being planned by some very rich people. They intend to use a crypto-coin, which presumably will gain currency within the local community. Would that crypto-coin be "basic money"— even without the threat of prison? Yes, it might, *in that community*. When you're there on the flotilla, you could pay for a massage, rent a mask and snorkel, and maybe even buy a bungalow. Not bad, given the crystalline waters and glorious surroundings.

But you can bet the adventure-set rich, who will be wealthy in dollars or euros or other government moneys (or assets denominated in such moneys), won't be converting their whole fortunes into the local crypto-money. For its part, it would be limited to local uses—for the massage and the snorkel. But just as a camping trip depends on the resources and money provided by larger society, any larger value it has in terms of government-issued money or assets would be parasitic on those governments.

The community will at any rate operate in the shadow of the Tahitian government. It gained permission to exist in relative autonomy, but it *needed* that permission. These days, almost no livable part of the planet counts as common property of the sort that a squatter community could just take over. Governments are now everywhere, covering just about every inch of land or water on the planet (excluding areas designated as "international" waters, etc.). If a government's money will predominate within its territorial jurisdiction, and we're stuck with a global state system, money will always and everywhere be some government's money, with few exceptions.

But could a delightful water-world utopia be a harbinger of

things to come? Might it prove that the state system isn't really necessary, in part because it isn't needed for money? Could the anarcho-billionaires join and finally rouse the anesthetized proletariat, now zoning out into their phones, to bring on the revolution Marx predicted?!

Probably not. The state and state system will always be needed to protect us from each other—not to mention foreign armies with advanced weapons (including hooligans riding Jet Skis, as in the 1995 cheesy dystopian film *Waterworld*). Governments pay armies and police forces in their moneys, which have currency, due to those very forces, under threat of prison. This basic reality of modern life won't change any time soon. So crypto is destined to play second fiddle.

The fear of prison is a powerful thing. As we've seen, it means a sovereign government can simply issue its chosen money into wide currency. But that's only the start of its remarkable powers for self-enrichment. As we'll see in the next chapter, with its money established, a government can keep spending new money into existence, from nothing, by simply deciding to make more promises.

CHAPTER 2

SPENDING FROM NOTHING

How does the United States pay for an aircraft carrier? Including all the steel, the engineers, the welders, and so forth?

The process seems almost magical. Congress authorizes the necessary spending, for labor and materials. And the Treasury spends. How does it spend?

It simply cuts a check drawn on its account at the central bank, the Federal Reserve, or asks the Fed to credit the banks of designated suppliers and contractors directly. The managers and workers then pay their bills with those credits. They simply "draw" upon them (hence the word "draught" or "draft" as a synonym for "check") in building the vessel on some agreed-upon schedule. And that's it! An aircraft carrier is willed (and built) into existence.

While we citizens have to get money in order to buy things, the same isn't true for the federal government, which after all issues the very money that's used in payment. It can snap up anything for sale in dollars, by way of steel and welders and so on, by issuing its own dollar IOUs, from nothing.

That's exactly how the United States pays for all of its wars. And how it builds interstate highways, post offices, and school buildings. And how it pays for retirement and health benefits. The federal government, by the numbers, is more or less a social insurance scheme with a standing army. How do we pay for it all? By deciding to make the payments and spending the dollars into existence.

Where, you may ask, does the United States get the money it spends? The answer is: nowhere! The government creates money *in the very act of spending it.* The very act of keystroking dollar credits into bank accounts *creates money.*

Don't think here of officials wheeling out a printing press in order to put cash in circulation, or of unusual "money-printing" measures. *All* spending by the government, in *every* season, creates new money. And don't think of tax revenue being collected and only then spent. The taxes don't have to be there in order for the government to spend. The money is always issued afresh. Taxes later mop up some of that money to avoid overissuance— i.e., inflation.

This works because the United States has its own bank, the Federal Reserve. This central bank, which powers the banking system from its core much as the sun powers the planets, *generates* the money. How? By doing a bit of simple bookkeeping.

Bankers once kept the books with a fountain pen on a paper spreadsheet. Assets on one side of the page, liabilities on the other. Adjust the totals with "credits" and "debits," the one offsetting the other. Mark up numbers here, mark down numbers there, always ensuring that assets and liabilities sum to zero. That's still how banking is done, except now bankers change the records electronically, tapping numbers into a computer keyboard (or writing a program). It wouldn't be far from the truth to think of the central bank as a big public spreadsheet, with constantly changing numbers.

So how do we get the money for an aircraft carrier? Bookkeeping actions! Once the Treasury authorizes various payments, it lets Fed officials know, usually by requesting electronic payments. Fed officials open the Treasury's account at the Fed and adjust numbers up or down. For the $13 billion in new expenditure, the number *13,000,000,000* is typed in as new liabilities. There may be credits from tax payments or other sources in the account already. Or not. Either way, officials type in the numbers.

At the same time, the officials type numbers totaling $13 billion into the asset column of commercial bank accounts, usually at the twelve "reserve banks," which are authorized to lend dollars and run the payments system. Those banks are required by law to keep accounts at the Fed, with mandatory "reserve" deposits. The Fed credits those accounts, typing in the numbers, creating "high-powered money." Now with extra credits in their reserve accounts, the various banks make the $13 billion available to the appropriate municipalities, firms, and workers in their own accounts. They then spend from those accounts into the larger economy.

This works because the central bank does the Congress's bidding. The Fed simply "monetizes" the decisions handed down to it. The Treasury and Fed coordinate in an elaborate dance, which we'll come back to. But, ultimately, the Fed won't refuse to make any payments the Treasury asks for. At what point would it refuse? It has discretion over some matters, such as interest rates. And it is "independent" of electoral politics in ways we come back to in Chapter 14. But on public spending, the central bank is the Congress's handmaiden.[1]

How is this possible? Well, all sovereign governments have the legal authority to issue money. Many choose not to. Ecuador, for example, uses the US dollar. Germany, Greece, and the eurozone countries traded their sovereign moneys for the euro—in what appears to have been a fateful decision. But among the governments that do issue their own money, such as the United States, England, Canada, Japan, Switzerland, Australia, China, Brazil, and Turkey, among others, they are constantly spending it into existence, routinely, on a daily basis, from nothing.

This isn't exactly news. It was explained plainly in the 1940s.[2] If it sounds surprising, you may be thinking the federal government is like a private household, which again does have to get its money from somewhere. In which case, welcome to the weird, wonderful world of "fiat money"!

TAXES DO NOT PAY FOR SPENDING

Many people seem to believe that the government must "get" its money "from" somewhere, the way persons, families, or companies do. They assume the federal government must first tax people to get their money from them, or borrow from them, in order to spend money on anything. The question, they assume, is only who will have to pay those taxes, or what lenders, if any, will be willing to lend and at what price.

This picture has things exactly backward. A government that issues its money doesn't need to "get money" or "have money" in order to spend it. It simply *issues* it, at will. That is the original source of any money the people have. (Remember that dollar-bill inscription—"Federal Reserve Note.") There's no big pile of money sitting around in a warehouse that could be used up, no vault anywhere on US territory being filled or emptied. When the United States pays for an aircraft carrier and social insurance benefits, crediting bank accounts, it doesn't lose any ability to make further payments in the future. At the direction of the Congress and Treasury it issues fresh promises—which is to say, new dollar IOUs. It never runs out of promises, or loses the ability to issue more of them.

Dollars are not inherently scarce. They are *kept scarce* to prevent unhealthy inflation. The trick, as we will explain moving forward, is to steer a course between deflation and healthy inflation, i.e., between making too few and too many promises.

Ever wondered what happens to your dollars when you pay them in taxes? Where do they "go"? Nowhere! They are in effect destroyed. In legalese, debts paid are simply "extinguished." The Treasury presents your check to your bank, and, once honored, the Fed removes the amount from your bank's reserve account and credits a Treasury account (or reduces its liabilities). The units are then deleted from the "money supply" statistics.[3] If you dropped off physical, tangible, cold hard cash at the Treasury building, the bills might simply be shredded. Or if they're still in good shape, they may be reissued into circulation as if they are new currency—which, as new spending, they effectively *will* be.

If this is hard to visualize, go back to why a sovereign's money gains currency in the first place—i.e., becomes what is "counted" on a "current account." In our Chapter 1 example, the government of Eudamia spent happies into existence. It was the tax *liability* that did the trick in getting them widely "accepted." Not a penny of tax *revenue* had to be raised and received by Eudamia's treasury. Because, again, knowing you're being held liable to pay taxes in a money is reason enough to get your hands on it. So you'll accept it in payment from others, including the issuing government itself. The fear of prison is a powerful thing.

And where, after all, would those intent upon avoiding prison procure a government's money if not ultimately from the government itself? Governments hold a *legal monopoly* on all issuance of the money needed to pay the taxes they demand of people. Children and criminals will wonder why they shouldn't set up a home money-"printing" operation down in the basement, even just to pay taxes. The answer is that even the most "advanced" countries punish counterfeiting harshly, handing out decades-long sentences in prison. For many centuries it was a capital offense, and still is in many jurisdictions.

Notice a key *consequence* of all this: a government *has* to spend the money it issues into the economy, or authorize private banks to issue it, *before* we can pay taxes in that money. What happens is a sort of circular flow. Dollars are continually spent into existence by federal spending and bank lending. They are then pulled out of circulation by federal taxing and "borrowing" (i.e., sales of Treasury securities). Dollars are constantly being created and destroyed, in hopes of keeping just the right amount of money in circulation.

So, strange as it may sound, tax revenue does not "pay for" or "fund" public spending at all, functionally speaking. Taxes may still be necessary and important. They have *other* functions, aside from drawing money out of the economy. They shape incentives and affect the distribution of wealth and purchasing power across an economy, for example. A tax lawyer will tell you that this is in fact what the tax code is principally *for*. But as long as a government issues its own money and mainly borrows in its own money, while keeping a flexible exchange rate for other moneys, its spending does not require or "come from" tax revenue.[4]

"BORROWING" IS UNNECESSARY

All taxes remove dollars from the economy. When dollars are left in circulation after taxes, the government can coax more of them out of private bank accounts by "borrowing" them. The Treasury issues a security, i.e., a Treasury note, Treasury bond, or Treasury bill (or "Treasurys," for short). You give it your dollars and it promises you a safe asset and a bit of interest, or a "coupon."

We call this government "borrowing." That is pretty misleading. The apparent analogy to personal borrowing or private-sector bond issuance obscures a deep truth. The government isn't trying to raise funds. Ask yourself: Why would the United States borrow dollars if it can create them at will? If *you* could issue dollars because counterfeiting became legal, why would you ever borrow dollars from anyone?

What US Treasurys are is a handy policy tool. They pull liquid dollars temporarily out of bank accounts, so that people can't spend them at times when we want there to be less spending. That helps the Fed manage the overall supply of spendable money in circulation, steering a course between deflation and excessive inflation. By buying and selling Treasurys, the Fed manages "the interest rate," the rate at which private banks lend to each other overnight, which in turn influences how much money the banks are lending into circulation.

Even that tool isn't necessary any longer, now that the Fed takes a more direct route: it just pays private banks "interest on reserves," or "IOR," to keep funds in their reserve accounts at the Fed, at an adjustable rate of interest. The rate is functionally equivalent to a Treasury bond "coupon"—the rate you are paid just to "park" your money.[5] By raising or lowering the rate, the Fed makes the banks more or less interested in parking funds with it, and more or less interested in borrowing or lending. So the Treasury doesn't have to "borrow" or even issue Treasury bonds, strictly speaking.[6]

And how are these Fed operations "paid for"? Fed officials just type in the numbers. Every dollar created is a liability of the US government, and added to a liability column of some part of a US government spreadsheet. In practice, the Fed and the Treasury are like a married couple with a shared bank account—in this case, the United States' *sovereign balance sheet* (a consolidation of twelve different balance sheets for different departments). Being part of the government, the central bank can book liabilities under its own name.

All those interest payments on bank reserves, they just go on the Fed's balance sheet. All those trillions in credits that mopped up the 2008 crisis, they went on the Fed's account as well. The Fed was planning to move the numbers elsewhere. Recently it decided to leave them there indefinitely. The $13 billion for the aircraft carrier could be parked there as well, if we changed a few rules. Same goes for anything else we choose to spend money on, whether it be the cost of shoring up Social Security benefits or investing in green energy.

Unlike bonds, absent a decision to pay interest on reserves, there is no interest owed on those central bank liabilities—just as there's no interest owed on a dollar bill, which is also a liability of the central bank. The numbers can in principle stay on the Fed balance sheet, interest-free, indefinitely. Traditionally, the liabilities wind up over on the Treasury balance sheet. But they are liabilities of the US government either way. And why should it matter *which agency spreadsheet they appear on*?

Think of that next time you hear some politician or pundit say we must cut Granny's Social Security benefits because we "can't afford it" by either tax revenue or Treasury "borrowing." There's always a third option: just credit Granny the money and leave the liability numbers on the central bank spreadsheet. That's sometimes called "monetizing debt" or "printing money." But all that's happening is liability numbers are left on the balance sheet of the central bank instead of the Treasury. And, again, that way they can be interest-free! Quite the bargain! So try explaining to Granny why this option is unthinkable, except maybe temporarily. If she knew how *little is at stake*—which government spreadsheet the numbers get posted to—she'd surely take offense that cuts to her modest benefits were even being contemplated.[7]

Why don't we load up the Fed balance sheet with everything but the kitchen sink, then? Mainly because of convention. The Treasury and Fed relationship evolved in a different direction over the years. The formal power to issue dollars was transferred from the Treasury to the Federal Reserve in the 1913 Federal Reserve Act (though they technically count as liabilities for both). From there the 1951 Treasury-Fed Accord divided Treasury and Fed responsibilities amidst inflation fears from heavy spending during the Second World War and the Korean War. Since 1981, the Treasury hasn't been legally allowed to overdraft on its account at the Fed at will. Even so, it spends first and "finds the money" later.[8]

When credits in the Fed account from previous taxes don't cover new spending, the Treasury will "borrow" to make up the difference. That *looks* like taxes or bonds are "paying for" spending. But at this point the Fed *could* simply "buy" those bonds directly. It would just move the liability numbers on to its own balance sheet and add offsetting credits to the Treasury account— by so many keystrokes into a computer. Et voila, paid for! No taxes, no bonds.

The Fed isn't legally allowed to do that at the moment, but for

a long time now a work-around has been standard operating pro-
cedure. The bookkeeping comes to much the same thing, except
private banks are let in on the action. The Fed simply buys Treasurys on the market—in "open market operations." That pulls
dollars from private bank accounts and loads up the Treasury's
account at the Fed. Certain banks ("dealer banks"), pursuant to
"a common understanding," will buy any Treasury securities on
offer and then sell them on to the Fed, pocketing easy money.
And when the interest rate at which banks lend to each other is
diverging from the Fed's target rate, the Fed has little choice but
to buy them (or take other measures—such as paying interest on
reserves, as suggested earlier). Why the Kabuki dance? Mainly to
help the reserve banks stabilize their reserve account balances,
which is to say, for technical reasons.[9]

If Fed operations seem dizzying in their complexity, what's
really going on is still just bookkeeping. It's just that nowadays
the entries are made in roundabout fashion.

CAN SOCIAL SECURITY GO BROKE?

What are the odds, then, that Social Security will go broke, as
opposed to being cut for political reasons? Exactly zero. Social
Security payments can *always* be paid in dollars in the very same
way they are paid today. Just spend new dollars into retiree bank
accounts, with checks in the mail or electronic credits.

Can it really be that simple? Take it from Alan Greenspan. In
2005, Greenspan was asked during a congressional hearing by
Representative Paul Ryan to comment on the solvency of Social
Security. Ryan had the floor and invited Greenspan to agree
with him that personal retirement accounts would "improve
solvency"—implying that Social Security might not keep its
promises otherwise. In reply, Greenspan flatly denied that Social
Security is "insecure." "There's nothing to prevent the federal government from creating as much money as it wants and paying it
to somebody," he explained.[10] In which case we can always sim-

ply decide to keep paying Granny $1,300 per month, for rent and basic necessities, instead of leaving her to exposure and death by uncertain causes. (Poverty rates were very high among the elderly before Social Security, which is why this venerable institution is sometimes called "old-age insurance.")

Greenspan went on to say that the real question is not the "security" of Social Security payments, but inflation management—making sure the retirees who receive the money have real goods to purchase. That point applies equally to aircraft carriers, interstate highways, or indeed anything the government might pay for in dollars. The government can pay for whatever we want it to pay for, as long as it manages the total amount of money spent.

Can there be too much public spending? Yes indeed, when the money supply grows in excess of our productive capacity. When workers, factories, technologies, and other resources aren't being newly produced or enlisted, we won't get extra new goods or services to absorb the extra money. That's when we get "too much money chasing too few goods"—inflation.

Inflation as such, by itself, isn't even a problem. A growing economy needs a constantly growing supply of money. Prices can and should gradually rise as long as the new money is used productively (in ways that mobilize idle resources or deploy new technologies that make resources more productive). That—our real productive and hence money-absorptive capacity—is the *only* real "speed limit" on money creation.[11]

But can't the United States nevertheless rack up "too much debt" and go bankrupt? Nope. A dollar is indeed a liability of the Fed. Any new dollars do add to the government's total liabilities, marked down on a government spreadsheet. But there's no inherent reason why they shouldn't exceed total government assets. A government that *issues* the public's money is not at all like a household that *uses* public money. The United States has run large and growing deficits on its balance sheet for most of its history. It's never defaulted. Why not?

Greenspan told us: "A government cannot become insolvent

with respect to obligations in its own currency. A fiat money system, like the ones we have today, can produce such claims without limit."[12] Meaning, if a government borrows only or mainly in its own money, it *cannot* go into default, except by its own stupidity.

Imagine bond payments coming due. Officials can make them almost effortlessly, by typing numbers into a computer. But now they are wondering, *should we go ahead and press the buttons*? Well, what would stop them from keeping the government's promises, short of craven idiocy?[13] The United States hasn't ever defaulted because officials can and always have simply made the payments.

But what if public debt climbs to a seemingly high level, and eye-popping figures are blared loudly in the financial news? Could that undermine the government's money, *as* money, by undermining "confidence"? Nope. "Borrowing" costs may rise with investor "jitters." But people will always widely accept dollar payments—as long as the government in effect has a gun to their heads. That, again, is why a sovereign's money ultimately enjoys the "confidence" needed to be money. It's not because investor "jitters" were soothed, or because its debt instruments were perceived as a good "store of value" compared to other assets. It's because people need the money to avoid garnished wages and incarceration, which itself underwrites money's status as a "store of value" in the first place.[14]

A FREE LUNCH?

All this means we have a hearty buffet of policy options. Let's see, should we opt for very small government—with few guns and scarce butter—and pay low taxes? Or should we have heavy guns and light butter—still with low taxes? Or should we have big government—with fleets of aircraft carriers and lavish social insurance benefits—and *still pay low taxes*?

These are all feasible options if we really must have low taxes. Because, again, taxes do not "fund" spending! *All* spending—on guns *or* on butter—simply creates new money, from nothing. Taxes may be needed to manage inflation, or to adjust the distribution of wealth and thus power, or to save democracy from plutocracy. But that may or may not require high *income* taxes, which of course tend to be a bone of contention.

These are not utopian yearnings for an ideal world. So far, we've been *describing* how public money and banking *already* work in the United States and many other countries that issue their own money.[15] Our point, for the moment, is that governments aren't constrained in ways that we often imagine—and some pundits want us to imagine—unless they impose those constraints on themselves.

So is there a free lunch, after all? Alas, no. None of the foregoing means a government can spend without limit. Our productive capacity, beyond which new money creates an unhealthy amount of inflation, does limit how much we can spend, as we've noted. But officials have been far too cautious when gauging where that limit is. Economists tend to agree that some inflation is healthy, but then reflexively set a conservative target rate (now a 2 percent general rise in prices). They do that without really clarifying why it is necessary, and without counting the lost opportunity of even a slightly higher target. If the Fed went for 4 percent instead, for example, would the wheels really fall off the money wagon? As we'll see later on, the Fed can install a fully reliable monetary brake system. When fine-tuned based on observable data, hyperinflation becomes *impossible for practical purposes.*

If history is any guide, there is little reason to worry anyway. The usual bogeymen of inflationary spending—Weimar Germany, Zimbabwe, and Venezuela—are very different from Japan and the United States where money's concerned. The United States and especially Japan have been struggling against *deflation*, failing to hit their low inflation targets from below for a decade on end, or over two decades in the case of Japan. Millions were still out of work in the United States—including those who stopped looking (who are therefore not counted in the unemployment statistics)—

even before the 2020 pandemic spiked job losses. So the country is well below its productive capacity. And with lessons learned from the aftermath of the 2008 crisis, the Fed now has many effective techniques for tracking and managing key prices. We can spend far more than we now do without risking unhealthy inflation.

For now, we're merely describing how a fiat money system works. Nothing we've said so far in this chapter tells us the ideal level of spending—on guns and butter. That is a different, political question, a matter of political philosophy and public policy.

THAT OLD-TIME RELIGION

Things were different under the "gold standard" of a long bygone era. Once officials committed themselves to limit the money supply by the supply of gold, they did indeed have to "pay for" any spending with tax revenue or borrowing. In order to spend money, they had to get it from someone—in order to keep their gold promise. Which meant, in effect, a strange Cyclops rendition of the "resource constraint" noted earlier, except that only *one* resource matters, i.e., gold. But the gold standard—which J. M. Keynes called a "barbarous relic"—was always a starvation diet of too little money. Gold stocks increase slowly, so there usually wasn't enough new money for a growing economy. That point is now widely appreciated. Yet somehow the ideal of a "balanced budget" lives on in the gold standard's shadow, under the more dignified name of "fiscal austerity." "Metallism" and fiscal austerity are the same thing: self-inflicted money-starvation diets. Yet to many the one is a needless disaster and the other a hallmark of virtue.

That's just one of the many confusions that plague public understanding of money. Perhaps the worst of them is the notion that a money-issuing sovereign government should be run like a household or municipality. Yes, a *household* requires income in dollars *before* it can buy stuff in dollars, unless it borrows against future dollar income. Here a "balanced budget" is indeed virtuous, at least over the longer run. The same goes for the great State of California, the great State of Louisiana, every local government, and every business, school, and individual subject to US tax authority. We merely *use* dollars, and so must "live within our means," or risk going broke in dollars. But that is simply not the US government's situation: it *issues* the dollars.

The word "balance" certainly *sounds* pleasing and harmonious. (Who doesn't like harmony?) Talk of getting our fiscal house in order sounds innocent and serious, like checking in to a detox or rehab after a bender. We have a good feel for our personal and household finances. And righteous anger about the "growing budget deficit" and irresponsible politicians can bring a pleasing feeling of moral clarity and individual probity. President Barack Obama went so far as to call George W. Bush's driving up US public debt "unpatriotic." But these sentiments are usually based in confusion: the United States is nothing like a household or city in its finances.

Even serious economists sometimes say confused things such as, "The problem with deficits is that the money has to eventually be repaid." But of course, as they well know, Treasurys are constantly paid off and newly issued, and this can be done indefinitely. While any *given* bond payments must be made as they come due, the *total* debt outlay need not ever be "repaid." Indeed, total debt typically grows over time with the economy—actually helping both to *fuel and accommodate* that growth. Again, the United States has run growing deficits throughout most of its history, and it can do so in perpetuity. The few times that it hasn't, recession and even depression have followed.

So the real question is: What could be good or virtuous—let alone patriotic—about preventing a government from supporting its people?

Paul Samuelson, the great twentieth-century economist who defined today's orthodoxy as much as anyone, gave us a frank answer: a balanced budget requirement is a "superstition," like so much "old-fashioned religion." Samuelson nevertheless thought the superstition usefully scares legislators:

> There must be discipline in the allocation of resources or you will have anarchistic chaos and inefficiency. And one of the functions of old-fashioned religion was to scare people by sometimes what might be regarded as myths into behaving in a way that the long-run civilized life requires. We have taken away a belief in the intrinsic necessity of balancing the budget if not in every year, [then] in a very short period of time. If Prime Minister Gladstone [a prominent figure of the time] came back to life he would say, "Uh-oh, what have you done?" . . . I have to say that I see merit in that view.[16]

Samuelson would probably make an exception for wartime spending. He's presumably worried mainly about hyperinflation, which can indeed wreak havoc upon society and does require discipline. But whatever the merit of balanced budget religion in other times and places, by now we've crossed the fine line between Plato's "noble lie" and a destructive taboo. When people start believing the lie with righteous certitude, losing all sense of its essential purpose, the old-time religion can work *too well* in the cause of self-denial. Struggling against deflation as we have been, the cost of old-time religion is mass money-starvation. When there's too little money in the economy, too little inflation, and hence too little transacting, productive activity dwindles and the economy languishes. Productive public spending is then exactly what the economy needs. And balanced budget superstition all but guarantees the wrong course of action.

Can we assume things will "work out" in the "long run," as economists often do? Not if, in the meanwhile, the social compact is broken, politics radicalized, and democracy crippled by insurgent authoritarianism. That situation is not entirely hypothetical; it is very much our situation today, or could easily be our future.

Balanced budget religion is a big part of why we are where we are, and why our future might still be much worse than it has to be.

Samuelson only notes the benefits of monetary superstition. The human toll of austerity seems to him unimportant or over-ridden in the name of "long-run civilization." This is, in a way, downright Strangelovian. To General Ripper, the worst part of the Commie fluoridation plot (aside from compromising his own bodily fluids and manly "essence") was the threat to the children's ice cream ("Mandrake . . . why, there are studies underway to fluoridate salt, flour, fruit juices, soup, sugar, milk," he tells the British officer Mandrake." "Ice cream. Ice cream, Mandrake, chil-dren's ice cream"). For the sake of civilization's children—Amer-ica's children, at any rate—a nuclear dust-up was necessary. And the cost of all those mushroom clouds? Ripper wasn't bothered, presuming serenely that awful things are justified in the solemn name of long-run civilization.[17]

On the other hand, Samuelson's hesitation is fair in one way. Can we really trust legislators, prone as they are to spend like drunken sailors, to resist the siren song of spending in their bids for reelection? Wouldn't we be wise to "tie their hands to the mast" somehow, to encourage self-restraint? Perhaps, but old-time reli-gion is the wrong method. Ulysses instructed his crew to tie his hands to the mast to avoid the sirens' temptations; he didn't go for castration, which would also have been rather effective. There are far better ways of keeping shortsighted politicians from maiming monetary policy.

One is already well established: the central bank should remain "independent" from short-term political pressure. This was rightly celebrated by the monetary economist Milton Friedman. But Friedman was too skeptical of the Fed's ability to advance even its own original mandate (stable prices *and* full employ-ment). Central banking techniques are constantly progressing, as bankers experiment and learn from each other. They've improved greatly since Friedman's day, in part thanks to lessons learned from the 2008 crisis. Nowadays there is much the Fed can do in the service of outcomes that nearly everyone endorses, without taxes and regulation that many find unacceptable. We lay out the tools in Chapter 12.[18]

No matter how sound the tools, the paranoid style of argument will no doubt come to old-time budget religion's rescue. What better way to scare people than with simple, exaggerated, moralistic language—if not talk of "preverts" and "perversions," as in *Strangelove*, then talk of the Fed "printing money" and "debasing" the currency. After all, people can be cowed into intellectual submission; if you scare the bejeezus out of 'em, they won't feel any need to understand.

That good ol' way of enforcing monetary religion may indeed explain our shaky grasp of public accounting. Which is all the more alarming when you consider the rudimentary facts even sophisticated people seem ignorant of.

Take a case in point: as a simple matter of bookkeeping, public debt just *is* private wealth; they are always equivalent (holding fixed a country's relation to the rest of the world).

When a dollar liability is added to the Fed's books, it is a dollar asset in someone else's pocket or bank account. When the United States issues debt in Treasurys, each Treasury is somebody's asset—a safe bond, perhaps being saved for Grandma's retirement. Public debt, private wealth—one and the same. This is not a point of controversy, by the way. It's a point of algebra, of basic accounting. "Liability" makes no more sense in the absence of "assets" than "right" makes in the absence of "left."

In which case, what about all that public debt being "left for the grandchildren," which Serious People crow so loudly about? It is equivalent to *private wealth*—much of which is . . . *being left for the grandchildren*. Which is great, right?!

When trying to frighten people, consistency is perhaps not paramount. Yet public ignorance about this key point of accounting has come at an extraordinary cost to our society.

To want a government "surplus" is effectively to want the

private sector—banks, businesses, households, etc.—to be a net debtor, literally to have *negative net worth*. And that means real risks of bankruptcy or financial crisis. Indeed, private debt build-ups were the tinderbox of the 2008 implosion: private banks lent too freely and families were living beyond their means in an economy long afflicted by stagnant real wage and salary incomes. The same bad cycle of public surplus to private deficit and private bankruptcy has happened more than once in US history. Why? In part because people believe the superstition that a public surplus is virtuous, when it is generally a menace to society—a case of too little money to accommodate growth and avoid the starvation that causes stagnation.

When budgetary debate in Washington, DC, isn't confused—which is to say, almost never—the argument isn't about public debt, per se, anyway. It's about whether *the other party's spending priorities are worthy*. The money always seems to be there for guns, aircraft carriers, and foreign invasions. But for extra butter—things like free or cheap college, better and affordable health care, or a green energy revolution—the immediate question is always, "Sure—but *how are you going to pay for it?*" This is said despite the fact that guns and butter are in fact "paid for" in *exactly the same way*: with authorized payments, as the Fed keeps an eye on inflation.

By now Republicans have led millions to believe Social Security won't be there for them. Ryan's message in his exchange with Greenspan—before Greenspan set him straight—is part of a larger discouragement campaign. It often has Republicans playing Cassandra about the "deficit" and "debt," styling themselves champions of "responsible," "balanced budgets," at least when social insurance benefits come up. When their own spending priorities are at issue, all that goes out the window: they spend freely. Here they show a better understanding of public finance.

As former vice president Dick Cheney once put it, "Reagan proved that deficits don't matter." Under president Ronald Reagan, the United States increased military spending, cut taxes,

and increased public debt markedly. Was there unwanted inflation as expected? Nope. And after trillions more in wars, tax cuts,
more wars, and more tax cuts, did we get inflation? Nope. Again,
decades on, in the United States, as in Japan, the worry is about
deflation, not *inflation*.

Cheney wasn't quite right. Deficits *do* matter, because it matters *what we spend money on*. It matters if we spend too much in
the wrong places, inflating prices too quickly. But he had the right
sentiment. "Balance" on the public ledger does not matter *inherently*, and it's often pernicious.

The Democratic party has been slower than the Republicans
to catch on. Long attacked as "tax-and-spend liberals," having
spent decades trying to establish a reputation for fiscal rectitude,
Democrats are only starting to reconsider their one-sided commitment to a "balanced budget." But better health care, cheaper
college, and green energy can be funded the exact same way the
military is. We just decide it is important enough, have the Treasury and Fed credit bank accounts, and have the Fed manage any
risks of inflation.

Some politicians understand this but won't admit it publicly.
Others live in a fundraising fog of confusion. Still others know
better and sow confusion anyway, banging on about "debt being
left for the grandchildren."

This turns out to be pretty good politics, in the sense of being
persuasive. The rest of us, we tend to believe the rhetoric. By now
we've all heard it said over and over and over that taxes must "pay
for" any spending on guns and butter. We cannot simply make
butter, we are told over and over. And could everyone really be so
confused? Could all the hair-on-fire yelling about "the debt" on
cable news, all the self-righteous posturing in the financial media
about "fiscal responsibility," all the hand-wringing about economic "uncertainty" and "confidence," the dark specter of "bond
vigilantes," and so forth, be founded upon ignorance, confusion,
or opportunism? Yes, it can (probably all three of those). It's just
the paranoid style in American politics, once again.

The fact is that we *can* have guns and butter. If we prefer, we can have low income taxes as well (since, again, they really just do not "fund" spending). In later chapters we explain how our banking system can serve us butter on a digital silver platter.

CHAPTER 3

PROMISING FROM NOTHING

Each workday, well-dressed officials show up at the New York Fed building in lower Manhattan. Still holding their morning pastry and coffee, they decide to create new money. They aren't running "the printing press," creating tangible cash or currency. That's the job of the Treasury. What they're doing is crediting bank accounts—pressing buttons at a computer terminal.

But wouldn't money created by an official at a computer—coffee in the one hand, tapping buttons with the other—have to be "backed" by something? Once we swipe back the *Wizard of Oz* curtain, peering into the Fed buildings, we see only office chairs, water coolers, wastebaskets, and computer screens. *Where's the money?* Where's the substance behind the spectacle? Isn't something missing? (And could it perhaps be gold?)

Nowadays dollars are issued "by fiat," which is to say, created out of thin air on the authority of the Fed's decisions, when officials press those computer buttons. Is that mysterious, fishy, even outlandish? It shouldn't be. We do much the same thing all the time ourselves in our daily business. If you wish to meet a friend, you might issue her a promise to meet for coffee at 2:00 p.m. at Starbucks next Tuesday. You've exercised promissory authority, in hopes of having the meeting. That is exactly what Fed officials sitting at the computer are doing, in hopes of influencing the economy. There's no sleight of hand when they tap the buttons. The magic of money is just the ordinary reality of promising.

WORDS AS DEEDS

Spoken words can be idle, fluff, cheap, a waste of breath, no better than noise. But certain words, said at the right time and place, by the right person, are deeds of consequence. When you say the words "I promise," "I apologize," or "I bet you," you aren't just *describing* what you are doing. You're *performing* a sort of action: making a promise, giving an apology, placing a wager.

The philosopher J. L. Austin explained it this way:

> If a person makes an utterance of this sort we should say that he is doing something rather than merely saying something. . . . Suppose, for example, that in the course of a marriage ceremony I say, as people will, "I do"—([viz.] take this woman to be my lawful wedded wife). Or again, suppose that I tread on your toe and say "I apologize." Or again, suppose I have the bottle of champagne in my hand and say "I name this ship the *Queen Elizabeth*." Or suppose I say "I bet you six pence it will rain tomorrow." . . . In all these cases . . . in saying what I do, I actually perform that action. When I say "I name this ship the *Queen Elizabeth*" I do not describe the christening ceremony, I actually perform the christening; and when I say "I do" . . . I am not reporting on a marriage, I am indulging in it.[1]

When such "speech acts" are performed in the proper manner, things suddenly are not as they were before. The couple didn't have to marry, or maybe shouldn't have. Yet once the minister declares them married ("I now pronounce you . . ."), that marries them. And now, for better or for worse, they owe things to each other they didn't before. The ship didn't have to be named the *Queen*

Elizabeth. Yet once it was so christened in a public ceremony, it was from then on wrong to call it the *Generalissimo Stalin*.

The philosopher John Searle, a student of Austin, explains it this way: "We change reality . . . [and] succeed in doing so because we represent the reality as being so changed."[2] That makes a speech act sound almost miraculous: we change reality by declaration, much as God is said to have created the world ex nihilo with four simple words, "Let there be light!" But of course a guy at a bar who declares that Paris is located in Belgium won't change the reality; he's just wrong about where Paris is. It's just that in marriage and in christenings—and actually in a lot of social settings—things do get decided because, in the right moment, the right person made certain authoritative pronouncements. And what could be more ordinary than two people becoming married on a Saturday?

When you promise to meet a friend for coffee, you have all the authority you need to create an obligation for yourself and give your friend a new claim against you. If the friend sees you catching a plane the day before your scheduled meeting, she has standing to demand answers: "Where are you going? You'll be back in time, right?" Had you never promised, she'd be a meddling busybody for asking, or have to pry apologetically. But in agreeing to meet her, you changed what claims she can make upon you if you show signs of wavering.

Technically, you could create that sort of obligation and reciprocal claim "for no real reason," even on a whim, just by deciding to. Maybe you didn't have to promise to attend your friend's daughter's birthday party. Perhaps you should have suppressed the sudden feeling of conviviality, which made you accept the invitation. But the fact is you *did* promise, and that itself changes things. Whether we've made a promise for bad or good reasons, we remain bound "by our own word" in any case (within reasonable limits). We're bound, that is to say, by little more than the authority of our own say-so.

At the Fed, the people behind the computers act in an official capacity. The Fed has an unusual role in our lives, which we'll come back to. Yet when its officials credit the private banks, they're acting like the minister or christener: they're exercising authority we've given them for an important social purpose.

That should settle the silly question that comes up whenever someone brings up a worthy spending proposal—"But where will we get the money?" To ask this of the United States, which issues its own money, is as silly as asking a friend for help with an internet connection problem and then wondering, "But where will he get his promises?" The friend has the authority to tell you he'd be happy to come take a look at your internet router. He is the issuer of his promises about his future conduct, just on his say-so. And, just so, the Fed "has dollars" because it has the authority to issue its own promissory notes.

GETTING RICHER OR POORER "OUT OF THIN AIR"

The Fed's actions are supposed to make people richer. Can one be richer in promises? Yes indeed.

"Sure, I'll clean the bathroom," you might tell your spouse or roommate. If she doubts that you, of all people, would actually clean a bathroom, you might add, "No, really, I *promise*." Just saying those magic words, in that moment, is a deed of consequence. Just like that, out of thin air, now you're obligated to clean the bathroom. Your spouse or roommate has a reciprocal claim upon you that you actually do it. If later the bathroom is still as dirty as it was, there's an immediate change in your relationship bookkeeping. As of today, she has an asset in her claim against you, and is a bit richer for it. And in being obliged to clean the bathroom, now you're your bit poorer for your liability. She's richer, you're poorer—just like that, "out of thin air."

She's richer because now you can't just change your mind and give "fair warning." If you try to say, "Hey, turns out I'm not cleaning the bathroom after all, lol," she could rightly retort, "No, you promised!" She can lay claim to your doing the cleaning as though she *already* owned your action. Because, in a way, she does. You gave her the claim against you already. She has it, and she can hold it, *holding you to it*, even holding it against you, until you either do the cleaning or she releases you ("That's okay; it's nothing").

You're slightly poorer for the liability, because the time and energy needed for cleaning won't be available later for other things you might then like to do. And if you never do clean as promised, you may have to make that up to her. So maybe you buy her lunch, which costs money. Or just give her money to pay a housekeeper. Either way, your promise is costing you time or money. As the poet Robert Service put the idea, a promise made is a debt unpaid.

Private banks create most of the money in our economy. They create in it the very act of "lending" it. When you propose to borrow for a home or a car, you make a promise of repayment, signing a promissory note. By the power we invest in banks, and on the solemn authority of a loan officer's decision, your private IOU becomes a public IOU. The officer stamps your loan application, dropping the hand to the table. In that "stamp act," the officer declares you credit worthy, and things are now not as they were before. You gain an asset in the new dollars keystroked into your bank account, which is the bank's liability. And the bank gains an asset in your promise of repayment with interest, which is your liability. And, voila, money—enough real, spendable dollars to buy the car or house. (We explain this "swap" of liabilities fully in Chapter 9.)

All this is regulated by the Federal Reserve System, which has final authority over all private-bank lending activity. As we noted before, the main private banks all have accounts with the Fed, much as we have accounts with them. So as new claims are noted as assets on a private bank's balance sheet, the liabilities are noted on the Fed's balance sheet as well. But then, as we explained in Chapter 2, the Fed also creates money directly. When Fed officials sit down at the computer and mark up sums in bank accounts, the

Fed takes on liabilities and creates new assets—by hitting those buttons. If that's a credit to Bank of America's account held at the Fed, then Bank of America makes the funds available in further "demand deposit" accounts, which people or firms can withdraw or spend from.

So far that's only a change in bookkeeping. The Fed's accounts are marked down, a private bank's account is marked up—as so many numbers are typed into spreadsheets. Yet much as with that fateful promise to clean the bathroom, now things are not as they were. As long as dollar promises are generally credible, the new dollar assets sitting in the bank account can be used to lay claim on real goods and services. In the larger US economy, we all accept them, selling things for them, buying things with them, dividing our labors, and growing richer together. We're talking real money.

PROMISE MANAGEMENT

At some point in a young person's life, a certain dilemma presents itself. On the one hand, standing before an open vista of possible futures, one wouldn't want to "tie oneself down too much" with inflexible or permanent work or personal relationships. One should "see what's out there," "keep the options open," you know, explore far lands, the bohemian parties, or new opportunities for public service.

On the other hand, getting invited to those parties, and hopefully meeting the good musicians and artists around town, will require you to build relationships. That means bearing obligations and debts to others, which do "tie one down," at least temporarily. You won't be able to avoid your relationship with society, and the debts you owe to it, entirely. (Good luck lasting very long on a desert island.) And anyway a life without debt, obligations, and promising is an impoverished life. With too few promises, you'll grow less than you might. So there's a real risk of *undercommitment*, especially early on in what is hoped to be a long life. But then one shouldn't *overcommit*, either. If one can't live up to all of one's promises, they'll lose their value, being "discounted."

So what to do? Well, just figure out what the sustainable rate of promising is and learn to live with that.

This is roughly the Fed's predicament, and its solution. The central bank does much more than issue US dollar promises. It also oversees the entirety of the economy, managing all the dollar promises being made. Which is to say, its job is to steer a course between deflation and unhealthy inflation—meaning, to ensure there aren't appreciably fewer or more dollars' worth of promises out there than can plausibly be redeemed.

There are dangers either way. Undercommitment is a danger, on the one hand—because too few promises relative to a given base of resources will mean too little productive activity that *could* be underway actually is underway. Then people are left unemployed or underemployed, consuming less than they would like to and otherwise could. But overcommitment is a problem as well. Too many promises relative to the same resource base means either that some of the promises won't be redeemed, that prices will rise artificially, or both. That tends to end in distrust, "discounting," and, in the end, underpromising.

The cycles of boom and bust, bubble and crash that so profoundly upend our lives and our politics are just fluctuations between over- and underpromising. It's no way to live. So our central bank tries to maintain stability—to "smoothen the cycle"—by overseeing the quantity, quality, and "directionality" of promising across our economy through time.

Although deflation is as bad as or worse than inflation, nowadays the fear of inflation somehow grabs all the attention. Which is strange, considering that major economies such as Japan and the United States have been struggling against *deflation* for years on end. The Fed has barely hit its low 2 percent target from below. And yet to those who comment on money publicly, "hyperinflation" always seems to be just around the corner. Even the outside *possibility* of inflation, however unlikely, seems as much as anything to encourage the suspicion that there is "nothing to money," unless it is tethered to something else, something *solid, there anyway*, like gold.

Promises can be made too freely, of course. But we know this about ordinary life, and so manage all of our promises, on a daily basis. The Fed's task in managing inflation is vastly more complicated. But, at bottom, it is what we do in managing our daily schedules: making or withholding promises to ensure good faith with our overall commitments.

A friend has plenty of space in her schedule and promises to meet you for a walk. You can take her on her word and presume her good faith, assuming she'll appear as agreed. Just so, we trust a newly issued dollar by default, unless or until there is further cause for concern. A dollar isn't like the Man Who Promised the Impossible in one of Aesop's fables. A man lying on his deathbed promises the gods a lavish offering if they let him live. The man's wife is at his side and asks him, "And where are you going to get the money to pay for all that?" The man says: "Do you think I might get better so that the gods can call me to account?" His promise to repay misfires from the start—which is what's funny about the fable.[3]

Of course, your friend's promise can be trusted only by default. Maybe she "double-booked" you in a "stacked" schedule. She never should have agreed to meet with you, and will probably have to cancel in any case. Once you get the news, seeing that she's the type that overcommits, you might "devalue" any of her promises out of suspicion that she won't follow through. Even then she's not like Aesop's man making incredible promises from the start, however. Maybe she'll still show, after all, despite her stacked schedule. And maybe, even so, you should trust her a bit less. Because her credibility is less about the seriousness she attaches to her promise to you than about that promise's *relationship to her overall commitments* and ability to keep faith with all of them.

The same goes for an economy: Money inflation is all about a pretty complicated *relationship* to the rest of an economy. In a slogan, "INFLATION is a RELATION."

Think of that slogan the next time you see an eye-popping figure for certain spending outlays and some politician acting shocked by it for TV. So what if the Fed issued *1 trillion new dollar promises* this year? What would that mean? Could we conclude *anything* at all about whether there are now "too many dollars," or even the slightest risk of overcommitment? No, we couldn't.

For starters, if the $1 trillion somehow wound up in your personal bank account, and you simply didn't touch it, thinking it some kind of typo, it would have no effect at all on the economy. The money has to be spent, and it matters where the money goes.

So say a trillion new dollar promises are spent. Even that won't be "inflationary" if they summon available resources and create new goods and services. With new goods created, we won't have "too much money chasing too few goods." The extra $1 trillion in new money, per se, implies *nothing* about trends in key prices or the dollar's credibility *automatically*, in and of itself. Not any more than your promise to attend a friend's daughter's birthday party implies that you can't be trusted to actually be there.

You may have read one of those op-eds, penned by a man (these types tend to be men) prone to pompous Man of the World posturing. He'll deride government spending without commensurate tax increases or borrowing as "printing money." Having called up images of worthless paper notes in Zimbabwe or Venezuela, he'll insist that this is "inflationary," automatically so. Then, after snooting about "debasing" the currency, he rests his case, acting as though he's given an argument. He could just as well have claimed to be protecting our "precious bodily fluids," as in *Strangelove*. The careful reader will notice that he's merely pummeled a straw man. Why is inflation supposed to be *even remotely likely*? That was always the question. He simply ignored it.

As we've seen, the Fed has no *automatic* problem when it

makes new promises—no more than you would in promising to meet a friend for coffee on an easy weekend. Inflation, again, is a pretty complicated *relationship* to a larger economy. So, yes, we'd see inflation if money creation were allowed to outrun our productive capacity—because we aren't pulling enough spent money back out of the economy, with taxes or "borrowing" or Fed operations. As we put it before, that's the true "speed limit" on spending money into existence. So an honest argument would have to estimate where inflation trends are headed in light of some package of management actions (targeted taxes, Treasury "borrowing," Fed operations, etc.). We'd need further cause for concern, which should be explained plainly, even in the breezy op-ed pages.

THE FED IS EXTRAORDINARY

Our authority to promise just by deciding to, "by fiat" or "from nowhere," doesn't itself "come from nowhere." We accord it to each other in our relationships. If relationships and reciprocity are the fabric of a good life, we also need the freedom and authority to determine what promises bind us.

As a legally created institution, bound by its mandate, the Fed is as embedded in relationships as we are. It's also an extraordinarily important part of a government that rules over our lives. And it is here that the analogy with a person's promise ends. When the Fed explains its own "dual mandate," it immediately notes the extraordinary importance of its decisions for our livelihoods. Its two objectives, "as mandated by the Congress in the Federal Reserve Act," the Fed website tells us, are to promote:

> (1) maximum employment, which means all Americans that want to work are gainfully employed, and (2) stable prices for the goods and services we all purchase. In this way, the Fed's monetary policy decisions *truly affect the financial lives of all Americans*—not just the spending decisions we make as consumers, but also the spending decisions of

businesses—about what they produce, how many workers they employ, and what investments they make in their
operations.[4]

How can monetary decisions be so consequential? Again, the
dollar has a sturdy source of "credibility": the fear of prison. If
people will reliably get ahold of dollars, offering them back at tax
time in order to lay claim to their freedom, the Fed's role, first
and foremost, is to ensure there's enough dollars for us to avoid
prison. From there, the central bank has a profound influence on
our money and prosperity. The fear of prison being so reliable,
people will keep on using dollars in order to keep paying fines,
fees, and taxes, year after year, buying their freedom with dollars. In which case the Fed can keep on issuing dollar promises,
at will, for any purpose we give it, as long as it doesn't grossly
overpromise—because it holds inflation to a healthy level. We'll
keep chasing dollars to "buy" our freedom, as long as they are
neither way too scarce nor way too plentiful.

This is an extraordinary power, though not by any spooky
magic. If the old sovereigns with unchecked power put on wiz-
ardly robes, while the priests spun tales of divine purpose, the
hope was often just to stave off revolt. In time, people caught on
and began to ask the modern question of political authority: How
could any man's rule over our lives be legitimate, rather than simple tyranny?

We've come a long way, but still have to ask of our government: Given its remarkable powers of money creation, what does
the central bank owe to us? The answer is that it had better issue
money in the service of a larger promise—a "social compact" that
justifies the very threat of prison itself.

Our democracy is in crisis, in part because so many of us do
not have enough money. But then, why not just give people more
money? And if you're somehow still wondering "Where would
we possibly *get the money*?" we'll say it again: the Fed can simply
issue dollar promises to people, directly.

Later we'll explain how the Fed can improve standards of living from the bottom, restoring the middle class with more secure and higher incomes, surer work opportunities, and more (and more flexible) time for family and leisure. For now, our point is just that *we have the money already*. We have all we ever needed: the full faith and credit of the United States. The Fed is *already* monetizing that credit by making promises—that's all a dollar is. And so repairing the social contract really can be as simple as Fed officials hitting the right computer buttons, directing new dollars to the right places. We need only allow the Fed to do that while also managing inflation.[5]

We'll explain later (in Chapter 12) how the Fed can reliably put the brakes on unwanted inflation—as reliably as the brakes in a well-serviced car we trust with our lives on the freeway. But, just for the sake of argument, grant us for the moment that the central bank *can* give us money directly with little or no risk of unhealthy inflation. In that case, ask yourself: Why *shouldn't* the Fed be doing it?

Short of an obviously better option, wouldn't the government owe us that much to us? After fifty years of failed alternatives, decades of broken promises, wouldn't it be obliged to finally make good on the promise of shared prosperity? Doesn't our democracy now depend on it?

CHAPTER 4

DEMOCRACY'S DOLLAR

Suppose a budding despot has somehow become president of the United States. He's angling to line his pockets and keep power in any way possible. If we didn't have a firm principle of central bank "independence" from politics (as we do, thank goodness), the wily fellow could twist a few arms and force the Federal Reserve to give him money to use as he wishes, with zero regard for the public interest. The Fed would simply credit his personal bank account with tremendous sums in dollars, which he'd then spend or transfer to a bank in Panama or the Cayman Islands.

That should strike one as patently illegitimate. But why would it? That is how the kings of yore operated, after all. So what's the problem? Well, in short, it's a betrayal of the dollar as a public money, which was established for our general prosperity.

WHAT'S OWED TO US

Political authority used to be rationalized as the divine right of kings. The guy in sovereign robes was presumed to have total power over his subjects. His subjects, for their part, had absolutely no rights against him. The taxman needn't even pretend that peasant subjects have rights; he'd just flash his sovereign badge, demand whatever coins he's after, and calmly say "Pay up or else."

To our modern ears, this is nothing but a raw exercise of power, and no more justified. It is no better than the mobster's "offer you can't refuse" or the highwayman's "your money or your life." It isn't political legitimacy, or even legitimate coercion.

It was here that Thomas Hobbes's 1651 masterpiece, *Leviathan*, had a fresh notion, which came to define modernity: political authority can instead be founded upon a "social contract" amongst people themselves.

To Hobbes, we make a deal with each other to empower a "sovereign" strongman for our own security. Then we can all rest easy being assured that anyone will think twice before attacking us—because the sovereign will come after him if he does. We can go about the arts, industry, and commodious living, being spared an awful "war of all against all," in which "the life of man is solitary, poore, nasty, brutish, and short."

In that case any rational person would happily pay the sovereign's taxes, in his chosen money. With the sovereign's money in currency, he could pay an army and police forces and establish peace. But then the taxman isn't quite like the mobster or the highwayman, who should just leave people in peace. When the taxman appears at your door, on behalf of the true guarantor of security, you really are liable to pay up as the "price of civilization." That's the social bargain.

But will it be a fair price? There's the rub: There's no telling. You're liable to the sovereign but he owes you nothing in return. In Hobbes's story, we made a deal with each other to empower him for our own security. The strongman himself, he wasn't in on the agreement. So while we have obligations to each other, he has no obligations to us. Once he secures peace, if he taxes us arbitrarily, or twists the banker's arms in order to fund his pleasure palaces, Ferraris, and Lamborghinis, that's entirely up to him; he never owed us anything else. And if he bumbles us into unnecessary wars or cruel policies, that's just our tough luck. The sovereign is under no obligation to us to serve the public interest, not even a little bit.[1]

Is that a sucker's bargain? If "war of all against all" really were the only alternative, one would probably settle for despotic rule and lay low—hoping the trains at least run on time. To Hobbes, that was our forced choice, either anarchy or absolute monarchy, war or peace. Only in passing did Hobbes note the ancient possibility of democracy. Philosopher J. J. Rousseau—who read Hobbes very carefully—ran with that nugget. We aren't forced to choose between anarchy and authoritarianism; there's a further option: If we are already making a social contract to avoid anarchy, why not just decide to rule ourselves, together?

DEMOCRACY ... JUST THE WORST

Democracy was tried in ancient times, unsuccessfully. Few had thought it possible since. Suddenly in the mid-eighteenth century, well over a thousand years later, Rousseau, a runaway from Geneva with no formal education, dreamed anew of a democratic polity. The idea of a new "social contract" caught ablaze.[2] With the help of English philosopher John Locke, who had a big influence on the New Englanders, the French and the American revolutions quickly followed. By the end of the twentieth century—only a few lifetimes later—the world's governments were mostly democratic republics. Not bad for a self-taught kid from Geneva.

Rousseau was inspired by his beloved city—or at least what he'd heard about it in tales of a bygone golden era. The Genevans didn't exactly return his affection; at one point his books were burned and he was stripped of citizenship. (Truth be told, he was probably an asshole, technically speaking, if only for recklessly fathering multiple children and sending them off to an orphanage.[3]) Yet his early life in Geneva helped him imagine something better than what he'd seen of the hierarchies of status, power, and money among elites after he moved to Paris, where he was an outsider and always felt like one. The inevitability of monarchy, the aristocrats' petty status contests, their utter indifference to the plight of everyone else, intellectuals serving their patron masters, the usual rationalizing stories of divine right, stale tradition, or political stability—suddenly none of it looked acceptable any longer.

There would have to be a new "social contract," an understanding as among equals. No one would be ranked, as either superior or inferior, in comparison to others—except maybe in jobs or friendship or marriage, where qualifications do matter. In our basic political union, we'd each be counted a citizen like any other. We'd be ruled by laws and not by any particular men— whether kings, lords, philosophers, or businessmen. And though the law would threaten us with force, we'd all be freer for living under legal obligations (being "forced to be free," as Rousseau put it in one famous zinger). With civil rights and secure property, the citizen would be free to go to a play or a dinner for the evening, feeling assured of not being harassed physically, confident of not having to defend the home from intruders. And we could all better trust agreements amongst ourselves, including all the agreements we make using money, for work, business, and leisure. In deciding our affairs together, we'd each listen, learn, and argue, appealing to common reason, ideally reaching a rough consensus, or at least narrowing our differences. And then, we'd vote—all of us would vote, from a steady sense of obligation. Not everyone would actively consent to the laws or institutions—not even "tacitly," as Locke suggested. But we'd all have a say, deciding upon our laws through a government with no authority beyond its ability to speak for our common reason.

Democracy is said to be the worst form of government—except for all of the alternatives. The old quip, once invoked by Winston Churchill, definitely soothes the nerves after an ugly election. But there's more to be said for the beautiful idea that swept modern history. At its best, it can sound rather wonderful, like a flowing conversation among friends, a sort of civic friendship. Why do we beam with pride on the way home from the voting booth, even in our very flawed political system? For having done our bit in the democratic project—a very good project, which we are fortunate to have. It makes sense to labor for its improvement, and worry in our bones about its corruption. And maybe the city's great cathedral is permanently under construction. What might command our allegiance is not the democracy we have, or might quickly attain, but the ongoing project itself, the experiment in living and deciding together.

A REPUBLIC OF PROMISES

When the American founders took up the project, they got started with public declarations. The Declaration of Independence and the Constitution were promises—declared joint commitments, which everyone was to take for granted, uphold, and rely upon. Being subject to the collective power of the body politic can make anyone nervous. So we'd all have rights against the government, which are the government's obligations to us. The government's rule over us would be only as good, only as legitimate, as its continued faithfulness to the many obligations it owes to all of us.

We said earlier that every dollar comes with the promise of being accepted back in tax payments. That promise is not offered just on the United States' good graces. *It is owed to us.* Anything less is illegitimate, no better than tyranny. We tend to forget about the routine obligations that organize a functioning republic—until they suddenly aren't kept. So it is worth noting some ways a malevolent or careless government can mess with us with respect to our money.

Say the United States declares tomorrow (perhaps in a presidential tweet) that all tax payments shall henceforth be paid in certain rare gems, which only very few could get their hands on. Initially there is public outcry. But after some administrative rulings and deferential court decisions, the IRS only recognizes the gems. If you can't get your hands on them by tax time, well, that's tough luck for you—you haven't paid your taxes. The police can and will be instructed to come after you.

Or suppose, as in our earlier example, that IRS officials simply refuse your dollar check, arbitrarily. Or maybe officials cashed the check and, feeling lethargic, never quite got around to crediting the sum to your government account. Tough luck for you—you're still subject to incarceration for not having made payment.

Officials couldn't do this too often; people would stop using dollars and simply revolt. But the dollar would be fine if the police single out only a few dissidents or undesirables who have the wrong skin color. Messing with them may send a clear message to dissenters. Officials can simply spin the events as "minor accounting errors" or discount them as "fake news."

Or maybe officials at the IRS accept your dollars, but then some judge garnishes your wages or demands your arrest anyway, after you've paid what you owe, for no further offense. The court-ordered officers are there at your front door. And can you prove you've paid? What if they have a doctored IRS computer printout that says (incorrectly) that you didn't? And what if, after they've put you in jail, the IRS officials are busy, and so not inclined to clarify the matter?

This is all of course a rank and unjustifiable exercise of the state's power over people's lives. But real governments do such things. The United States, for its part, is still something of a working republic, thank goodness. But to keep its basic legitimacy, it must keep on recognizing and fulfilling its many obligations to us. That is all that separates the United States from an authoritarian state with the mere pretenses of "democracy," such as Russia, Hungary, or Venezuela.

So while the United States still has the right to demand tax payments in dollars, it equally must make those dollars available, recognize timely tax payments in dollars, and, once the taxman cometh, leave us alone. Anything less would violate what the government owes to us in our most basic liberties—the very thing the French and the American revolutionaries fought for so fiercely.

And a democratic republic isn't just about civil and political rights. It's also about providing its citizens with a decent life—

"life, liberty, and the pursuit of happiness"—and generating enough money to pay for it. Money is not just another value, or a mere instrument to something else of value. It's a crucial public institution. Defined by our government—along with its central bank and treasury—the dollar is bound up with what we promise each other in business, work, many of our life choices, and the promise of shared prosperity. Our money is in on our social contract, and a big part of why we might all keep faith in our union.[4]

THE GOLDEN GOOD OL' YEARS

When Rousseau imagined a modern republican democracy, it was but a dream of a possible future. To many of us, it's a nostalgic image of what America was not too long ago, during the two or so decades after the Second World War.

In those "golden" years, millions had risen into the middle class from poverty because of New Deal and wartime spending. Some still had more money than others, of course; America never promised material equality. But the size of the gap between rich and poor was low compared to the earlier Gilded Age—and to the new Gilded Age we've entered since. In those days President John F. Kennedy could say—with a good measure of public trust—that inequality brought a "rising tide" of growth that "lifts all boats," yacht and dinghy alike, to everyone's steady benefit.

Eventually racial tensions, Richard Nixon's criminality, and the Vietnam War exploded the illusion. But still, the dream of postwar America is rather wonderful, is it not? It's a good dream: harmonious cooperation in good faith, for nearly everyone's mutual benefit, with assurance of fair treatment felt all around. What's not to like?

Rousseau grew up on similar stories about the golden good ol' days in Geneva. They got him dreaming of democracy for the modern age, and the world has never been the same since.

THE DOLLAR "SOCIALIZED"

What made America's golden age possible? Money, the US dollar. The "almighty dollar" is like God in at least one respect: many of us assume it was always there, immutable from the start. The fact is, though, it took a long time to ascend to its almighty status, by the painstaking labors of democracy.

At the country's founding, the British pound was quickly rejected. The "dollar" and its symbol $ was chosen as an official unit of account. But as we explain more fully in Chapter 8, the dollar would have to wait almost a century to become a truly national currency. In the nineteenth century, private banks each issued their own dollar notes. It was only after a protracted period of trial and error, repeated crises, and much suffering, that elected legislators "nationalized" money issuance in the early 1860s. That didn't quite work, either. So in 1913 they finally just "socialized" the dollar in a public-private partnership. A new central bank, the Federal Reserve System, would now issue the dollar and embody the United States' "full faith and credit." The "almighty dollar" came into adulthood, not only by a democratic process, but also for a democratic purpose: shared prosperity in a more stable economy.

Even in these golden years of American capitalism, the "free market" was never fully trusted. The country made sure to share the growing economic pie around. Chancellor Otto von Bismarck had already established social insurance in Germany—partly in order to fend off hardcore socialism. In the decades before the war, the United States had followed suit, establishing social insurance for unemployment and eventual retirement with health care. Workers began to have "cradle-to-grave" relationships with firms. Unions were strong and steadily nudged up wages and benefits. With standards of living rising and bright prospects, the implicit "social contract" felt like a bargain.

But it was a bargain you could believe in only because the US economy had found new stability. The great promise of American democracy was always prosperity, shared widely. And the dollar, issued and managed by the Fed, made that possible.

Later in the 1980s, the Prime Minister of England, Margaret Thatcher, seemed to have forgotten her history. "There is no such thing as public money; there is only taxpayer money," she said. Perhaps she never looked carefully at the pound note, which bears an image of Queen Elizabeth. The dollars in your pocket are of course yours, your private property. But the dollar, itself, is indeed a "public money." The dollar is ours—our public institution. It's owned by all citizens and established by elected representatives for our shared prosperity. Like it or not, that much "socialism" is baked into American (and English) capitalism like leaven in the bread you thought you were buying on the free market.

BACKSLIDING

Today, "prosperity" for most of us is always just over the horizon. Wages and salaries have stagnated for most people now for almost fifty years since the late 1970s—the entirety of many people's working years. Millions who "worked hard and played by the rules," believing the postwar era promises, never did see the money.

America is still the richest country in human history. Although we now often hear about rising inequality, most of us don't quite realize how rich the richest have become. Imagine getting a *monthly* paycheck of $200,000, which means $50,000 each and every week. That sounds impossibly extravagant, and yet it comes to just $2.4 million per year, a rather modest income among today's superrich.

At this point 90 percent of the country's total wealth is held by the richest 20 percent of families. The richest one percent of the population alone holds 40 percent of it. And everyone else, the bottom 60 percent, holds a mere one percent. And, no, the rich mostly aren't heroic entrepreneurs, whether lucky or deserving.

Sixty percent of total private wealth held in the United States was simply inherited.[5]

People do of course get the general picture. One can understand why many working people have lost confidence, become contemptuous, and voted for disruption—in hopes of change, or at least of breaking things. One can see why, amidst rising distrust, the paranoid style of politics would be back in fashion.

The twentieth century gave us the rise of democracy. The twenty-first century has us sliding back into authoritarianism. While trust has been in decline for decades, the global financial meltdown of 2008 brought a complete collapse of confidence. Authoritarians are feasting on the unravelling—in Russia, Poland, Austria, Hungary, Turkey, Venezuela, Brazil, the Philippines, and even the United States of America.

Not that democracy is being openly rejected, exactly. It's being hollowed out, eroded from within.[6] The new authoritarians even pay homage to Rousseau's vision. Like the Jacobins in revolutionary France, they claim to speak for "the people" while shredding the very norms and institutions that give the phrase real meaning.[7]

Money was always how despots gained and kept power—and often why they often lost hold of it. Monarchs and dictators would levy taxes to be paid only in their chosen money. Instead of investing in the public, they'd issue money to pay off the generals and other key supporters, poach talent from the rebels, divide the opposition, and of course line their own pockets. It's a delicate game, keeping new rivals for power at bay.[8] That only gets easier if you've co-opted the bankers and can issue money at will.

Similar methods still work in today's kleptocracies. Rulers seize control of the country's oil, gas, diamonds, or other common resources, along with its banking system.[9] That's a big part of why authoritarian states such as Russia or Saudi Arabia have survived the rise of democracy over the previous century—and why they are now subverting the major democracies. Russia, a country condemned by the "resource curse" in oil to remain underdeveloped in other sectors, can't count on getting ahead by robust economic development. Its leaders can't use that promise to hold on to their essential supporters, beyond measures of intimidation. So, instead, they've sown dissent and corruption in liberal democracies abroad, if only to look less bad by comparison.

It's hard to say exactly where or when things went wrong for America and many other Western democracies. It was apparently some mix of globalization, technological change, hollowed-out communities, deregulation, declining unions, elite indifference, predatory self-dealing, institutional capture, political opportunism, bogus economic ideology, media capitalism, and political polarization, to name just a few causes. Now, in reaction to these trends, even in the supposed land of liberty, that alleged bastion of republicanism, millions have been wooed by the authoritarian's siren song. Many are honestly asking themselves: What's so bad about authoritarianism anyway—as long as your guy, or your tribe, holds power? The old philosophical question has become as urgent as ever: Is a democratic republic really necessary? And if so, can money help preserve it?

CAN WE RESTORE FAITH?

Among those in today's electorate who bother to vote, many—maybe most—vote with very little information. People also tend to be easily distracted, too trusting of the familiar, and prone to rationalize away inconvenient facts and focus on confirming evidence.[10] With all the ruthlessness, tribalism, fevered antagonism, naked contempt, petty childish grievance, schoolyard acts of domination, and performative cruelty, one needn't be a cynic to honestly wonder about the very possibility of republican democracy, and whether enough of us are fit for it.

How was democracy ever supposed to last in the first place? The philosopher John Dewey suggested education: "Democracy has to be born anew every generation, and education is its midwife."[11] Here he echoed Rousseau's cautiously optimistic view of human nature. We can be either vicious or sociable, according to how we are treated. If most of us aren't exactly angels, and probably can't be made into them—especially not as adults—society should start early, giving everyone a decent upbringing, helping us accept responsibility, manage temptation, soothe unsociable feelings, listen to and respect others, and play fair. If democracy is to last, from one generation to the next, weathering the shocks and setbacks, it is because it manages to generate its own support from within.[12]

But of course the youth need more than schooling. They also need hope for a nice future, which requires money. Rousseau mainly lamented the preoccupation with money in his own time: "What will become of virtue when people must enrich themselves at any price? Ancient politics talked incessantly about morality and virtue; our politicians talk only about business and money."[13] It's a fair point about greed and shallow obsessions with luxury. And we definitely need a modicum of morality and virtue. But lasting democracy also depends on who has what money. Rousseau became famous for his vivid depiction of a collapsing democracy. A spiteful, hateful politics of status, property, and business sets the stage for a despot's rise to power.[14] That seems startlingly prescient now. Yet what Rousseau never quite saw is how a better sort of politics of money and business, geared for shared prosperity, could also stabilize democracy.[15] It actually happened once, in postwar America. So it can happen again.

To the cynic, the postwar decades were an accident of history, a confluence of circumstances that are unlikely to be repeated. The postwar promises were always going to be broken. "Backsliding" into authoritarianism was inevitable. To an awful lot of us, those who are different from us do not deserve to be accepted as equals, with equal rights and influence.

Is this just human nature, if we are realistic about what people are like? The "authoritarian personality," as psychologists call it, readily organizes people by hierarchy, first and foremost by in-group and out-group, as us and them. That shapes racism or sexism, but goes well beyond it, and in some cases helps explain it (racism is sometimes more accurately nativism). Ranking people by their relative status, given their talent, beauty, wit, power, wealth, race, gender, or sheer similarity to ourselves, has always been common, in and beyond the United States. No surprise it can be activated by blood-sport politics in high-stakes electoral contests.

We all rank people in hierarchies in sports, at work, or in other specific settings. Nearly all of us operate with egalitarian feelings as well, in relationships such as friendship or business partnerships. So the question is how far our hierarchical instincts can be contained. Can they be muted only in close, personal relations, and then only temporarily? If so, a large democracy founded upon a mutual affirmation of our equality will not last.

This was Rousseau's original problem. What explains the ills of civilization? The destructive ways we compare ourselves to each other, competing for status as superior or inferior.[16] We are naturally capable of pity and compassion. We can understand the reality of others' lives and occasionally even empathize with them. And yet, acutely self-aware, we compare ourselves to them, and love or hate ourselves in light of how we think we appear in their eyes (what Rousseau called "amour propre"). Feeling inferior or superior, we become vicious—conceited, selfish, hateful, or cruel. Not exactly for its own sake. But in order to prove our status or power, so that we can love ourselves.

When the Declaration of Independence called us "created equal," the hope was to send a message. As self-conscious creatures, we constantly adjust the image of ourselves we catch in the gaze of others, or merely project on to them. In the flattering light of equal citizenship, we find it easier to love ourselves and take pride in our station, without having to put others above or below us. We can more readily acknowledge the equality of others, in part for being assured that, in society's estimation, each is counted as an equal, a citizen. And because we all need constant reassurance, even a well-run republic will have to reaffirm our equal standing, year after year, election after election, in all public business and speech.

In that case, while America never promised equality of power or of money, the disparity we now all see in everyday life and business should never have been allowed to grow so large or conspicuous as to call anyone's status as an equal into serious question. With the size of the gap between the rich and everyone else rising to and beyond Gilded Age heights, the economy is sending a conflicting message. If we are all "equals" officially, "some are more equal than others," as the pigs in George Orwell's *Animal Farm* said. The notion of our "equality" before the law and polity has begun to feel like an absurd fiction. Accordingly, the sense that one is presumed to be inferior can cause one to want to break things, even when nothing good will come of it. "Blind rage" needn't be baseless rage or unjustified rage; there can be good reasons for it.

Indeed there are plenty of reasons to worry about inequality, even if you aren't worried at all about material equality per se. When the rich command a very large share of society's resources, this can slow economic growth, or even fuel instability, leaving most people worse off that they could otherwise be. The rich among us may benefit more from the public services—street repair, sanitation, and schools—to which everyone is entitled. For those with less, the disparity may become a stigma, because they are too poor to appear in public without shame, humiliation, or a full sense of self-respect. And if the idea of "equality of opportunity" is supposed to legitimate our very different fortunes, that notion becomes a sham when a person's chances in life are determined mainly by what family or class he or she happens to be born into rather than his or her own free choices and efforts (which are also shaped by fortunate or unfortunate upbringing). Finally, the well-to-do may have too much control over the lives of others, not only in private dealings, but in politics as well. They may buy influence over politicians, veto popular laws or measures, or have too much influence over public deliberation, for instance, by media ownership.[17]

Yet shouldn't one just shrug it all off as the sad way of the world, you know, just focus on what's in your power, even if that's just your attitude, like a good Stoic? Was it not ever thus? The rich "winners" of the capitalist money game will keep running ahead, often breaking laws but evading accountability. As the ancient historian Thucydides put it, "The strong do as they will; the weak suffer as they must." Isn't comparing yourself to the winners just "envy," or worse—what philosopher Friedrich Nietzsche, influenced by Rousseau, called "ressentiment"? For, feeling inferior, one finds someone else to blame—if only an imagined scapegoat. That helps soothe the pain.

But if we are expecting people to cooperate more or less in good faith with a political and economic system, we need to do more than merely soothe the pain of resentful compliance. As Rousseau would agree, the real question is how we might address our basic need to be seen and treated as an equal. And we could do that, for instance, by giving people a fairer shake.

SURELY SHARED PROSPERITY WOULD HELP

When postwar Americans had a general sense of shared material prosperity, this sent a clear public message of everyone's equal standing. With a sense of comity and confidence, people could more easily believe they weren't fundamentally in competition with each other. Sure, others might do a bit better than you, but you or your kin could still do better or as well yourselves. To feel recognized as an equal, you wouldn't need to resent the accomplishments of others, finding ways to "own," dominate, or humiliate them, or supporting people who do. You wouldn't need to assert your superiority in order reassure yourself of your worth.

The postwar decades were far more racist and sexist than today. What's happened recently, it seems, is that those who once felt comfortably in charge saw their status slipping. In part due to changing demographics, this brought a new sense of political competition, which required staying ahead of the perceived up-and-comers. Was the cause "racism" or "economic anxiety"? The answer is both.

Yes, it's about perceived power or authority along racial or perhaps nativist lines in politics and culture, which isn't essentially about money. Yet broken economic promises and increasing competition, not to mention the sight of communities in economic decay, only exacerbates the competition for power and its symbolism. And whether it is power or money, what's ultimately at stake is status.

Now it's all too easy for political entrepreneurs in power or on cable TV or social media to enlist a perceived hierarchy of gender, tribe, or race and inflame a wounded sense of grievance. Many white Americans evidently love the idea of being preserved in greatness—or at least of cultural and political prominence and felt superiority. But if so many Americans seem to feel this way, so strongly, can we hope for a greater acceptance of our fundamental equality, the most basic principle of republican democracy?

We can, and should. Rousseau's big idea was that human nature is neither fixed nor fluid. If we have a latent disposition to hierarchy or tribalism, it must be activated by our circumstances. And so it can be deactivated as well. Our politics are malleable. Psychologists easily shift them in surveys. When people are "primed" before they answer questions about their political preferences, "liberals" become "conservatives" and "conservatives" become "liberals," all rather quickly. The big factor is simply whether they feel fear. A cough in the room makes people trend "conservative." Imagining being a superhero who cannot be harmed makes them trend "liberal."[18] The constant priming we receive from our families, friends, tribes, parties, and media consumption steers us to more or to less democratic ways of thinking. Our cultures are being deeply divided, quite deliberately, by those who profit from it. Political entrepreneurs do it for money, power, status, and the sheer fun of it. As ordinary folk, we mainly go with the cultural flow. We adapt to our different communities of trust.[19]

If the decline of trust has exposed the worst in our natures, the cause of distrust was partly about money—about not having enough it, or not as much as promised, whether for oneself or in one's collapsing community. Which suggests a bold if obvious solution: New money would help restore faith. Money is a powerful symbol of status in our culture—part of our cultural "score-keeping" as we put it in Chapter 11. Ensuring that people have more of it would affirm everyone's standing as an equal citizen, easing the strains of status competition, rebuilding communities, and restoring a bit of hope. Those who feel inferior would find reassurance. And those now nervous about their slipping superiority would have a softer landing as reality asserts itself.

Where we can better advance shared prosperity though monetary policy, we must. But in a time of resurgent paranoia, we'll have to bootstrap our way up to a new set of promises that engender new trust. Since money is a kind of promise, we can make it at will, just by deciding to. In a real sense, the decision is up to us. But it will take enough of us being persuaded, and for that to happen we'll need a clearer picture of what money really is and how our economy really works.

THE MONEY CONTRACT

We learn about money through mixed messages—of silver coins, gold bullion, paper currency notes. It's all pretty confusing, so one can feel unable to grasp how monetary policy could be put to new uses—short of "printing money" in reckless excess. The deepest obstacles to progress are not technical; they are *philosophical*. Just to comprehend our real options, we need to dig deeper into history, philosophy, and economics and clear our heads.

Part II looks further back in history. It shows that money was always a kind of promise. Orthodox economists, who have never quite understood this, fail to see why money matters as a cause of the wealth of nations, and so fail to see how monetary policy could promise to help restore shared prosperity in the future. Once we have a better sense of money's nature and importance, we'll return to modern banking in Part III. Then we can fully appreciate what our central bank makes us capable of.

CHAPTER 5

A VERY (VERY) BRIEF HISTORY
OF FINANCE—I.E., CIVILIZATION

We often think of tangible items when we cast our minds back to the history of money. Popular histories only encourage this; in all the colorful stories of coinage, silver, and gold, it can seem that money *used* to be something you could hold in your hand. Our new age of "fiat money" can seem fishy, airy, or less trustworthy by comparison.

This shows how confused we are about money and its history. Money never was mere coinage, gold, silver, currency, or indeed anything you can touch. It has always been a certain credit-and-debt relationship, a way *we account for what we owe each other* in human relationships, as we suggested in Chapter 1. The history of money is partly a history of confusion about money. So we should review a few high points, to get the story straight.

"BABYLONIAN MADNESS"

In the beginning was the promise, along with the trust that it pre-supposed. It was the earliest form of "credit," which comes from the Latin *credere*, meaning "to believe." This trust or faith alone, even without paper (perhaps before any notion of it), moved life along in the cradle of civilization.

Eve wanted the garden swept. Adam said he'd get around to

it, and Eve believed him. He gave her his word and, in effect, an IOU—he now owed her the sweeping. She banked on it, trusting him to appreciate his obligation to do as he promised. And if he wasn't getting around to it, she could lay claim to it later: "When *are* you going to do it? I mean, come on, you did promise!"

And so humanity discovered finance. What is "finance"? Just the means by which people who at the moment lack something necessary for an activity come to secure access to it, temporarily, from those who have resources.

Adam liked to sweep with Eve's favorite whisk. So he borrowed it, in exchange for his promise to put it back later, right where he found it. Which is to say, Adam borrowed *on credit*, on the strength of a promise. He "repaid" his debt, fulfilling his promissory obligation, when he returned it to the place Eve normally keeps it.

Eventually, complex civilizations, with complex divisions of labor, were up and running. In ancient Mesopotamia, sticks were broken into fragments—"tally sticks"—to represent debtor and creditor in verifying the existence of a debt obligation. Later on, clay bars proved to be a sturdier medium. But what mattered wasn't the bars or the sticks: it was who owed what to whom in the accounting.

What are debt and credit, then? Two sides of the same coin, so to speak. In 1913, A. Mitchell Innes explained economic "credit" in plain terms:

> It is simply the correlative of debt. What A owes to B is A's debt to B and B's credit on A. A is B's debtor and B is A's creditor. The words "credit" and "debt" express a legal relationship between two parties, and they express the same legal relationship seen from two opposite sides. A will speak of this relationship as a debt, while B will speak of it as a credit.[1]

But of course outstanding debts have to be *settled*, at some point. Both creditor and debtor have to agree that payment has been rendered. So, Innes suggested, people would go to the religious festivals or fairs. Not to "truck, barter, and exchange," as Adam Smith would say, but to *settle* or *clear debts* at a common "clearinghouse." If the baker owed the butcher, but had to pay the candlestick maker because the butcher owed her . . . well, you can see this is already getting complicated enough that it might be best to meet at the fair and settle things in person. Or just turn the bookkeeping over to an honest banker. The banker is just the person they ask to do the accounting.

And what if a debtor can't make payment, and can't get further credit, after a bad growing season? Well, these may have been the very festivals where Friedrich Nietzsche says debtors were made to "pay" by suffering a flogging or other cruel treatment. The spectacle of the debtor's humiliation and the creditor's pleasurable feeling of superiority were counted as "compensation" and payment of the debt.[2] It took a while for bankruptcy law to give debtors another way out. In time judges would order settlement in the public money. What we now think of as crass "cash compensation" was actually a big advance in humane civilization.

Centuries after tally sticks, clay, and early forms of metallic coin, J. M. Keynes read Innes, but worried that Innes hadn't documented his historical examples, which included the Hammurabi code and the Mesopotamian system of accounting. So Keynes studied the matter for himself. After emerging from a bewildered state of "Babylonian madness," as he called it, Keynes decided that Innes was right.[3] Money is a credit-and debt-relationship. Keynes's followers even use the term "credit-money" instead of "money." With that insight, Keynes, the foremost economist of his day, laid the foundations for post-Depression economic policy and the postwar global economy.

And there you have it, a very, very brief history of money.

It's a pretty good history if only because it leaves out coinage, gold, silver, or other precious metals, certificates, or paper currency. But then how do those tangible items figure into the story of money? The answer is: they are just accounting devices, ways of representing credits and debts, which is to say, tokens of promises.

To see how, let's fill out the story further.

ANCIENT MONEY

Returning to the ancient Near East, we find promissory IOUs being developed into what we would call "claim checks." Claim check in hand, you could prove that you'd met certain obligations—for instance, to make your grain contribution. Much as in the biblical story of the young Joseph, ancient societies commonly stored grains in "fat years" so as to be well provisioned for "lean years." Dependent on agriculture, but subject to the whims of nature, communities were wise enough not to leave grain storage to the wisdom of individuals alone.

Much as with today's insurance for old age and the premiums paid into Social Security, growers were required to make "grain deposits" into a community pool. When you "deposited" your grain per this requirement, the local authority who received your deposit (usually a religious authority) gave you a token, a signal that you'd made it. The tokens were like the hand stamps we receive today upon entering a nightclub. It shows the bouncer at the door that you've paid the fee for entry should you step out and then return.

In time, these early tokens began to circulate as currencies. One can see why they would. Maybe your neighbor has very good land that produces great crop yields. Your land is less good, but you are a very good shoemaker or toolmaker. You neighbor has a much easier time producing grain, while you have an easier time making good tools and shoes. So you both benefit from letting your neighbor "deposit" extra grain at the community grain-store. He can collect extra "receipts" for having done so, and then give you those extra receipts in return for your making tools or shoes for her. You do what you're best at, she does what she's best at, and both of you produce more overall.

Thus grain "receipts" became money, which improved over-all productivity. We see much the same cooperation today in the market for "tradable pollution permits" among firms that run factories, or what's often called "cap-and-trade." This may seem novel, but, in fact, money in IOUs, represented by physical tokens—receipts, claim checks, permits—has always improved economic activity when such systems have been well managed.

The obligations and receipts of the ancient world had every-thing to do with promising. Members of a society (or their deity) would recognize the authority of a "governmental" agent (or priest) to requisition grain during fat years for provisioning during lean years. And that authority, for its part, would in turn recognize "grain receipts" as proof positive that the members of society had met their grain depository obligations, discharging their obligations to the community. The authority had an implicit commitment to recognize those receipts as verification. Because, otherwise, how could people trust it? Millennia before philoso-phers started talking about "social contracts," there had to be an unspoken promise, perhaps conveyed in a shroud of religious symbolism.

With such a commitment in place, explicitly or implicitly, the "receipt" acquires the characteristics of a claim. And not just a claim to having the authority recognize that one has indeed "paid one's taxes." Once those lean years commence, it would also become a claim to procure grain from the grain-store—in order, for instance, to make bread and eat. And then, once "tax receipts" become "claim checks" in this sense, it is only a matter of time before they begin to circulate as currency. Everyone needs bread, and so needs to be able to claim some share of it. So every-one accepts those claims as payment, not just for grain, but tools, shoes, and other things too. And so the claim checks gain currency and come to represent "basic money," as we defined it in Chapter 1.

The "claim checks" were currency, and they stood for money. They still weren't money itself. What stood for money changed over time. The Mesopotamians moved from wooden "tally sticks" to clay tokens. And the promissory claim took on new and different representations as civilization advanced throughout the Mediterranean region and across the Eurasian continent through Anatolia, Persia, India, and China, among other places. But the money itself was the claim, the promissory IOU, all along. The grain "claim checks" showed that, in depositing your grain quota, you'd discharged your obligation. The fact of the discharge was what ultimately mattered. How you proved it was in an important sense incidental.

This is precisely why it will be possible, in the future, for central banks to issue cryptocurrencies in lieu of paper currencies. The medium, again, is simply a matter of convenience and technical feasibility; what is essential is the "message"—the debt and credit information—that the medium conveys.

HOW TO DO THINGS WITH STAMPS

The history of confusion about money perhaps begins with coins in "precious metals," which became particularly widespread for a while. To this day many think of gold, silver, platinum, and other metals as somehow "inherently" precious, and thus "natural" stores of monetary value. The truth is the reverse. These metals become "precious" in part because they came to be used widely as material representations of money claims. For a while, they were the best media, the "high tech" of "claim information" for the day.

And what was so special about these metals? Their relative malleability and durability. A soft metal could be easily stamped with official images and code words, and would resist corrosion. Perhaps it was now Tarquin or Caesar in Rome, rather than the pharaoh or high priest in Egypt, who was requisitioning taxes from the citizenry. But if the climate wasn't dry enough to rely upon clay tokens not to disintegrate, it was natural to seek some durable substance into which Tarquin's or Caesar's image could be stamped when it came to issuing "receipts" to taxpayers who'd paid their taxes. Plus, rulers have often enjoyed having their name and image placed flashily upon things people use and see.

And so "coins," as they came to be called, began to circulate as a stand-in for money. And soon after coins began circulating, the counterfeiting of such coins—by stamping fake images of Caesar or whomever on them—became a capital crime. After all, if the coin of the realm couldn't be trusted because too many good copies were in circulation, the reliability and hence utility of money itself would be undermined.

The stamps were a stamp of authorization, the public record of a deed that vouched for claims and obligations. It is not unlike what banks still do today in giving you a home or a car loan. At one point there is a stamp of approval, sealed in an act of stamping and a notary's signature for public verification. In that moment, they declare you creditworthy, and a remarkable "swap" happens: your personal IOU (your promise to repay the loan) and signed promissory note becomes a public liability—something you can then spend at the car dealer. (We explain how today's central banks authorize this in Chapter 9.)

SEIGNORAGE

This basic truth about authorization did not change with the evolution of who was doing the authorizing. With the collapse of the Roman Empire in the first millennium c.e., Europe fell into a period of domination by warlords. Descendants of Roman equestrian soldiers known as "knights," who later came to be known simply as "lords," owned the most advanced weapons of the time. And they came to own large landed estates or "manors," which they could defend with those weapons.

To those willing to work their lands and make them productive, the lords could offer protection and some semblance of social order. And so "peasants" worked the manorial lands for their lords. The lords would in turn make crop requisitions upon them—not unlike those made by priests, monarchs, and emperors in earlier ages. They issued tokens as receipts.

The economy of a manor would often become as developed as the economies of the ancient world before. A lord, lady, and family needed more than just simple foodstuffs. They needed clothing, weapons, horses, and many of the finer things in life too. Their peasants produced these things for them—manors had not only farmers, but also weavers, cobblers, metalsmiths, and more. And so manors developed fungible moneys, along with "coins of the realm" with wide currency between different manors. Just as in the ancient world, these currencies came to be understood as fulfilling obligations: they came to embody promises.

It's thanks to this period that we have our money-word "seignorage." The Old French word for "lord" is *seignior*. (The same Latin root was the basis for the modern French, Italian, Portuguese, and Spanish words for "mister"—itself derived from the English word "master.") The requisition receipts—i.e., currencies—issued by seigniors served as universally usable moneys upon their manors. So seigniors could issue such moneys not only to serve as receipts, but also to enable them to purchase things made on their manors in excess of what was requisitioned. They could issue in order to spend, in what became known as "seignorage."

Even today, the United States grows ever richer in just this way. When the Fed earns returns on the transactions it conducts to control the money supply, we call those returns "seignorage." And in the world economy, the United States enjoys those same advantages thanks to the dollar's status as de facto global reserve currency. As we'll explain in Chapter 6, other governments hold on to dollars and other dollar-denominated financial instruments such as Treasurys as "safe" assets, held in reserve for rainy-day use. And they're willing to pay for the service, giving the United States what 1960s French finance minister Valéry Giscard d'Estaing called an "exorbitant privilege."

BREAKING THE BANK

Later in the Middle Ages, metalsmiths began to offer storage services to owners of precious metal coins and bullion. They'd issue "claim checks" to the "depositors." These begin circulating as money claims in their own right, at first in standardized denominations—one ducat, five ducats, ten ducats, etc. By the late eighteenth and early nineteenth century, you could "write out your own amount," or write "cheques" much like the paper checks we write out today. Though we don't do it as often, the checks themselves could be endorsed and then circulate like currencies.

All through the medieval period, small towns and then cities emerged under manorial protection. Manorial economies grew more complex, with a more specialized division of labor. The first towns, with workers on diverse tasks toiling in close proximity, became "factories" for the many different products the manors needed. (The term derives from the Latin *facere*, meaning "to do" or "to make.") And once you have people in such concentrations, they steadily begin to exchange their products among themselves, in addition to trading them to the lords in exchange for protection. And so the lord's receipts—the money-tokens issued by the lord—became the currency of the village, town, and then city as well. Once again, money, productivity growth, and sovereign or quasi-sovereign promising were interconnected.

As the towns and cities grew very large, the volume of intra-town transactions began to exceed those of manor-town transactions. People were selling and buying many products and services to and from one another, and of course needed to pay each other. But manorial coins were heavy and hard to lug around. So relying on metals such as gold or silver alone became inconvenient. Plus, lugging big bags of gold around made you a target for brigands and footpads. So a new practice developed: the practice of using paper.

Italy had been the site of the Roman Empire, at its core. It had never fallen as far behind as had peripheral Europe, population-wise or technology-wise, in the Middle Ages. And perhaps also because its climate was so good, its cities were among the first to emerge from the so-called "Dark Ages" of the medieval warlord period. They grew more quickly than others and developed more complex economies more quickly as well.

In time, people with surpluses of metal coins began to avail themselves of a new service offered by metalsmiths. The metalsmiths had strong safes in which to store their own metals. So they were able to take others' coins "for safekeeping" in return for a fee. And thus was born what is known to this day among English-speaking lawyers as "bailment."

The one who "deposited" her metal with the metalsmith of course wanted proof that she'd made the deposit. So she demanded and "received" a "receipt." The receipt would need to be durable but also lightweight. In time, it was fibrous paper, or materials somewhere between paper and cloth, that proved most economical. The Italian metalsmiths seem to have got the idea from China, to which certain enterprising Italians in the late medieval period traveled. By Europe's late medieval period, China had already developed an advanced civilization and economy—on which Marco Polo famously reported in the thirteenth century after extensive travels.

Our word "bank" derives from this period. Metalsmiths in medieval Italy did their work upon benches, as many traditional craftspeople still do. The Old Italian word for "bench" is *banca*, which is of course cognate with the English word "bank." This all stems from the fact that the issuance of receipts for stored metal eventually became much more profitable for the *banca* occupiers than metalsmithing itself.

It's not hard to see why. Suppose you're a metalsmith and your "receipts" begin circulating widely as currency, because they are sufficiently trusted. It doesn't require a stroke of genius to realize that you yourself can now just issue currency when you want to buy things, rather than earning it by metalsmithing. The shoe-maker or baker will take your "receipts" as money, since they'll assume they can spend it somewhere else. So you can simply pay them for bread or shoes in "receipts." And that's not all. You can also profit in making loans to others by issuing your currency to them. You just make them pay you more when they pay you back—charging "interest." Thus currency issuing and lending became the primary occupation of many of these late medieval metalsmiths. *Banche* became what we now call "banks" rather than metalsmiths' benches.

We have another word from this era—a word that signals an inherent danger in the banker business model just described. The word "bankrupt" derives from the Italian and Latin phrase *banca rupta*, meaning "broken bench." Use of the Latin root "rupt"— the same concept that we find in the English words "disrupt" and "rupture"—stems from city officials' practice of ceremonially breaking the benches of bankers who ended up not being able to "pay" when their depository obligations came due.

And what would break the bank? Well, if the banker issued receipts that began circulating as currency, she could earn sei-gnorage just as the manor lords did when they issued their coins. She could either spend her own notes, or lend them out at inter-est. And she could issue lots and lots of such notes—far in excess of the gold that she had in her safe to hand over should people come to her door all at once with receipts. As long as they didn't, she was golden. But it's a rather tempting situation, being able to enrich oneself almost at will. Many bankers really like money and are not especially circumspect. So they push it, wittingly or unwittingly, "going for broke."

RESERVES—AND NOT HOLDING ENOUGH BACK

By itself, the ability to issue notes in excess of what they represent is harmless—at least up to a point. Indeed, it is helpful to a society.

For, up to a point, the availability of more currency in circulation enables far more transacting—and hence far more promising and producing—than would otherwise be possible. Money enables much more productive activity than can occur without money.

But only "up to a point." What point? Precise answers are the subject of actuarial science, but we can often estimate. Suppose our banker—let's call her "Caterina"—starts by issuing one paper receipt per gold coin she holds in the vault. She then notices that, on any given day, only one-tenth of those receipts at most are actually brought in to exchange for gold. Then an idea might come to her: Why not issue ten or just under ten paper receipts for each gold coin in the vault? Then she could worry less about not being able to pay out—and hence going "bankrupt." And she'll increase her local money supply tenfold. She'll earn a great deal of seignorage, and her local economy will produce and grow much faster than it otherwise would.

Perhaps not surprisingly, there came to be many Caterinas in late medieval Italy. In time, bankers spread across Europe and all over the world. Their practice came to be known as "fractional reserve banking," so called because only a fraction of the total issuance is held back "in reserve"—"in the vault," so to speak. That's where we get the word "reserve" in our central bank's name, "Federal Reserve System." Only now it's not gold that is held in reserve, but something else—something we'll come to soon.

But with the opportunity opened by fractional reserve banking comes the risk of overissuance. There might be an excess printing of gold claim checks. In addition, there might be an excess issuance of credit in the form of loans measured in such checks. It costs Caterina nothing in the short run to issue more checks or credit, and each such issuance yields real monetary seignorage benefits to her for as long as people are able to pay in her currency. With the gravy flowing, when should she stop?

You can see here already why banks are, in a certain sense, inherently untrustworthy. The bank's "business model" is inherently dangerous unless carefully overseen. There's a constant temptation for banks to put too much money and too much credit into the economy. They can too easily make more promises than they can possibly keep even on a single day. And when they do overextend themselves, and people come rushing back—in a "run"—to redeem their receipts for the gold, the banks' paper suddenly loses its value and the money supply suddenly shrinks.

The classic Frank Capra film of 1946, *It's A Wonderful Life*, depicted a run on the Bailey Building and Loan, a small bank owned by George Bailey, played by Jimmy Stewart. It certainly wasn't the first bank run. But Stewart's character pointed out what hadn't quite been appreciated: "You're thinking of this place all wrong, as if I had the money in the back in the safe. The money's not here. Your money's in Joe's house, that's right next to yours. And in the Kennedy house and Mrs. Macklin's house and a hundred others."

But the run was on, and the town would fall into what economists call a "liquidity crunch" or "contraction." Productive activity, which proceeds on the strength of the promises memorialized in paper currency, grinds to a halt. People are thrown out of work, nothing is sold or produced, and all members of the community quickly grow poorer. No wonder city officials "broke the benches" of bankers who overissued their currencies. Overissuance imperiled everyone. It wasn't just the bankers and their depositors who were vulnerable—it was everyone who depended on the "common currency" and associated "payments system."

And thus "bank regulation" was born. You wouldn't need a paranoid conspiracy theory to see the need for it. It first tried to ensure that bankers' "reserves" were adequate to meet daily withdrawal needs. Later it began monitoring other activities that could put banks and broader economies in peril. The urgent need for this never really went away. These are just the sorts of regulations the United States imposed after the 2008 crisis. And, alas, the new regulations—the "Dodd-Frank" reforms—are now being weakened again.

"GOLD STANDARDS" AS PROMISES

In a way, things didn't change very much in the basics of banking and finance from the late medieval Italian period to the early twentieth century. Manorial coinage morphed into sovereign nation-state coinage, which in turn merged with private bank issuance. The result was a system in which sovereign currencies served as reserves, while bank currencies "multiplied" those reserves in keeping with the fractional reserve model.

In this system, private banks would be simply given deposits of sovereign coins. Some such coins even came to be called "sovereigns." The banks would then issue paper receipts in excess of those coins. The receipts would first be given in exchange for the coins, and thus act as claim checks, and then be issued in excess of coin reserves as extensions of credit. And so Europe as a whole came to enjoy the benefits of what came to be known as "an elastic currency" that had been developed and enjoyed earlier by Italian goldsmiths.

This is the profitable system of leveraged promises about which the industrialist Henry Ford, of Ford Motor Company, said: "It is well enough that people of the nation do not understand our banking and monetary system, for if they did, I believe there would be a revolution tomorrow morning." He didn't just mean the bankers enriching themselves almost at will, which they did. He was also describing the ever-present danger posed by over-issuance. More promises might be made than could possibly be kept. Much as it was with the medieval Italians, the overissuing, overpromising banker could always turn short-term profits. What would hold the greedy back?

During the nineteenth century, many societies saw devastating boom-and-bust cycles. Many of these dovetailed with wartime overissuance inflations and wrecked government budgets. No wonder conspiracy theories about corrupt bankers—including the Rothschilds in London and politicians willing to do their bidding—found a firm footing.

A dramatic foreshadowing of the danger occurred very early in the eighteenth century, courtesy of the Scottish economist John Law's ingenious plan for financing the wars and other ambitions of France's King Louis XV. Law was a remarkable character, combining a brilliant theoretical mind with a rogue's eye for danger. A formidable gambler thanks to his mastery of probability theory and penchant for quick mental calculation, Law had to leave his native Scotland in haste after killing a fellow cardplayer in a gambling dispute. Fleeing to France and the Netherlands, he applied his talents to the rapidly growing securities exchanges of both countries, then quickly becoming the largest in Europe.

On the markets, Law came quickly to understand the monetary attributes of credit, and developed a plan for national money systems on this basis. His *Money and Trade Considered: With a Proposal for Supplying the Nation with Money*, published in 1705, was effectively the first systematic plan for a credit-money-issuing central bank that could finance government operations, simultaneously supplying the full national economy with an elastic currency that would facilitate rapid growth in the private sectors as well. He first pitched the plan to his native Scotland—once the warrants for his arrest had expired—but the "thrifty Scots" at the time were uninterested. Louis XV of France, however, was another story.

Law's plan worked wonders at first, rendering France for a time the most rapidly and dynamically growing economy in the world. We owe the word "millionaire" to this period (ever wondered why it sounds French?), and hence to John Law. But as luck—or should we say "greed"—would have it, both Louis XV and financial elites before long began using Law's credit-money to finance expensive but unproductive wars and hyperinflationary speculation on North American land and foreign trade, respectively. The upshots were the infamous Mississippi and South Sea bubbles, the crashes of which led to Law's having to flee France just as he'd fled Scotland.

Law understood well what we've tried to communicate thus

far: that money is really a credit-and-debt relationship. But he hadn't yet mastered the need to root money growth in productivity growth in the ways we elaborate in Chapters 12 and 13. Nor had he thought much about the need to regulate finance "macroprudentially," again in the ways we discuss later. This took a while—until some then orthodox economists (alas, very few!), like Irving Fisher and J. M. Keynes early on in the twentieth century, finally saw fit to incorporate the insights of real market-watching "heretics" like Henry Thornton, Karl Marx, A. Mitchell Innes, and even, to a lesser extent, Sir James Steuart and the Baron de Montesquieu.[4]

Even before Keynes and Fisher, many governments had had enough of banks and the financial mood swings they fueled. But without Keynes and Fisher around to set them straight, they came up with a cure just as bad as the disease. They sought to "impose discipline," on both themselves and their bankers, in a very odd way. The real dangers, they thought, must have come from fractional reserve banking. With the banks using indefinitely extensible sovereign bonds in lieu of rare metals, something had to be done.

An idea took hold. Just require banks to hold back metal, which is inherently in short supply, among their reserves, or at least to increase their ratio of reserves to lent funds, or both. This was the job of "the gold standard."

Really there were various gold (and silver) standards. But the general idea captured imaginations and fostered great confusion about money. Many began to assume that money had always had some connection to gold. A "gold standard," they surmised, simply recognized this deep fact of monetary metaphysics. And so a fundamental error became conventional wisdom in the bad sense—the sort of thing worldly people think they know and stop questioning.

This was despite the fact that a gold standard has been used only rarely, even in the post-Renaissance era. So part of the problem was bad history. There was also a larger and worse confusion: the idea that the gold standard was somehow outside of us, "exogenous," acting as some sort of "external" limit on our over-issuance of currency. That has never been the case at any time in history, anywhere—and never will be.

When it has been adopted, a "gold standard" was always the sovereign's standard, or "the people's" standard, or both. There is absolutely nothing "natural" about gold's functioning as, or limiting, "the money supply." It's always been a matter of law or convention or both. It is not the natural order of things, but one of society's most important decisions—and often a fateful one. It is a very deep confusion to suppose otherwise. The same confusion still besets a small number of "crypto-utopians" who think cryptocurrencies must be inherently limited in supply in order to be "more reliable" than other currencies.

Even during the rare periods when "gold standards" have been in effect, gold has never been the sole circulating medium. It's never been the sole material representation of promises that function as fungible claims, since that would be much too inconvenient. Remember, the stuff is too heavy, and too easily stolen. At most, gold has functioned as "base money." Other and more convenient money forms—like paper notes—form an inverted pyramid on top of the gold supply even in the "gold standard" systems of the distant past. But the ratio of pyramid-pinnacle volume to full pyramid volume has always been the product of decision—the decision of how much "reserve" to require of governments or banks.

There's simply no getting around it: all monetary "standards" are choices. And, in short, a "gold standard" *was always itself simply another promise.*

It was a promise by sovereigns not to issue or to allow issuance in excess of some stipulated level. The level was just a multiple of a somewhat rare substance, where the key thing about it was that its supply couldn't be quickly be changed on a whim. In a world where gold had often itself circulated as a heavy and durable form of currency, that was a natural way to signal commitment that the supply of money would be modulated. It was a natural way of making a promise credible. But it was always just a signal. And in time we came up with better ways to show credibility in our promises.

And there you have the history of finance and banking—or the story of how we learned to create money by promising "from nothing."

CHAPTER 6

WHY MONEY CANNOT BE PRINTED

If you wandered into an economics class at a major US university, you'd likely hear your professor explain money through a simple parable. For, you see, there was a time before the invention of money. In those days (the professor never says exactly when or where), people did business by simple barter. They'd trade apples for oranges, work for bread, squirrel pelts for spices, haggling, bargaining, and swapping goods and services.

As the story continues, we learn this was all very inconvenient. If you happen to have a dead elk, and you'd like to find someone who'll trade you for a suit of clothes, you might be hard-pressed to find takers. Or if you have five apples and hope to trade them for two oranges, a banana, and lima beans, finding a willing trader may not be easy. Certainly not as easy as paying prices in some common "universal equivalent" or "medium of exchange." So at some point (it is never said exactly when or where), people began to swap some commodity that most people wanted. If this sounds shaky, your professor might quote philosophers Aristotle and Adam Smith, who made similar comments about the origin of money in barter.[1]

The professor might add, though never explaining very clearly, that the medium of exchange then also became useful for accounting (a "unit of account") and for savings (a "store of value"), among other functions. But still, money was originally, perhaps primarily, a transaction technology. Here the professor might quote the neoclassical economist Paul Samuelson, who wrote: "Even in the most advanced industrial economies, if we strip exchange down to its barest essentials and peel off the obscuring layer of money, we find that trade between individuals or nations largely boils down to barter."[2]

Feeling more confident now, the professor teaching your economics class might explain that people often suffer from "money illusion": they confuse the face values of their notes or credits with what these things actually buy them.[3] And, much as in the professor's original parable, money does not make a real difference to what people are willing to trade. It's just a convenience, a transaction technology, in which case, we can ignore it.[4] Money is "neutral," as the saying goes, a mere "veil," which overlays the "real" economy, where the real productive action is.[5]

There probably isn't time left to discuss banks. But if a student asked in the minutes remaining, the professor might quickly say they are "neutral" as well. The early bankers in Renaissance Italy simply took deposits and passed accumulated capital between hands for a fee. And little has changed to this day. Banks are "intermediaries" between lenders and borrowers. Their job is to "allocate" resources already on hand. They don't create money themselves. They don't create new "demand" in "the real economy."

As you pack your books and notes at the end of class, you'd be left with the impression that this parable has something to do with the real history of money and banking. But it doesn't. It is just another model—one that happens to be wrong about what money and banking have always been.

THE ORIGINAL DEBT

Some people might well have traded squirrel pelts for spices on the Silk Road, occasionally. But anthropologists and sociologists have confirmed that people rarely engaged in barter, even in the distant past. What they did, mainly, was borrow on credit—that is, by making promises. They'd barter and bargain mainly when markets broke down, in order to avoid the inconveniences of money. Until recently, for instance, the Lhomi people, who live near the contemporary Himalayas, preferred barter over money, in part because there just isn't enough government money flowing into their region.[6]

And why again was barter supposed to be so inconvenient? Enough so that it would seem *easier* to lug around heavy gold or silver?

Economists routinely fall into Adam Smith's big error about the origin of money—the one we noted in Chapter 1. Smith insisted the baker and butcher *had* to establish a common "medium of exchange," overlooking a far easier option: they just exchange on credit, borrowing on the strength of a promise to repay later.

But perhaps the money-from-barter story isn't supposed to have actually happened, as ancient history or as a subject for social scientists to investigate. It's just a "conjectural history"—a way of framing things in a suggestive way—of the sort you might hear over in philosophy class. In that case, the economics professor should be more careful not to confuse students. And really, the philosophy class offers a far better parable.

In *On the Genealogy of Morals*, Friedrich Nietzsche invited us to consider the unsavory origins of the feeling of personal obligation. What he called "bad conscience" derives from "the oldest and most primitive relationship there is, . . . the relationship between seller and buyer, creditor and debtor. Here for the first time one person moved up against another person, here an individual measured himself against another individual."

He added, "To breed an animal with the right to make promises . . . With the aid of the morality of mores and the social straightjacket, man was actually made calculable." Man would be fit for "the contractual relationship between *creditor* and *debtor,* which is as old as the idea of 'legal subjects' and in turn points back to the fundamental forms of buying, selling, barter, trade, and traffic."

At the very dawn of society, Nietzsche tells us, "original tribal cooperatives," in "primeval times," devised a useful fiction. They invented the notion that we owe our very selves to the tribe and its ancestors. People bought the story, and the rest was history. For then we couldn't *but* "give back," endlessly, in community service. There would be "sacrifices, . . . festivals, chapels, signs of honor, above all, obedience—for all customs, as work of one's ancestors are also their statues and commands." We'd have a debt to society, in other words, but of a magnitude we can never repay.[7]

That was the "stroke of genius" in Christianity, as Nietzsche put it. Because then God can be offered as the only possible redeemer. Being redeemed looks like freedom from heavy debt—and that is how Christians talk about it. But really it isn't—not if, by the same gesture, humanity incurs a debt of gratitude to the one who paid off one's other debts, which can never be settled. There's no paying God back, no way to be debt-free.

From this Nietzsche concluded that morality is a psychological burden that one should free oneself from. We ultimately shouldn't be accountable to others—at least not by any traditional or transcendent standards. Better to be a heroic creative, an authentic original, or an unaccountable asshole.

Might that be slightly rash? Why must moral accounting be cosmic and theological? When Dostoyevsky wrote that without God "all is permissible," surely he didn't mean it literally. A waiter gives you good service as you visit a foreign city. You leave a nice tip. Why? Because it's her due. You owe her a tip, in all fairness, even with no expectation of future reciprocity. Is it morally okay to stiff the nice woman? "Sorry, Miss, no tip; God does not exist." Insofar as God does exist, surely even God would prefer that we tip waiters properly—not from simple obedience to *Him*, but because of what we owe to *them*.[8]

Morality is about far more than money. Yet money is not so far off from morality as it may seem.[9] Nietzsche understood its essence, which is about debt, obligation, and how we *account* for what we owe each other. That is how money matters, on the strength of our promissory claims against one another. (We explain how that works in Chapter 7.)

THE "VEIL"

When orthodox economists call money a mere "veil," which overlays the more fundamental phenomena of the "real" economy, they mean the "real economy" is where all the productive action is. That isn't just a suggestive metaphor, an innocent simplification for ease of classroom instruction, which is left behind after Econ 101. It changes how many professionals think about real-world economies. Because money is primarily just a useful "medium of exchange," the thinking goes, it has *no lasting significance for economic production*.

Most economists will agree that money can be a cause of instability. Bad stuff happens—inflation crises, deflation crises, and other shocks to mundane daily commerce. Some insist that there is little if anything we can or should do about these extraordinary, unfortunate events; we can only reassure ourselves that, for all the suffering in the short run, we're better off in the long run. Others admit that steps can and should be taken to secure or re-establish the stability of "normal" circumstances. Yet, according to today's orthodoxy, when things return to "normal," money does not make a lasting economic difference. At most, "printing" extra money brings a one-time boost, a "sugar-high" temporary improvement. As long as we avoid big disruptions, money can be safely ignored. Again, it is a mere "veil" for the "real economy," where the productive action is.

This way of thinking has had catastrophic consequences for public policy. The 2008 crisis began in the banking and "shadow banking" systems. While a few attentive speculators, forecasters, and heterodox economists saw gathering signs of trouble, the orthodox crowd was caught unawares, because their basic way of thinking about economic reality obscures the crucial role of money and banking.

As the crash of 2008 has now made plain to everyone, private debt liabilities can build up and cause financial market crashes and then long recessions or great depressions.[10] But believe it or not, for a long time, key central bank models *didn't bother to track those buildups*. (That includes the workhorse "dynamic stochastic general equilibrium" or "DSGE" models.) Look closely at ortho-dox economic models and you'll see that they typically assume a "barter economy."[11] There are no money payments or financial institutions of any kind.[12] After the 2008 crisis, more recent DSGE models have included money and banking—but *still* not in a way that significantly changes projected economic outcomes. Money still makes little or no difference.[13]

There's nothing wrong with a model, per se; it can clarify ideas. But the models used by central banks and other monetary authorities are generally supposed to have something to do with real-world economies. And how apt can a model be if it ignores not only banks and other financial institutions, but even *money, credit, and debt themselves*? Are they not part and parcel of *capitalism*? Indeed, for Hyman Minsky, capitalism is nothing more than an economy that relies upon finance and money (and inher-ently unstable for that reason).

It's a striking irony, which goes back to the classical economists of the nineteenth century. Never were there bigger fans of capital-ism. None deny the workings of financial markets. But they tend to see finance as a sort of "add-on" to productive economic activ-ity. It does little more than *reallocate* resources, ideally in an "effi-cient" manner, at least more efficiently than central planning. Or as the idea is put in op-eds and classrooms: "The role of financial institutions and markets is to allocate a society's savings to their most productive uses."

Financial institutions do "intermediate" between savers and borrowers. But as any banker will tell you, they also *create money*. Banks extend credit simply by deciding to, on the strength of their well-considered trust in a promise of repayment. With the public's imprimatur, those new deposits—which are simply typed into accounts by computer as credits—get counted as real money. That is the "alchemy" of finance, which makes real money in a physical sense ex nihilo, and in turn shapes real economic activity, what we can buy, who can buy it, and who gets richer. Yet as we explain in Chapter 9, there's really no magic in bank chemistry: it's mainly just promises and bookkeeping. Money matters on the strength of contracts and promises.

Economists of the modern monetary theory school do take money and banking seriously. But MMT is still relatively new and treated as "heterodox," if not "marginal," by mainstream economists. That's a pity. For the self-styled orthodoxy renders itself almost useless, if not ridiculous, when it ignores money and the banking institutions that constitute the backbone of our money, credit, and payments systems. Money is absolutely crucial for understanding, let alone predicting, how an economy will actually function, *especially* in a capitalist economy. If the 2008 crisis brought many lessons, one of them is: Never ignore money and banking. And never trust the economic wisdom of people who do.

This was J. M. Keynes's original beef with the big classical economists of his day, Alfred Marshall and A. C. Pigou. They treated money as just a "neutral link" between transactions, as Keynes put it, which doesn't itself "enter into motives and decisions" for exchanging one thing or another. That *had* to be wrong about a modern capitalist economy, however. "Money is not neutral," Keynes insisted; it "plays a part of its own, it affects motives and decisions" all on its own. [14] Or as we say today, money makes the world go 'round.

Plus, Keynes noted, the classical school never explained how a hypothetical world of bartered dealings was supposed to be adapted to a real-world economy that uses money. The thought experiment just *assumes away* even the possibility of booms and depressions—"having assumed away the very matter under investigation," in Keynes's words. What was needed was a story—indeed, a *better model*—of how booms and busts were possible and real and reoccurring, in accord with the plain facts before our eyes.

Keynes went on to deliver just that in his celebrated 1936 *General Theory*. No book of economics was more influential—at least until the United States faced the horrors of 1970s "stagflation" (high unemployment combined with quickly rising prices). That came with the rise of a new high priest of the economics cathedral, one Milton Friedman.

Friedman explained, quite rightly, that there is no absolute right amount of money. The money supply must grow with rising transaction volumes, lest deflation starve an economy of money needed for rising production. Still, for Friedman, the best way to steer between deflation and inflation is to simply lock in a steady increase in the quantity of money and try to "avoid wide swings." "'Fine tuning' is a marvelously evocative phrase in this electronic age," he said, "but has little resemblance to what is possible in practice."[15] Yet Friedman's skepticism about central banking capacity wasn't a conclusion drawn simply from formal economic doctrine or empirical data. It had as much to do with his *philosophical* libertarianism, which opposes much of government management in principle. That part of his view was no better than amateur philosophy—he was trained only as an economist. But it was no matter. Many were happy to trust the oracle.

Central banks are constantly learning. They've progressed since Friedman's day, and will do even better in the future. Better "fine-tuning" is *exactly* what we propose central banks do. And surely Friedman, the worldly man of social science, would keep up with the steady advancement of practical knowledge. His "monetarism" never was entirely opposed to "Keynesianism" anyway; it was he who coined the slogan—which Richard Nixon later cited—"We're all Keynesians now." Friedman was *largely* right about money. He perhaps just never considered the new tools for inflation management we lay out in Chapter 12.

REAL AS VIRTUAL

If money has a slippery sort of reality, it shouldn't be so puzzling in the age of the internet. It is "virtual" but perfectly real—*real as virtual.*

For those who still find the internet puzzling, it may be helpful to think of the US presidency. What is it? It's an office and a person, or rather a person who holds an office (for being duly elected, mentally fit, etc.). To be president is just *to be the kind of thing that fills a social role.* The president is *whatever,* or whoever, happens to fill a role appropriately. And in this case "appropriately" is defined by the US Constitution, which lays out personal criteria like age, place of birth, and so forth, as well as procedural criteria like the rules by which elections must occur.

So it is with money. As suggested in Chapter 1, to be money in a community is to be something that parties to the communal relationship recognize together as settling accounts between them. Whatever it is, that's their money. In that case money is definitely *something*—something founded upon a special sort of agreement or social contract. It only seems like nothing because what people "recognize together" is an intersubjective matter rather than simply a physical object, like a planet, a tree, or a puppy. As one *Onion* headline has it, "U.S. Economy Grinds to Halt as Nation Realizes Money Just a Symbolic, Mutually Shared Illusion."[16] The joke works because we know that money is not an "illusion." It is a perfectly real matter of fact, albeit an "intersubjective" sort of fact.[17]

Money is no less real than our relationships, including the relationship that is our nation-state. *All* relationships are intangible and merely in "all of our heads," along with the accounting we do in them. You can touch your friend with a finger. But you can't touch your *friendship* with a finger. You can touch some part of US territory, its buildings, its flags, and so on. But you can't touch the *United States of America*—the larger relationship that organizes all the buildings, flags, and so forth.

A promise made is plenty real, but not something you can

touch in the way you can touch a physical substance, like gold or paper. When you "have" a trusted a friend's promise, do you ever worry, in a state of philosophical perplexity, whether she'll meet you at the movie theater as promised, because, after all, *where is this promise, anyhow?* If you check your pockets, you won't find the physical place (perhaps next to your keys?) where this supposedly "real" promise is located. No one worries in this ridiculous way. No one is so confused as to think that a promise can't ever be *relied upon*. A promise by a trustworthy person or institution is as real socially as anything else.

As so it is with money. A. Mitchell Innes explained the point colorfully back in 1913:

> The eye has never seen, nor the hand touched a dollar. All that we can touch or see is a promise to pay or satisfy a debt due for an amount called a dollar. That which we handle may be called a dollar certificate or a dollar note or a dollar coin; it may bear words promising to pay a dollar or promising to exchange it for a dollar coin of gold or silver, or it may merely bear the word dollar, or, in the case of the English sovereign, worth a pound, it may bear no inscription at all, but merely a king's head. What is stamped on the face of a coin or printed on the face of a note matters not at all; what does matter, and this is the only thing that matters is: What is the obligation which the issuer of that coin or note really undertakes, and is he able to fulfill that promise, whatever it may be?[18]

"PRINTING MONEY"

Those who scoff at the idea of solving important social problems by issuing money often deride it as just "printing money." "We of course can't just print money," is often asserted with a smug chuckle. This is usually said as though it is something everyone of any worldly wisdom takes entirely for granted. Few notice that the saying is confused to the point of incoherence.

Odd as it may sound at first, *money cannot be printed*. Only *representations* of money can be printed. We can indeed print *cash* or *currency*. Or one could make a computer screen printout of electronic dollar credits. But to *print money* is simply impossible.

And yet somehow the phrase "printing money" itself never raises an eyebrow. The saying is either incoherent, like talk of "round squares," or it is elliptical for "printing representations of money." It's a shorthand we think we understand. Except that it has created centuries of confusion, obscuring what money is, the real difference it makes, and how money might be used most productively.

Those who deride "printing money" are often raising the specter of hyperinflation, of the sort that ravaged Zimbabwe and Weimar Germany. To the paranoid mind, the very mention triggers righteous scoffing and disgust. Hyperinflation is indeed a scourge, and we'll have much to say about how we can always prevent it in Chapter 12. For the moment, just notice that this way of dismissing money *issuance* is based in confusion.

The economist's "veil" metaphor is right in one way: *currency* or *cash* is not money, but a mere representation *of a promise.* Though metals like gold have on some occasions *represented* the promise in money, that promise—the obligation and the corresponding claim—is where the money is.

To fixate on gold or green paper or any other material representation of money is to confuse the thing with its *representation*. It's an error akin to a fetish or idolatry. The icon is not the saint, but merely the saint's physical representation. The Christ is not the Mexican Jesus candle purchased down at the 99-cent store for the bargain price of $1.16. The Jesus candle—not including the Kanye West knock-off version—is but an icon or depiction.

Or since economists tend to respect mathematics, here's a math example. The numeral *7* is not the number seven. The *numeral 7,* which you might write down on paper, represents the number seven. But if it were itself *the number seven*, there would be literally countless numbers seven out there, which is absurd. There is only *one* number seven—the integer between six and eight. Currency stands for money much as the numeral 7 stands for the number seven, or as an icon might stand for a saint. The money itself does not "stand for" something. It *is* something—a kind of promise.

You can print a representation of a promise. The dollar bill is indeed a promissory note. A roommate might scrawl out "IOU" on paper, which will henceforth stand for his promise to you to clean the bathroom. But "printing a promise"—meaning the promise *itself*—is impossible. It's as impossible as the Christ being incarnated as the Mexican Jesus candle. It's as impossible as *writing down the number seven* (instead of just writing down the numeral 7, which we do often). It simply can't be done, metaphysically speaking.

If this point seems pedantic or merely terminological, note that mathematicians were for a long time not very good at answering the question "What is the number seven?" They worked just fine for millennia with the number seven, along with many other numbers, puzzled all the while by *what numbers are*. A good account of the nature of numbers emerged only by the time philosophers of mathematics began to develop good definitions of "number" in the late nineteenth century. Alas, such is the slow progress of human knowledge, aided by philosophy.

To this day, many economists are in a similarly perplexed state about money. Yet their confusions have proved far more harmful than any confusion of pre-nineteenth-century mathematicians. Which is all the more reason for them to do what the mathematicians did as regards arithmetic: work through the philosophy.

So promises are plenty real, plenty capable of creating economic activity. Money is as real as all of the contracts, and all of the socially enforced promises, on the strength of which people do or make all that they wouldn't have done or have made without them. And that's why orthodox economists are wrong to ignore money: money is definitely part, in fact the biggest part, of the real economy itself.

INTERNATIONAL MONEY

During stretches of the twentieth century, before the current orthodoxy settled, economists did think deeply about money. It made an enormous difference to the world economy, and it's an important backstory to the 2008 crisis. Here, as so often, history can help us deconstruct misconceptions about what money is or has to be.

Today different moneys are mainly issued by national governments, with one very important exception. The governments of the world themselves have their own money. The International Monetary Fund ("IMF," "the Fund") is a quasi sovereign of 190 or so governments. By international treaty, it was given jurisdiction over its sovereign member governments for monetary purposes. At fewer than two hundred members, it's a small community— smaller than most elementary schools. And much as many schools have "brownie points," the IMF community has a working money of its own—the Special Drawing Right, or "SDR." (If the name sounds odd, recall that the legal term for a check or cheque is "draft" or "draught"—the latter word being the past participle of the English infinitive "to draw.")

The SDR is an excellent example of why money—an authorization to spend, to "draft a check"—needn't be "based on anything" beyond a special sort of agreement or understanding. It shows why money can be "virtual" and still matter, in this case, for the whole course of world history.

Back in the 1950s and '60s, Robert Triffin, the Belgian American economist, was a persistent man with a big idea. Some academics—the "foxes"—dabble in this or that idea without any one driving theme. Others—the "hedgehogs"—labor away on one big idea their whole lives, hoping that something good comes of it. Triffin was a hedgehog and made a whole career of pointing out a flaw in the postwar economic system. The needed fix, he argued, was for the IMF to follow through on Keynes's original plan for the postwar global economy and establish its own money.

Keynes's original plan never was adopted completely. Well before the Nazis and the Japanese were defeated at the close of the Second World War, Keynes, the Englishman, and Harry Dexter White, an American, hammered out a plan. Over two weeks of negotiations at Bretton Woods, New Hampshire (the resulting "Bretton Woods system" is named after the place), White had the upper hand. It was to become the American century, and despite Keynes's charisma and stature as the world's leading economist, White was caught in the wash of America's new prominence. Over Keynes's objections, White insisted that the dollar be the world's new "reserve currency"—meaning the money in which most countries save.

The two men agreed on setting up the IMF, but as little more than a lender of last resort. Governments facing a crisis often need somewhere to turn for short-run loans. Since financial crises spread rapidly, the IMF would be something of a global fire department: emergency loans would keep the flames from spreading from country to country. That was progress. Even the *assurance* that funds are available helps reduce the risk of a crisis erupting. Lenders would be less likely to flee in fear of default on debt payments.

The Bretton Woods system, which included other institutions for development and trade, worked almost too well for over two decades after the war. There were virtually no financial crises in that period. Which, in effect, put the IMF out of a job. So, looking for work, it moved into development alongside the World Bank. This did not go swimmingly (so-called "structural adjustment programs" were pretty bad for many developing countries). But, eventually, after the 2008 crisis, the IMF returned to its original mandate as a lender of last resort, when the need for a global fire department become obvious again.

Triffin never lost sight of the IMF's importance. To really work as it should, he urged, the IMF always needed to go beyond short-run crisis management. It should issue a money for interstate transactions, much as Keynes had suggested in his original plan (Keynes called it the "bancor"). That would help prevent unsustainable imbalances in national accounts, prevent crises from erupting over the medium to longer run, and make the world safe for equitable growth, high employment, and democratic prosperity. By the mid-1960s, Triffin finally won the argument. The IMF established the Special Drawing Right.

When first told about the SDR, it is easy wonder how it could possibly be a money. Where is the gold? Where's the cash? How can a simple "drawing right," or "right to draw," whatever that means, be a money? Yet the "drawing" here is no different from drawing on an account at your local bank. The IMF simply confers "a right to draw" upon its members *by agreement*. The member governments then credit one another up to some designated amount. The credits are measured in drawing units, or SDRs, which are booked as an asset or a liability in government accounts. They are what governments mutually recognize as settling accounts between them. And there you have it, money.

FROM CAUTION TO CRISIS

The existence of international money has real import for government finances. All governments save for a rainy day, storing up precautionary "reserves," which are just "safe" assets parked for use when the rains come. Governments once sat on gold or other precious metals for that reason. But as any good investor knows, it's prudent to diversify instead of putting all one's eggs in one basket. The SDR is valued as a "basket" of various strong currencies, including the dollar, the euro, the yuan, and others. So having them on a government's books brings diversification automatically. No need to put all of one's eggs in a *dollar* basket, or indeed into *any* particular national currency. Governments can simply bank on SDR promises, with the full faith and credit of the international economic community.

In the nineteenth century, governments started holding foreign currencies along with gold in order to "hedge" and create stability. But when White successfully placed the dollar at the heart of the postwar global economy, things took a dramatic new turn. Governments started banking mainly on dollars—meaning lots and lots and *lots* of dollars (usually by purchase of US Treasurys). The dollar's preeminence was never a recipe for stability. A national money was being asked to facilitate a global public good—financial stability—despite the fact that no national money, which is subject to domestic needs and pressures, is very well suited to the task. A crisis was always just a matter of time.

By the 1990s, China and other governments had been holding huge reserve accounts in dollars. That "glut" of savings was a key cause of the US real estate bubble and its ultimate collapse in 2008 (along with banking deregulation, large private-debt outlays in the United States, and many other factors). The crisis Triffin feared back in the 1950s and 1960s had finally come to pass. And the 2008 crisis is *still* upending our politics, causing peril for the very future of real democracy.

Sad as it is to look back upon the road not traveled, there was a more stable, more orderly way of doing things, which Triffin himself had mapped out for us. Though the SDR was formally established in the mid-1960s, it was never used very widely. Today we can at least hope that governments are starting to get the message. SDR allocations were considerably expanded in the wake of the 2008 crisis. Not by enough, but it was at least a step in the right direction. We can at least see how the SDR might gradually "dethrone the dollar" as the world's reserve currency. The global economy might become much less prone to crisis, which would be very good for everyone.[19]

So money matters. But we've only begun to fathom how it boosts economic production. For that we need to probe its foundation—accounting for what we owe each other.

CHAPTER 7

WHAT WE OWE EACH OTHER

How do nations grow rich? We divide our labors. When we "specialize" in our jobs and chores, each of us produces more than we would if we did everything ourselves.

That was the idea Adam Smith celebrated in his 1776 masterpiece, *Inquiry into the Nature and Causes of the Wealth of Nations*, which the banker, political economist, and later member of the British Parliament David Ricardo refined in his 1817 theory of "comparative advantage." It's often seen as the signal achievement of two hundred years of economics, which no serious economist would question.

Yet, for today's economic orthodoxy, money is not an essential part of the story. It may aid economic cooperation at first or temporarily—or, more likely, it may cause temporary disruption. But, again, in the orthodox picture, money is but a "neutral veil" that makes no lasting "real" difference to economic activity. In which case it doesn't explain why specialization makes us richer.[1]

In this way orthodox economics tends to overlook the single most important way money matters, both for our lives and our politics: it helps us grow ever richer, steadily advancing the wealth of nations. *How*, exactly, do we divide our labors and work together more productively? On the strength of our promises and contracts. Money is why many developing countries are

now quickly reducing poverty, making good on the basic promise of capitalism; why so many of us already enjoy the comforts
of advanced-world living; and why we can hope to become even
richer in the future, in a lasting democracy founded upon a common sense of shared destiny.

AN ECONOMY OF FAVORS

Since orthodox economists love models (and won't be convinced
without one), let's sketch a mundane little economy—a small
"favor economy." If any good model should clarify things, this
one makes obvious what many economists seem to forget. Money
matters not simply as cause of temporary disruption, but as part
of the prosaic "real" economy itself. It is precisely what allows us
to specialize and grow steadily richer together.

Suppose you have a sibling or close friend, and the two of you
regularly do each other favors or "good turns." Maybe it was your
sister's turn to take the garbage out last night. Seeing she was busy,
you gave her a hand and did it for her.

Afterwards your sister might say, "Hey, Brother, I owe you one!"
If she scrawled it on a napkin ("Good for one trash removal"),
you'd have her IOU as a promissory note—a representation of her
obligation to return the favor. A note might seem a bit excessive;
you both could easily "keep track" of your IOUs by memory alone.
If these sorts of favors happen often enough, you'd be "keeping an
account" of the favors you do for one another.

Now suppose she'd like to "call in a favor," as though asking for
payment on a debt. If your sister has been doing a lot of sweeping
or math problems as a favor for you lately, one day she might ask
of you, when it is she who is now short of time, "Hey, could you
take the trash out for me? You do *owe* me, right?" If you disagree,
you might sound like a banker: "Actually, we're *even*. I walked the
dog yesterday."

Or maybe the truth of the matter is that she really owes *you*,
in a big way. You've been doing her favor after favor in doing your

and her family chores, building up quite a "surplus" with her. So if you respect one another as more or less equally obligated to do household chores over time, you could hope to eventually "spend" from that surplus, to "cash in." So one night, when you're finally the busy one, you ask her, "Hey, Sis, I know it's my turn to wash the dishes tonight, but I've got a paper due in the morning—may I redeem some of my 'credits' with you and ask you to handle the dishes this time?" And if she's free tonight, she may say yes and do the dishes without saying "You owe me one." She won't say that, because she's paying back some of what *she* owes to *you*. She's "paying" her debt to you.

A MONEY CONTRACT

So far, our little economy runs on a loose sort of accounting. The siblings can easily remember where they each stand in relation to one another, duly noting relevant changes in their mental book-keeping. They don't really need anything so formal as a physical "currency," perhaps in IOUs scrawled on napkins. The essence of the story is in the "accounting," not in whatever physical things (neurons in this case?) they might use as memory aids to keep the accounts.

On the other hand, if keeping score becomes complicated, because the siblings were forgetful enough or things got too messy, then maybe they would begin to write things down—on a dry-erase board in the kitchen maybe. They'd keep a *ledger*.

By agreeing to the ledger, they've authorized something like a constantly updated contract, a public record to which they could refer back in order to check their balances with each other and sort out any disagreements or misunderstandings or memory lapses. They still may not have made *literal* "promises" or "authorizations" of IOUs or contracts—not in the legal or formal sense of those words. But it's easy to see a kind of agreement at work.

At the very least, the little economy runs on an implicit understanding, a latent promise, that the one will be "paid back," favor for favor. There's even a principle at work, as they might put it, that "one good turn deserves another—it's only fair." Both siblings accept the principle and feel bound by reciprocity. Each feeling confident in the other's continuing good faith, they each keep faith themselves.

But in that case the siblings have authorized something very much like what lawyers call a "relational" contract, such as a lease, a nondisclosure agreement, or a long-term supply arrangement or similar business contract. It's an agreement of the sort that endures through time and "covers" what may be an indefinite number of discrete interactions. It's the beginning of something like a *social* contract, which has moral force in the little "society" that is you and your sister.

And indeed here the little society *almost* has *money*. For the siblings implicitly agreed that certain actions shall count as "paying the debt" when either "owes one" to the other. Money, as we put it in Chapter 1, just *is* whatever parties to a relationship mutually recognize as "settling accounts" between them. In this case, it's the *chores*, done as a favor. Chores are what they "pay" each other in, and so those chores serve as their "legal tender."

HOW MONEY MATTERS

Eventually we'll want to see how this works in an economy with millions of people. But for starters, we can add just one more sibling, along with a few more ways the siblings come to owe one another. So, in keeping with our finance ABCs, meet three siblings, Aaron, Bob, and Catherine.

It's been a busy week for Bob at school. Aaron has done a bunch of his chores for him, so Bob owes Aaron. Bob might eventually "pay" Aaron by doing chores for Aaron at some later date. On the other hand, with a third person in the picture, there's another possibility: Maybe Bob did a bunch of chores for Catherine last week, in which case Catherine owes Bob. And if Catherine owes Bob as much as Bob owes Aaron, the debts might conveniently transfer over. Bob could just authorize Catherine to "pay" Aaron, in lieu of his own payment. And why not? Bob owes Aaron anyway. "Just pay Aaron," Bob might say. "I owe him. So it's all the same to me."

In that case we've got something even more like a genuine economy. It's larger in population, but also larger in the variety of ways to get "credits" that can be "spent" in the discharge of "debts."

Even with a mere three people, what's important for the moment is that keeping track of things is already getting complicated. The three siblings will need to find a good way of "keeping accounts" among the three of them, even on their dry-erase board ledger. They'll need some reliable, public way of regularly transferring "credits" and "debits" to and from one another as chores get done.

So here's an idea: As the three swap chores, maybe the *term* "chore" begins to take on new meaning. It starts to refer not to this or that job within the family, but to a "unit of account" as well—much like the dollar, yuan, or euro. Then the three siblings will start owing and paying each other in these "chores," perhaps storing up a surplus, or going into chore debt, measured in that more abstract unit.

And if on a given day Bob owes Aaron two chores, while Catherine owes Bob three chores, the accounting will already look a lot like the accounts in a large firm, a government, or a central bank. This is fascinating if you're an accountant, or you find yourself up late at night reading about double-entry bookkeeping. Many people—including many, maybe *most*, economists—are definitely *not* interested in how bank accounting actually works in practice. They really should be. But we can all agree that it's entirely understandable to find the matter a bit boring when you consider that, even in our very simple case, the books then look something like this:

1. Bob has liabilities in the amount of two chores (both owed to Aaron) and assets in the amount of three chores

(owed him by Catherine). He's one chore in surplus—his "account balance" is net positive by one chore.

2. Aaron for his part has no liabilities. He does have assets in the amount of two chores (Bob's liabilities to him). So his "account balance" is a positive two chores.

3. Catherine, finally, has no assets. She does have liabilities in the amount of three chores (owed to Bob, hence Bob's assets). So her "account balance" is negative three chores.

And if keeping track of all of this seems exhausting and tedious and mind-numbing, be assured that you've entirely grasped our present point.

Worse still, much as in any economy, Aaron's, Bob's, and Catherine's accounts will change on a weekly or even daily basis. The patterns of obligations and claims between each of them will shift all the time, like flows of water rushing along bending tributaries. In this sense "money" will be "flowing" back and forth among them all the time too, as their "account balances" shift. Now imagine this happening constantly among hundreds of millions of people.

What's plainly needed here is a *public scoreboard*, like the scoreboard at a baseball game. The flashing bulbs or hanging cards indicate, plainly and visibly to all, where exactly things stand at any given moment of play. It would still be our little economy, only now with a public ledger, more people, and, with them, a greater variety of kinds of obligation that they might incur to one another.

And just so that people who may not know one another very well avoid misunderstandings, forgetting, confusion, or dispute, we should imagine them adopting a *formal* social contract: they "formalize" and "regularize" what sorts of obligations can be incurred or enforced by whom, and exactly what sorts of "payment" are authorized to satisfy such obligations. And, in fact, legal tender laws do just that.

But if things have to be more explicit and formal in a large society, the foundations of money—as mere IOUs in a system of social accounting—remain the same.

DIVIDING LABOR

Even with only three people, there's a lot going on. Whether or not any of the siblings are keeping track very carefully, the flow of money is in any case terrific for all three of them. Each can do things they otherwise couldn't.

Aaron, for example, can do much better on his homework— perhaps even write a research paper for "extra credit" at school— on some nights when he'd otherwise be too burdened with chores to do his best schoolwork. He just "spends" some of the "chore money" surpluses he has built up already. Or he "borrows" chore money from one or more of the others, hence incurring a "chore debt" to them. Catherine will be able to do likewise on some nights, as will Bob.

Taken all together, Aaron, Bob, and Catherine now become much more productive. They all get the chores done *and* produce much better homework and research papers. That is, if Aaron, Bob, and Catherine arrange this thing right, they'll not only get all of the chores done just as they would have done had they not begun "trading" in chores. They'll also get *other* things done that they *couldn't* get done before—such as the homework or "extra credit" research papers. They simply would not have been able to do those things as well if they couldn't sometimes "buy time" with "chore money."

This is just the sort of division of labor that Adam Smith marveled over, for its ability to make people more productive together and, in time, amazingly wealthy in vast numbers. But what we can see more plainly now is that money is a big part of it.

That's why economists are wrong to think of money as merely a "veil" behind which the *real* economy happens. Money itself, as we can see even in our small model, has a *creative role* in boosting production. It doesn't only enable us to buy what is already

produced. It allows us to *produce more in the first place.* And
not just for starters; at every stage of specialization, it allows to
divide our labors ever further, becoming ever more productive,
ever richer. This is the secret behind what a few—alas, thus far
only a very few—savvy economists call "the monetary production
economy." Money is not just "a veil," but a productive factor—or a
productivity booster—in its own right.

COMPLEXITY

If our chore economy is itself something of a chore to ponder,
the vast complexity of a proper economy is truly a challenge to
fathom. But we're getting there, and our model can help us probe
more deeply with just a bit of further complexity.

At the moment "chore credits and debits" simply circulate
among Aaron, Bob, and Catherine. But now suppose our three
siblings are able to give and receive from one another in ways that
go beyond merely exchanging chores, one to one. They can do this
in two further ways: first, by setting "exchange rates," and second,
by explicitly adopting a common "unit" of measure.

First, our siblings will compare chores themselves. Maybe
washing the dishes is a much less pleasant task than taking out
the garbage or vacuuming the floors. Having to clean the bathroom might be worse even than that. If that is the case, then
neither Aaron nor Bob nor Catherine might wish to "recognize"
vacuuming the floors on one occasion as adequate "payback" for
cleaning the bathroom on another occasion.

In that case, they might all come to agree that if Aaron, for
example, cleans the bathroom one night when it was Bob's turn,
Bob owes Aaron *either* one bathroom cleaning *or* two dishwash-
ings *or* three floor vacuumings *or* four takings-out of the garbage.
(And the same goes if Catherine must pay Aaron what Bob would
owe him.)

In effect, our three siblings are establishing what economists
call "relative prices" or "exchange rates" among qualitatively dif-

ferent chores. You may recall just such rates being posted for major currencies in the airport during international travel. But here, the worry is that a mere dishwashing may not feel fair in exchange for having gone to all the trouble of cleaning a bathroom. And once the group starts to worry about those relative values, they'll find it useful to devise some common standard by which all the chores can be compared.

So the siblings might settle on a unit of measurement—perhaps calling them "points," or "chore points." They can then assign prices by that common measure. Taking out the garbage "earns one point," vacuuming the floors "earns two points," washing the dishes "earns three points," and cleaning the bathroom "earns four points." To put this in the fancy idiom of economists, then their chore money is no longer just a "medium of exchange" usable in settling chore accounts. It's evolved: it now also serves as a "*unit* of account" in *keeping* such accounts.

The sibling economy might even develop one more important layer of complexity. Suppose the group moves beyond chores, to other spheres of activity. Bob might struggle with trigonometry, while Catherine is very good at it. Aaron might have trouble finding someone who shares his sense of humor, while Bob "gets him" and is always ready to banter with him in ways that keep both of them smiling. Catherine might have little fashion sense, while, unlikely as it may seem, both Aaron and Bob have a real eye for style and new trends. And perhaps all three siblings feel discouraged at certain times, while, at the same time, each of them is good at cheering up the others when cheering is needed.

In this ever more realistic scenario, Aaron, Bob, and Catherine will over time do all sorts of "good turns" for one another. Each might also sometimes do things that tend to irk one or both other siblings. Aaron borrows Bob's finest shirt without asking, then inadvertently ruins it by putting it on after surfing when he's wet with salty ocean water. Catherine calls Bob "an idiot" in frustration some evening when he's slow in the uptake of the trigonometry she's trying to help him with. And so on . . .

In that case we can imagine how the siblings might informally "keep accounts" with one another, in much the same way that they did with their chores, but now with an eye to all of these benefits and burdens. Aaron "owes Bob one" for the shirt, Catherine "owes him one" for the insult, and so forth. Aaron might then "pay Bob back" by doing one of his chores for him—perhaps one, perhaps two chore-points' worth. Catherine might offer to do three chore-points' worth for Bob owing to the hurtfulness—or injustice—of the insult. And so on.

But now suppose that our three siblings come to "account" in this way for sufficiently many benefit and burden types additional to chores. Then they might at some point stop counting their "money" in "chore-points." They might move to something more generic. Instead of "chore-points," it's "points," or "merits" and "demerits." At that point, their protomoney will have become *fungible*—or at least as fungible as it can be in a family "economy."

And that, in a microcosm, is how we all get richer together. Our siblings could "produce" more by being freed up to fulfill the aggregate chore commitment *and* now do lots more in the way of extra things, like doing their homework well and writing research papers for "extra credit" at school. Just so, in a larger economy. The institution of trusting, trading, circulating, and fulfilling promises—i.e., the institution of money—enables a society to produce much more than it could in its absence. And it does that at every stage of economic progress. Which is why the wealth of nations steadily rises.

DEMOCRACY'S MONEY

Every democracy establishes a money and uses it for the "common weal." To see how they do that, there remains only one more thing to note—or rather, to make explicit, since it was implicit all along. Where did the "chores" come from? Why were they obligatory in the first place? The answer is pretty clear, once you think about it—and once you do it explains why you might have detected a faint air of *Charlie Brown* in our sibling story. *Where are the parents?*

The siblings were obliged to do chores because the parents "legislated" them with all due parental authority. The siblings owed washing the dishes, or taking out the trash, or cleaning the bathroom, *to the parents*, who gave them chore obligations. That's a "vertical" obligation, if you will, between child and parent, which you could think of as a kind of tax liability. That explains why chores became "money" amongst the children, why they came to owe things to each other in the "horizontal" *child-child* relation as well. For when one sibling is obliged to take out the trash, and the other does it for her, she's less indebted *to the parents*. That was the "favor," for which a favor was then due in return.

This was also why "chores" and then "chore-points" took on a life of their own, becoming a medium of exchange and the unit of account as things went forward. As our story continued, the children also developed other means of "earning money" with one another, by doing favors in addition to doing each other's chores. If Aaron was especially inconsiderate to Bob, Aaron could "repay" or "make it up to him" by cleaning the bathroom. Yet all along it was the chore obligation to the parents that continued as a sort of touchstone. The chore obligation—that pesky "tax"—was an original money-form in terms of which the money-forms that developed later were valued and measured. For the *parents* still had to be paid in *chores*: someone at some point still had to actually take out the trash and clean the bathroom.

As any parent knows, parenting itself comes with a raft of obligations. If the parents are reasonable family members, they'll oblige *themselves* in assigning chore obligations. The chores will have to be manageable for the kids; they'll have to be fairly enough distributed; and they'll themselves have to *recognize* when a chore is completed, counting a child as having *discharged* his or her chore obligation. Without at least that much fairness, parenting is not loving authority; it's domestic tyranny.

When monarchs reigned across Europe, they were often

thought of as God-ordained parental figures. John Locke's celebrated treatise on government—the one that helped inspire the
American Revolution—was a polemical reply to Robert Filmer's
Patriarcha, which called the king of England the nation's "father."
To Filmer, it was "us" and "them," the ruled and the rulers. The
ladies, lords, or monarchs were the rulers, and everyone else saw
themselves as "subjects," for being subject to their authority.

In the first modern democratic republics, established in France
and then America, the "them" of governance could only be "us,
the people"—as in "we, the people" who constitutionally "ordain
and establish" our very own government. Then "subjects" are not
simply subjects. They are *citizens* who are subject in an important
sense only to *themselves*. But if government is supposed to be "of,
by, and for the people," we haven't yet fully appreciated what it
means for *money* to be of, by, and for the people.

So now just think of our "chore economy" as a small democracy. Now Aaron, Bob, and Catherine are not children, but adult
roommates or members of a college fraternity or sorority or a
business partnership. They "ordain and establish" a government
among them, taking turns discharging governmental functions
in the form of, say, a rotating "governorship." They each remain
subject to the "them" that they constitute, which is something
"over and above" any one of them individually. Each is subject to
the delegated authority of the legitimate governor, whose turn it is
to govern at any given time, but with only a soft sort of authority,
the sort you find in a business partnership of equals. Each of the
partners owes obligations to the partnership. But they each partly
constitute that partnership, and they're equally *owed* obligations
by all the others.

Now suppose the roommates are laying out chore obligations
together much as the parents did, in order to live all together
and manage a livable household. And whoever's turn it is to be
governor at any given time will presumably remind any roommate of those obligations if they fall delinquent. If only by nag-
ging and cajoling, the roommates would thus impose and enforce

"chore" obligations on themselves. They'd live out a social contract defined by the promise of their shared "money," doing better than they otherwise could have for dividing labor and working together. They'd have a democracy—and democracy's money.

In a premodern monarchy, money was needed only to pay the lord or king, in order to meet a "vertical" obligation between serfs and rulers. The serfs didn't owe their tax payment "horizontally" to each other. In a democracy, we still have "vertical" claims and obligations between us and our government. But, as our model suggests, they ultimately run "horizontally" as well between *us as fellow citizens*.

The money we ordinarily use in economic cooperation, down at the liquor store, bike shop, or dentist's office, isn't just there by some historical accident. It's chosen for our shared prosperity. We first together determine what our tax obligations shall be and what moneys will be recognized in payment of those obligations. When the taxman cometh, we owe taxes in our chosen money, not to a lord or king or parental figure, but to the public treasury, and, ultimately, to each other as fellow citizens. Aided by a banking system, we then use that money with each other in cooperation, working together, dividing labor, and growing richer together. Then, even in the promises we make to each other in our private dealings, in marriage, work, or business, our public money becomes a sort of touchstone—an original money-form in terms of which other money-forms are valued and measured.

WHAT WE SHALL HAVE IN THE FUTURE

Which brings us once more to Augustine's puzzle about time. Time is elusive. So one can see why orthodox economists might tend to overlook it. Yet it is an important, undeniable truth: economies are about more than exchange at an instant.[2] Economic activity takes place in time. Promises bind present and future, and so does money: It converts the fruits of past production into augmented future production and national wealth. And so money, in the form of credit, is responsible for the generation of nearly *all* of the things that we have.[3]

This is why ignoring money, treating exchange as mere barter, can be a terrible error. An economy involves humans interacting and producing through time, with gradual credit and money growth fueling steady material growth. What *gets* produced, and what resources we *actually shall have in the future*, depends almost entirely upon who now gets to claim and deploy what from among what we *already* have, and for what purposes. The "real economy" of tomorrow, in other words, is a function of claims people have on the real economy of today. And those claims are money. That is how money takes an economy—takes *us*—from today to tomorrow.

In that case, *what we now do* with what society happens to have already in the way of material goods and services is as real as all the decisions we make daily, which steer what our future eventually brings. And what we *can* do with what society happens to have already is entirely a function of *who has what money*. That's how, if we choose to, we can now make a real difference in the future, making everyone richer, in a renewed social compact. We just change who has what money.

Reality does set limits, as we've said; we are constrained by what we have done and what we can now do. Money, as a claim on nonmonetary resources, cannot of itself make such resources. That's why overissuance of money—inflation, or *overpromising*—can in the long run undercut the credibility of money itself. That's why money can flip from fueling production to discouraging production, morphing from a credible promise to an incredible promise. All promising can be "overextended." But that doesn't mean that promises or money, when *not* overextended, are not real, or that they aren't what economists call "factors of production."

We saw the productive role of promises in our sibling story: Aaron and Bob in effect "borrowed time" from each other in order to produce more—in this case, brilliant research papers or other homework assignments. Time was an input in that productive activity. Borrowed time—hence also owed time—was effectively money. This is why highly abstract models of economies (such as the general equilibrium/DSGE models we noted in Chapter 6) dispense with *both* time and money. To abstract away from one in a certain sense just is to abstract away from the other.

Such models may help us analyze "marginal utility" and the comparative values we place upon various already existing goods and services. Yet they don't very well explain, or even describe, the *creation* of value, or the *production* of goods and services. Those things take time, and hence money, as *inputs*. A model without time or money will in that case have little to say on such matters—less than even our quaint little homework stories.

One great economist who *didn't* make this error seems to be more loved by conservative than by progressive-minded people. Joseph Schumpeter is likely best known for his oft-quoted celebration of capitalism's "creative destruction"—an observation that, ironically, stems from Marx and Engels (whose extolling the Promethean triumphs of capitalism in *The Communist Manifesto* would make even Donald Trump blush). Schumpeter made many signal contributions to economic theory, mainly from inside the so-called "Austrian" general equilibrium tradition favored by libertarians. But probably his richest and most insightful work is his *Theory of Economic Development* (1934), whose subtitle— *An Inquiry into Profits, Capital, Credit, Interest, and the Business Cycle*—already hints at his view of how time and money enable the process of production.

Schumpeter is very clear about the role of bank-issued credit-money in the process of production, and about the vulnerability of such issuance to bipolar ("boom-and-bust") cycles over time. His account of the process of wealth generation remains to this day the single best integration of theoretical insight with actual market observation. (Like Minsky, whom he taught, Schumpeter was also a banker.) Along with his insight into the indefinite "extensibility" of credit-money, he was a perceptive analyst of hyperinflations and deflations as well. He saw, in other words, why money is existentially important in any decentralized exchange economy. We can use it intelligently and creatively to build heaven, or unthinkingly and destructively to fuel hell.

PART III

BANKING FROM NOTHING

If public money makes us richer, America learned this the hard way through its tumultuous history. We already saw the promise and the peril of banks in our brief history in Chapter 5. Private banks have always been dangerously prone to overpromise. If the "gold standard" helped rein the banks in for a time, it also brought instability of its own—this time crises of underpromising. Plus, it confused almost everyone about what money is and how banks work.

That was the thick, dark curtain in Frank Baum's parable *The Wizard of Oz*—the one Toto the dog was supposed to have "pulled back," unmasking the machine behind the mythology. We eventually started to learn how things really worked, aided by the creation of a central bank. We learned that we *can* "smoothen the cycle," steering between under- and overcommitment, between starvation and excess. But we've yet to take the full measure of good Glinda's lesson that we've always held the power.

To see how true that is, we can study the days when America first began to catch on, creating the Federal Reserve System. We'll then see how much more the Fed is truly capable of.

CHAPTER 8

WHEN PROMISES GO PUBLIC

For almost a century now, the United States has had a public bank, the Federal Reserve System. These days anything so "socialistic" sounding as "public bank" prompts sneers, suspicion, and fears of the country careening in the direction of Venezuela. To many, the Federal Reserve is an alien presence in the economy, which is "taking" or "debasing" our money and should be abolished in favor of a truly "free market." "End the Fed!" is actually a slogan, on both right and left.

Never mind that those dollar notes in your pockets, those dollar credits in your bank account, are all *issued by the Fed*. They are just a promissory claim based on the Fed's public authority. If we were foolish enough to abolish the Fed and have a free market in money issuance, we'd immediately have a global financial crisis. Those "credits" on your Wells Fargo bank statement might quickly become worth less than the paper they aren't printed on. And let's just hope your salary isn't paid in the new "Wells Fargo dollars," which might be worth much less than your lucky neighbor's "Goldman Sachs dollars," and maybe not even accepted at the gas station or grocery store, except at a steep discount. You could very well be stuck with something like foreign currency in your own land, with *no truly national money* to exchange it for.

And the crises would keep coming. We know they would,

because a free market in money issuance was tried in the nineteenth century, in the "wildcat" or "free banking" era. What happened was crisis after crisis. As we explain momentarily, we gradually smoothed out the cycles of boom-and-bust by "socializing" the dollar and establishing the Fed. And are we so foolish as to repeat all the mistakes of the nineteenth century? Would we even relearn the lessons of history? There is of course no guarantee.[1]

Why have a *central* bank? Because we've had a long, awful history of failed alternatives. We stumbled into the present public-private partnership through a painful history of calamity and correction, of lessons learned and later forgotten. But looking back, the sad ways of the world reflect gradual, halting progress, what G.W.F. Hegel, the great titan of 19th century German philosophy, would call "the cunning of history."

THE FIRST CENTRAL BANK

Top warlords, who governed the peasantry and other nearby warlords, were the first monetary authorities. Some even regulated banks, shrewdly following the lead of late medieval and Renaissance Italian city officials. But as wars between nation-states or the dynastic families who ruled them dragged on, they often needed money, and often issue too much of it. That perennial problem gave rise to two institutional developments whose vestiges we live with today.

The first innovation was a way for states to finance their operations by issuing debt. If the crown had issued too much currency, it would draw some of it out of circulation by selling paper certificates on the market, promising to pay back the funds later, and then some. The certificates would bind sovereigns to pay their bearers regular interest charges over some period of time, and the remainder of the obligation—the "principal"—would be paid out at some stipulated date. The "binding" involved here was of course promissory (as in "Your word is your bond"). It gave the instruments the name they still bear—"bonds," or "sovereign bonds."

Eventually, corporations got in on the action, issuing debt instruments as well. The first of these were instruments of the state. The bonds themselves circulated as currencies in some cases, although that became unnecessary after the second financial innovation developed by nation-states—the invention of "the central bank."

In essence, sovereigns copied what private banks had done, or simply commandeered private banking. A bank that issued a currency of its own might be officially chartered, vested with sovereign authority. And as we explained in Chapter 1, once a sovereign levied taxes that could only be paid in that currency, or legislated legal tender laws that required its use, or both, the bank's currency quickly went *national* as well.

Central banks financed the critical operations of states, so they quickly became the most important banks in their nations. The Swedish Riksbank (*rik* is the Swedish for "empire," just as the German *Reich* is) is the oldest continuously operating central bank. Sweden had embroiled itself in multiple wars that could be fought only by "renting" foreign soldiers. This required a sophisticated money-raising system, which the Riksbank operated. A Dutch, then an English, counterpart quickly followed, and soon enough central banks spread all over the world.

Thanks to their closeness to sovereigns, these banks also emerged as reliable "banks to the banks." The public, in effect, gave privately owned banks a bank of their own. The banks could store their own reserves at the central bank, keeping accounts with them much in the way we keep accounts with the "private sector" banks themselves. They'd then use receipts for their deposits in supplementation or in lieu of gold coins or bricks as their "vault" money, profiting from a new kind of public-private partnership.

At first these paper IOUs were "backed up" by gold. Governments accumulated gold stocks, much in the way private bankers themselves had. But in very little time at all sovereign bonds, explicit promises, became the main backup. The promissory nature of bank- and sovereign-issued currency became obvious again. Any gold supplies simply made government promises a bit more credible.

What "backed up" a sovereign's bonds, and hence its currency, was ultimately its taxing power. The key here wasn't that it could collect taxes and then "pay out" the proceeds to bondholders, as many still assume today. It was that the sovereign could *requisition* taxes, much as the ancient grain-gathering authorities did. If you don't pay the taxes, people with weapons will come after you. For nearly all of us, that's reason enough to use the sovereign's money, as we explained in Chapter 1.

Once the sovereign is the chief money issuer, it faces the same temptations of overissuance as the private banker. Being well aware of its seignorage powers, it can wage wars, or undertake other excessively costly projects. But then when should it stop? It can "overpromise" with its notes just as the private banker can. To make matters worse, if private bankers are allowed to continue to issue their own currency, "backed up" by sovereign bonds and/or notes, they may overissue as well. There'd be *two sources* of overissuance in an economy: the sovereign itself, which might issue too many bonds and/or notes of its own, and the private bankers, who might issue too many notes and loans of *their* own on the basis of too little in the way of *sovereign* currency. Meaning we can easily have a very big mess.

BEING MANIC-DEPRESSIVE—WITH A BAD HANGOVER

And many messes there were, with much needless suffering, at least in the early centuries of sovereign currencies, sovereign bonds, and nonsovereign banks. With so many sources of money, public and private, the European economy saw tremendous growth *and* regular boom-and-bust cycles throughout the early modern period. The same unstable pattern held in the American economy after Europeans conquered and settled in America. It was only sovereign *central* banks that finally brought more coherence—though, as we'll see, that came late in America.

There was indeed tremendous growth, despite the many busts. With an abundance of sovereign instruments and currencies in European jurisdictions, private bankers could "lever up" even those abundant quantities by lending much more than they held. This brought rapid productive improvements and economic growth. More promises meant more productive activity predicated on those promises. And more such activity meant more improvement in material conditions—more "wealth" (a term which derives from the same root as do "weal," as in "commonweal," and "wellness").

And yet this same "elasticity," as it was called, also meant that the currency was often overstretched. Promising became overpromising. There was always a danger that promises could lose their value by being made in excess of any real prospect of redemption. And so began a common cycle of boom-and-bust, a cycle between overissuance and contraction, which ate away at the benefits of rising wealth.

An old song once had it that "love is like oxygen," inasmuch as "you get too much, you get too high," while "not enough and you're gonna die." That is the story of promises and credit—of money—in a modern economy. It is as real, vital, and potentially dangerous as are oxygen and love themselves.

Ah yes, the boom years—so easy and gratifying, the future seeming so bright. Productive activity is picking up and banks are making even more loans. Optimism is in the air. On the strength of anticipated production, an entrepreneur can approach the banker with big plans and promises. She explains that she plans to build this new "manufactory" (later shortened to "factory"), produce and sell this new product, and then pay back the lender later. Under the circumstances, this will seem plausible. The banker then opens or credits an account in the name of the entrepreneur, denominates the account in the currency of her jurisdiction, and then authorizes the entrepreneur to withdraw currency from that newly created account, or even just "draw on," i.e., "write draughts" (i.e., checks) against it in whatever amount one writes down. Thus checks emerged, as a "customized amount" sort of currency, drawn against promises.

When things were hopping, banks did a great deal of lending, and could expect repayment. They made money at it and so booms elicited their own financing: they attracted the very credit and money creation the booms needed to continue. The money lent served as claims upon current resources, which could be used in turn to produce greater future resources. Here again we see promises making a real economic difference—this time in fueling booming growth.

This is why certain economists (often called "heterodox") speak of money "coming from within." Money, credit, and finance need not come from "outside of" the economy itself—"exogenously" (with the "ex" here being the Latin for "out" or "beyond," as in "exotic," "exit," etc.). Money can also be generated from within— "endogenously" (with the "en" here being the Latin for "in"). It comes from within by promises made against expectations of future activity. (That's what's meant by the phrases "endogenous money," "endogenous credit," and even "endogenous finance.") And yet the point is still heterodox from the point of view of the economics profession, which is largely stuck on abstract theories and misleading pictures. As the great twentieth-century philosopher Ludwig Wittgenstein might say, "a picture holds them captive."

Endogenous money is *especially* susceptible to overissuance. Which explains why booms easily get "out of hand" and culminate in "busts." Busts were simply what happened when everyone suddenly realized the promises had been issued in excess of what could possibly be fulfilled. The "music stopped," and promises lost their redeemability and value. We saw it happen in 2008. It's happened *often* in economic history.

The busts could be utterly awful. When lots of people were left deep "underwater" with "debt overhang," owing more than they owned, the dire economic conditions would often morph into what are called "debt deflations," or what are now popularly called "depressions." This is the bubble's bursting. It's the steady decline, after a crash, of the "inflation," the credit-and-money excess, that had grown and then gone bust.

Boom-and-bust cycles became chronic conditions of modern economies. They were endemic to the mechanisms of promise making and credit extending—i.e., of money issuance—themselves. If money is a kind of promise, crises of credibility are the beast within.

A whole vocabulary developed around the pathologies, a vocabulary redolent of the familiar psychological problems of people. Booms became "manias." Busts became "depressions." It was almost as if the economy were as a single person with bipolar disorder, or what used to be called "manic depression."

Another colorful term—one of our favorites—was "revulsion." This is what markets experience after prolonged periods of "binging" or "credit excess." It is almost as if credit and money were alcohol—healthy and even life-enhancing (or at least party-enhancing) in moderation, but deadly when overdone. And the term "overhang," mentioned earlier (from "debt overhang"): It is reminiscent of "hangover," is it not?

Perhaps it's no surprise, then, that economic illness would breed mental illness, in oversimple delusions, suspiciousness, and conspiracy theory—all the elements of the paranoid cast of mind. And of course the problem remains to this day. The 2008 crisis and aftermath attest to that. At the same time, central banking has made great progress in taming the unstable cycles over the decades. There's plenty of room for improvement, but, ultimately, a strong central bank, functioning smoothly and transparently, does wonders for our collective sanity.

OF FRANCHISE AND FRENCH FRIES

The history of American money, banking, and finance largely recapitulates the earlier European experience, but over a shorter historical span. To get a sense of its peculiarity, it will help to pause and look again at the dollar bill.

Dollar bills are remarkable things. They're the same all over the United States. Take out money from a bank branch or an ATM anywhere and you'll get the same thing for your trouble: Whether in combination of green $1, $5, $10, or $20 notes, they'll all look the same. And they'll all be worth the same when their denominations are the same.

That's what sovereign-issued currency looks like, even when it is paid out by nominally "private" banks. The banks all deal in a national money, so they aren't as private as you might think. They are licensed by us, the sovereign public, to deal in our money—our "Federal Reserve Notes."

In effect, banks are franchisees. We the sovereign public are the franchisor. Our national money is the franchised good.

If our money has a uniform value and appearance, it's a bit like those golden arches you see all around. They let everyone know that the item in question is the same irrespective of just where you are in our nation. New York, California, Florida, Alaska . . . it's no matter: they are always and everywhere the same. The McDonald's burger doesn't have to be the best burger; it only has to be the same burger. The dollar may well be the best money; but it has value mainly because it has the same value everywhere.

If a bank abuses the dollar's brand by issuing bad loans or over-levering itself, it will risk losing its charter. Just so, a restaurateur who sells spoiled food risks being booted from the franchise. That's how franchises work. They are "quality control" pacts. Much as with foodstuffs and hotel rooms, the franchisees abide by the terms, the franchisor administers the terms. And where our money's concerned, we, the public, are the franchisor.

McDonald's and the dollar—what could be more American? But of course the golden arches were erected only in the twentieth century. And so, finally, was the dollar as we know it. Was it not with us from the start? No, not exactly. In the early days of our republic—until 1863—the dollar was a mere *unit of account*, *not a* currency. Sure, the Mint minted coins. But paper money in dollar "notes" was issued by so many private banks. That's why the paper currencies that circulated in the nineteenth century were and are called "banknotes." America's paper money supply was, for much of its history, a plethora of private banknotes.

HAMILTON'S BANK

That was partly for lack of a proper central bank. Things got off to a good start in the new American nation-state. Circa 1787, it had very little precious metal—what then was called "specie." The youthful country needed to finance its development, somehow, and the Founders knew they needed what they called an "elastic currency"—a currency whose supply could gradually increase to accommodate rising transaction volume as the new nation's economy grew. So the nation's first Treasury secretary, the brilliant Alexander Hamilton, developed a plan.

First, Hamilton arranged for the new nation's Treasury Department to issue sovereign bonds—still to this day called "Treasurys," the American rendition of what in other jurisdictions are still often called "Sovereigns." These would be "backed" by the taxing authority and function as "base money," in lieu of gold. On that basis, private banks could multiply money by issuing currencies of their own in amounts that were multiples of the Treasurys they held.

Next Hamilton persuaded Congress and President Washington to institute a "Bank of the United States" on the model of Britain's central bank, The Bank of England. It would sell securities of its own in return for what gold there was, putting those chunks of inert material in the service of national economic development. And these securities too could function as private bank "base money."

The Bank of the United States would also then issue currency of its own, "backed" by the confidence placed both in the gold that it held and by Treasurys. Much of that early money was spent on canal digging, roadbuilding, and other public infrastructure projects. The bank even helped finance an early form of "public R&D," in an "industrial development campus" near Paterson, New Jersey, which helped develop new products and manufacturing techniques. And, soon enough, the new United States had "leapfrogged" ahead of Britain and Europe in industry and commerce.

Hamilton's Bank of the United States, in effect, was a central bank, an infrastructure bank, and an industrial development bank, all in one. This was a success at home and influential abroad. Hamilton's blend of public money, public banking, and development finance was later used in Germany, Japan, Korea, and China—all of whom cited Hamilton's program as their inspiration. The program mobilized and channeled resources toward real economic and infrastructural development. It did that by diverting surplus capital that would otherwise inflate financial-asset price bubbles and bring further busts. It simply sent money and credit to the right places.

WILDCAT BANKS

In the Southern states, politicians distrusted Hamilton's program for the same reasons they'd been suspicious of the federal government itself. Industrial development sounds nice in principle, but since it boded ill for slave-based agriculture, it was deemed unacceptable. Once a politician of their own, Andrew Jackson of Tennessee, became president, they managed to kill the descendant of Hamilton's central bank.

What followed was a period in which the United States had a truly "free market" in money issuance. Private banks issued their own currencies with abandon, much as their Italian predecessors had done nearly one thousand years earlier. And, as you might expect, those who ignored history were doomed to repeat it, just as the proverb says.[2]

The notes issued were denominated in dollar increments, but

they weren't sovereign-issued liabilities. The banks were their own franchisors and franchisees alike. Their notes were their own private liabilities, each with a very different credibility. Two banks might both promise the redeemability of their notes for something more solid—gold, for example. But they might differ greatly in their ability to live up to those promises when you show up to claim the gold.

Banks differed in reliability for more than one reason. In part, bank regulation was just more technologically difficult in the nineteenth century. Regulators could be only so effective at exercising "quality control" over paper currency issuers. Another reason was that all banks were chartered and regulated by states rather than by our federal government. Banks for their part were kept local by the only public authorities that licensed them—subnational state governments.

We had in effect a "bank Babel," a cacophony of different dollars. The nation's currency supply consisted of thousands of distinct banknotes all trading at various discounts to their face value or stated par. A dollar note issued by Billy the Kid Bank or Sidewinder Bank might trade at 50 percent of par, for example, amounting to no more than "four bits," not a dollar. (A "bit" in the day was 12.5 cents, hence the term "two bits" one still sometimes hears in place of "a quarter.") A dollar note issued by Wyatt Earp Bank or Bald Eagle Bank might, by contrast, go for 90 percent of par, or even full par. And to make things worse, these different currencies constantly fluctuated in value, both in relation to the goods and services they could command and in relation to *one another.*

The seemingly simple question "How much money do you have in your pocket?" could be difficult to answer. Whose notes were you carrying when you wanted to buy something? They were all dollars, but of very different value. That hampered even the most routine purchase. Shopkeepers had to regularly update discount schedules behind their counters, instructing clerks how much to discount separate banks' notes in determining "how much" to charge buyers for goods, depending on what sort of notes they were presenting. If you carried multiple banks' notes in your pockets, making purchases at the general store could take you— and the store clerk—much longer than we're now used to.

Scarce wonder this period is often called the "wildcat banking" era. (Those who think this was a good idea call it the "free banking" era. It was free alright—it was pretty much value-free.) Private banknote money just didn't make for an efficient, trusty payments system. It was good that the nation had a *unit of account*—the dollar. But it still needed a truly national *currency*.

This "system," or rather its lack, posed two major challenges to transcontinental market integration in the growing United States. First, payment in one state out of accounts held in another state was fraught with uncertainty. The states differed in their regulatory competency, which meant dollars had different values in different states. The reliability of notes or drafts from one state looked "iffy" to the counterparties in other states. For a nominal dollar note issued by, say, Doc Holiday Bank in Kansas might circulate at par or near par while another nominal dollar note issued by Billy the Kid Bank in Texas might circulate at but 40 percent par. That ain't so good for Kansas-Texas cross-border transacting.

The second challenge was that, in states where bank chartering and regulation were lax, currencies varied in value in relation to one another even *within* states. Wildcat Bank's dollar might trade at 35 cents up in Concord, while Hawthorne Bank's dollar might trade at par in the same town. This had the effect of slowing intrastate transaction activity, and almost kept nascent interstate commerce from expanding. The dollar, though a national unit of account, simply could not be a bona fide national currency.

The free banking era was a tumultuous time. Banking had in a real sense returned to medieval times. Each wildcat bank was essentially a nineteenth-century American version of the medieval metalsmiths and claim checks described in Chapter 5. Was a bank reliable? The question was the same as in medieval Italy. Could this particular bank, in exchange for its notes, hand over metal coins or bars—typically gold, sometimes silver as well—if one appeared at the bank and claimed it? One never really knew. Each bank would choose its own "reserve" ratio between metals and circulating notes. And would they play it safe? Every banker had the constant temptation to overissue their paper currencies or deposits in relation to their metal stocks. After all, they could themselves spend any extra notes they issue, or lend them out at a profit.

Reliability came at the expense of profitability, and the appearance of "reliability" varied with the changing economic seasons. If people felt generally confident about the financial or broader economic environment, there was no problem juicing money creation. If people felt generally worried, they'd be much more prone to rush to the bank and to trade notes for metal, precipitating a banking crisis. And which season was one in? One couldn't really answer. One couldn't tell which banks were overissuing notes and at what times, which made it difficult to plan long-term productive activity with any confidence.

Unsurprisingly, bank runs were common. There were runs on offending banks and any other banks viewed as guilty by association. Given its once-again primitive financial system, the national economy was hamstrung. It swung through wildly bipolar boom-and-bust cycles for decades on end. A nation abundant in human and natural resources could not finance its own development. Despite aspirations of independence, it came to depend more and more upon Europe.

THE GREENBACK

That all changed in 1863. By that point the nation was embroiled in civil war. And for two reasons, the Civil War made a uniform national currency possible. For one, to wage the war the federal government had to be able to spend its own currency anywhere in the Union, and for that the dollar needed a uniform value. Second, the Southern slave states—which were the principal objectors to national monetary uniformity—had temporarily left Congress, thereby enabling the vote in favor of new national standards.

So Congress passed, and President Abraham Lincoln signed into law, a currency act, a national bank act, and a legal tender act in the years 1862 through 1864. These enactments together established, for the first time in our nation's history, a system of federally chartered "national banks," which all issued the very same currency, called the "greenback." It was the progenitor to today's very green US dollar.

The groundbreaking monetary policies of the 1860s transformed our interlinked banking, financial, and monetary systems. In very short order there were federally chartered banks in every state of the Union. All of them were subject to uniform regulatory standards. All of them were issuing a uniform currency with a uniform value.

These banks could also sell US Treasury securities. They became outlets for both of our federal government's principal circulating liabilities—greenbacks and Treasurys. And in no time at all, the "wildcat" banknotes left circulation. Why bother with uncertain private banknotes if the greenback could be used instead? Greenbacks and Treasurys, our two *sovereign* financial instruments, became the proverbial "only game in town."

The administrator of this national bank system was called the Office of the Comptroller of the Currency, or "OCC," and housed in Treasury. This was the "controller"—the administrator—of our first truly national currency system. To this day the OCC remains one of our principal bank regulators. It is the federal chartering authority—in effect, the licensor—for national banks. It sets the rules for how banks lend or invest. And it has final word on whether a national bank has gone bankrupt.

The comptroller was essentially the "quality control" agent through which the sovereign public maintained the dollar's quality. That meant maintaining the safety and soundness of the franchisee institutions—the banks. As distributors of the public's currency, the banks were in effect privately owned public utilities. They were locked into partnership with the public's agent, the Comptroller of the Currency.

Still, the new national system was not up to its challenges, for lack of a proper center. The Treasury Department lacked the authorization to expand and contract the money supply in response to oscillating "on the ground" economic conditions. Plus, the Treasury lacked the bank-regulatory expertise it needed to prevent national banks from over- or underissuing currency or loans. Though national banks proved much safer than their state-chartered competitors, the next fifty years still brought harsh booms and busts in 1873, 1893, and 1907.

The new comptroller improved the dollar as a means of exchange. But it couldn't maintain the dollar's stable value over time. For that, it would need to regularly readjust the supply of currency as transaction volume in the broader economy changes. But daily, even hourly modulation was not something the OCC was capable of within its mandate.

A healthy economy needed more than a *uniform* currency. It *also* needed an *elastic* currency. It needed a currency whose supply can be regularly adjusted to accommodate desired transaction volumes, so as not to squelch desired transacting needlessly. And, at the same time, it needed to be able to prevent overissuance of the sort that can spark inflation—the classic problem of "too much money chasing too few goods." The money supply must be capable of growing gradually, without growing so rapidly as to outpace that real growth. And it must also be capable of being trimmed back when credit expands at rates higher than that optimal rate. None of this was news by the start of the twentieth century. The "developed" world in Europe had long-established central banks and elastic currencies. The Founders themselves knew how important this was, as we noted. But slavery politics in the post-Jacksonian era would put off a true US dollar for more than a hundred years.

MONEY TAMED

It took fifty years after Lincoln signed the banking, currency, and legal tender acts of the 1860s, but by 1913 Congress had finally had enough. When the Panic of 1907 struck, enough US policymakers finally saw the urgent need for an active money modulator. And so the Federal Reserve Act of 1913 supplemented the national bank system with the Federal Reserve System—a network of regional banks across the country, with various regulatory agencies and committees, and of course the Fed chairperson we often hear from in the news. The dollar had come in from the medieval cold, joined the family of modern central banking, and returned to a semicentralized version of the original Hamiltonian system.

The Federal Reserve Act established the dollar that we all know today. Instead of the comptroller, the Fed would administer the national money supply. And instead of the Treasury, the Fed would take responsibility for the issuance and quantity of greenbacks and credit. That's why the "greenbacks" you now find in your pocket call themselves not "Treasury Notes," but "Federal Reserve Notes." We still use "banknotes" as currency just as we did in the nineteenth century. But now they are *public* banknotes—"central" banknotes. They are *Citizen* Notes, you might say.

The new Federal Reserve also commandeered the liquidity risk-pooling system that some banks had developed on their own. It was a system whereby one bank, if it began to run out of reserves in the form of Treasurys or gold during a temporary panic, could borrow such reserves from other member banks. This is why the Fed's full name is the "Federal Reserve *System*." It is, among other things, a reserve-pooling system maintained among Fed "member banks," which not only ameliorates but also helps to *prevent* financial crises. Any given bank is less likely to go bankrupt. With that assurance, there's less risk of a bank run.

The "greenback" was the start of the dollar as a trusted circulating medium. Much as Hamilton had hoped, it was a representation of common money. Private bank promises were steadily supplanted by national bank promises—private banknotes by national banknotes, private paper by public paper. We were well on our way to the ultimate public IOU—the Federal Reserve notes that are today's US currency.

Why did the greenback supplant private banknotes? Well, their uniformity and stability nationwide of course helped. Regulation also played a role—partly by enabling that uniformity and stability. The national banks had to be licensed. They were carefully regulated by the OCC, which kept the new currency stable and reliable. And as the federal government began levying more and more kinds of taxes during the late nineteenth and early twentieth centuries, it required payment in greenbacks rather than private banknotes.

And so we came to recognize that private banks have essentially public functions. The unruly "wildcat" banks had gone out of business or jumped through the hoops necessary to be chartered as quasi-public national banks. We relearned Hamilton's lesson. A growing economy requires a stable and *elastic* money—a circulating public promise whose quantity can be regularly adjusted, so as to avoid both underissuance and overissuance. To stay stable the Fed acts in concert with the OCC and other US financial regulators established since 1913: notably but not solely the Federal Deposit Insurance Corporation ("FDIC") of 1933 and the Securities and Exchange Commission ("SEC") of 1934. The system is the American public's primary money modulator. It gives us a franchised good—a sovereign currency—that is now reasonably uniform not only across space, but also across time.

Nowadays all claims we exercise over resources by spending money—all payments we make in dollars from bank accounts, whether they arrive there from deposits or lending—"clear" through our central bank. The Fed handles our modern rendition of the old "greenback" and manages private banks to protect the integrity of the dollar. Another regulator, the FDIC, assists with the regulatory task. Its establishment in 1933 put all of us—

the public—directly on the hook to compensate depositors when banks go bankrupt.

So we can view all of our ordinary market exchanges all at once, in their overall public purpose. The banks that hand you dollars when you withdraw from your account; the credits they give others when you write a check or swipe a plastic card; the credit to your account when you borrow—this all serves a public function. The banks are partner institutions acting on our collective behalf, via our central bank—the Fed. What the Fed creates and distributes through the banks, i.e., the US dollar, is ultimately just the monetized full faith and credit of the United States, measured out in increments.

RELEASING GOLD

In the first twenty years of the Fed's operations, our new central bank adhered to a "gold standard," much as the world's other central banks had done for decades. The Fed was but a fledgling central bank, which joined a global "club" of banks that hoped to ensure monetary stability during the first real modern "globalization," with cross-border trade growing rapidly. Of no mind to be "disruptive," officials wanted the new regime and new national currency—those Federal Reserve notes—to be quickly accepted and trusted by the nation's now many millions of market participants. And nothing signaled trustworthiness and financial probity in those days like gold.

It was after the crash of 1929, twenty years later, that the gold commitment became far too heavy to carry any longer. During a crunch, when credit is rapidly contracting and the money supply thereby vanishing, the monetary authority should act in "contrarian" fashion, putting out as much credit as private bankers are calling back in. That could be done, in theory, by lowering gold reserve requirements and thereby raising money multiples over those reserves. Yet making such cumbersome changes couldn't be done on the fly as market sentiment restlessly shifted in bipolar fashion. It was easier to supply credit and money directly during the bust, then rein it back in once "recovery" began.

And that was what FDR did in 1933, when he formally severed the dollar's domestic relation to gold. John Maynard Keynes had persuaded the Bank of England to do that ten years earlier, thereby bringing Britain out of recession. Of Roosevelt's decision, Keynes wrote in a *New York Times* op-ed that the president was "splendidly right."

And he was.

With the promise of gold out of the picture, we can better see what was true all along: Dollars are *our* claims—*our* promissory notes—issued in the name of us all to one another. They aren't just *my* notes issued to *you* or *your* notes issued to *me*. Banks are *distributing our product* and are responsible to us for its quality. Which is why we regulate them with the Fed's partner agencies, the OCC and FDIC. Our financial regulators may not always do their jobs well. All human institutions are prone to error, of course—and especially so when they or our legislators are unclear about their mission. But we can now see what these institutions are for: they're for maintaining the smooth operation of our promissory circulatory system, so as to ensure the stable, sustainable, and socially inclusive betterment of our material well-being through time.

CHAPTER 9

WHAT BANKS DO FOR US

Bankers sure seem to have it pretty good. Those with an eye for business might be curious: What would it take to get in on the action and establish a bank of one's own? It's easier than one might think.

You'd have to get a license from a regulator up front—what's called a "bank charter." What you don't need is a stash of money up front. As bankers know, you can get rich starting from virtually nothing if people are willing to bank on your promises. And they *will* do just that when the feds are backing you up with deposit insurance.

To go through the steps, consider a tale of two friends. Bob and Aaron had ideas for a new business. At first it was selling a slick online course called "The Seven Secrets of Banking That Will Make You Rich" for the bargain price of only $19.99 per month. Then Bob wondered: If they really knew the alchemy of finance, why sell an online course? Why not just *use* the secrets to get rich? Bob already knew how finance makes money out of thin air. Aaron was trained in moral philosophy and had no trouble seeing how money is created from nothing, on the strength of so many promises. So Bob and Aaron decided to open a bank.

The two friends both owned suits and cleaned up well. They could sound respectable when they needed to. They also had the right friends. One friend allowed them to use the stately old building on the corner in the town square. There they'd shake people's hands, look 'em in the eye, and decide who could be trusted. The building was mainly an old-fashioned flourish, a hipster styling of sorts; the whole operation could have been run online. What really mattered was a certain big bureaucratic favor by a friend in government. She knew Bob and Aaron well enough to feel sure they'd use the secrets of banking wisely and for the public interest. After Bob and Aaron asked her for help, she somehow persuaded her own friends in high places to waive many of the usual chartering formalities. And soon enough, "Golden Eagle Bank and Trust" was approved, chartered, and open for business.

Turned out Bob and Aaron had a good eye for sizing people up. A nice man, Mr. Jones, was the very first customer to walk through the front door. He needed $15,000 for a car. Neither Bob nor Aaron had *that* kind of money in their personal bank accounts at Wells Fargo and JPMorgan Chase at the time. They'd been unemployed until recently (and thus cooking up business ideas). Both were "running on fumes" with $3,000 combined in their personal accounts. Fortunately, that made no difference at all to the business. They simply wrote out a check to Mr. Jones in the amount of $15,000—being sure to write in the dollar sign, $— *in the name of Golden Eagle Bank.*

That IOU was then "swapped" for Mr. Jones's personal IOU and his signed "promissory note." This required a bit of bookkeeping (Bob and Aaron insisted upon using paper books and fountain pens, another old-fashioned flourish). So they'd mark down *$15,000* in the liabilities column of Golden Eagle's balance sheet, and mark up *$15,000* in the assets column of the balance sheet corresponding to Mr. Jones's promissory note. Golden Eagle check in hand, Mr. Jones headed out the door.

Good thing neither of them issued a *personal* IOU ("I promise to pay the bearer of this note $15,000. Yours truly, Bob"). Jones would have been out of luck. The owner of the car he'd hoped to purchase, Ms. Vega, would have to present that personal IOU to her own credit union for redemption in Uncle Sam IOUs, i.e., dollars. And surely the managers would stare back blankly, wondering, *Bob, Aaron—who are they, anyway? Why would anybody accept a promise from two recently unemployed academics?*

But since the IOU to Jones was issued by *Golden Eagle Bank and Trust*, which had received the US federal government's blessing, it *was* equivalent to Uncle Sam IOUs. The IOU had the public's imprimatur. With that, Ms. Vega and her credit union could accept it as readily as a check from JPMorgan or cash from the US Treasury.

When Ms. Vega's credit union accepted the check, it adjusted its books. Its bankers credited her "demand deposit" account with a $15,000 asset, which she was free to draw from as she pleased, to buy groceries or whatever. They noted a corresponding liability in her right to draw upon that account at will, and booked an asset in the "claim" the credit union now had on Golden Eagle (which corresponded with Golden Eagle's liability). Jones had made payment and the car was now his. The bank loan had worked—as money!

Jones paid back his loan to Golden Eagle Bank only gradually. Bob or Aaron always kept the books up to date, gradually reducing the liability numbers as payments came in. Those numbers whittled to zero after a while. Once paid in full, the bank was left with a 5 percent interest payment, recorded as a (still dollar-denominated) net asset. And, voila, Bob and Aaron profited from a promise! So of course they immediately withdrew the funds in new Uncle Sam IOUs (dollars), bought themselves drinks in celebration, and spent the evening talking about logic, Hegel, and the spooky way self-consciousness creates recursive collective action problems and financial crises.

Every Thursday, they'd meet for those drinks, paid for with a Golden Eagle debit card that incurred further bank liabilities ("debits," a.k.a debts). If the assets weren't there on the bank's books already, it was no problem; they'd just "pay off" the extra liabilities later, for instance as another borrower, Ms. Smith, repaid her small-business loan. With her interest payments, the bank would cover the cost of drinks, eventually.

Bob and Aaron carried on like this until the bank was earning steady profits. Soon enough, they could hire accountants and loan officers to handle all lending and collecting functions. They barely went to work themselves, though they never did miss a Thursday night meeting for celebratory drinks and philosophy, courtesy of Golden Eagle Bank and Trust. If you've ever heard of "bankers' hours," you know about the leisurely practice.

Was this some weird Ponzi operation—yet another way elites get ever further ahead and corrupt the republic? Well, yes and no. On the one hand, they were "getting something for nothing," profiting from nothing more than the authority to issue Uncle Sam's promissory notes and size up people's creditworthiness. On the other hand, what they were doing is exactly what *all banks do already*, including all those wholesome community banks and credit unions you hear praised by the same people who sing the praises of "small family farms." And if that sounds impossible or fraudulent, you may have some misconceptions about what banks actually do for us.

BANKS DON'T JUST "INTERMEDIATE"

If this story seems confusing, you may be assuming a conventional notion about what banks do, which goes like this. First, people get some money through work or whatever. They then "deposit" their money with the bank so they can later spend "out of" their accounts.

In this picture, the banks perform "deposit-taking," "safekeeping," and "payment" services. They're just *repositories of accumulated funds*. They may charge you for the account (if you don't keep a stipulated minimum balance). But they really make their money by loaning out those funds. They "intermediate" between people who save and people who borrow, taking a small fee.

You'd be forgiven for assuming this "intermediation" story is so much common sense. Mainstream economists, even famous ones, often reinforce the picture in their public comments and op-eds (Paul Krugman's *New York Times* column is a leading example of such rhetorical mischief). In what is sometimes called the "loanable funds" model, banks merely pass the scarce stock of capital between hands for a fee. So when a borrower gets more money from a bank loan, *some saver now has less money*. This "reallocation" from people who save to people who borrow is said to be "efficient," because capital is reallocated from less valued to more valued uses. But borrowing and lending are a *wash* for *overall* demand in the economy in this picture. Banks do not create new money; they simply pass it around. So goes the intermediation story.[1]

Banks of course take deposits and keep them, so you don't have to stash cash under the mattress. But that's hardly *all* that they do, or even the *main* thing they do. They also *create money* from nothing. With the public's blessing, they steadily grow "the money supply." That is the story of Golden Eagle Bank we've just told.

This will sound ludicrously freewheeling if you haven't freed yourself from misconceptions about what banks actually do for us. So let's more carefully walk through how banks pull the monetary rabbit out of the promissory hat.

CHECKING THE FINGERNAILS

Say you need to borrow $15,000 to purchase a car. The car will allow you to take a new high-paying job that requires a commute. You walk into a bank near your home one day, hoping to secure a loan. The bank's loan officer looks you over, up and down, seeing that you're respectably dressed and well groomed. No dirt under your fingernails, no obscenities tattooed on your forehead. She asks you to take a seat.

The loan officer asks you a few questions and likes your answers. Your new job sounds promising. That someone offered it to you speaks well of your prospects. She asks for your Social Security number and proof of your identity, runs a credit check, determines your prior borrowing and repaying history, whether you've been convicted of any felonies, whether there are any liens on your property, what previous jobs you have held, and so forth. Finally, she decides to approve the loan.

She then draws up papers—mostly boilerplate—that spell out the loan terms. There is the principal amount, for example, as well as the interest the bank will charge for the loan. There might be a lien on collateral—though in this case perhaps not, since the loan's collateral can just be the car itself, which the bank could later repossess. There's also a schedule of regular monthly payments which include both a principal and an interest component. And of course there are lots of documents explaining the consequences of any late or missed monthly payments. You read through these documents, and finally agree to their terms.

Now comes the interesting part. For this transaction to be finalized, you'll have to sign a promissory note. Your promise to repay is about to become money. It is about to become *Fed* promissory notes.

THE BIG SWAP

The word "note" on the document you sign is the same word you read when you read "Federal Reserve Note" across the top of a dollar bill. It is a promissory note and it represents two things. On the one hand, there's your obligation to the bank that extends you the loan. And on the other hand, there's the bank's claim upon you. The note at once signifies the bank's asset and your liability. But that's just one side of the agreement.

Viewed from the other side, the bank also takes on a liability, which corresponds to an asset that you will now have. The bank will soon open or credit a deposit in your name or cut a check in your name in conveying the lent funds to you, which is a liability for the bank. Checking accounts, a.k.a. "demand deposits," which can be spent at will, are bank liabilities. Banks are "liable" and obliged to recognize withdrawals or drafts drawn on them. It's a liability that's also your asset, in that very credit—that deposit—that the bank extends to you.

So, really, the note represents what the accountants who do double-entry bookkeeping would call *two* "balance sheets." One for each of you is produced by the lending transaction, and each one has two sides. It's a bilateral *trade*. Each party gets something. And each party gives something in return. You get the lent funds. You give your promissory note in return. The bank gets that note. It gives you the funds in return.

The transaction is a kind of "swap"—a swap of both assets and liabilities. The bank swaps an asset/liability to you in return for an asset/liability that you swap to the bank. You receive the asset that is the bank deposit, meaning the $15,000, which is a bank liability. The bank receives the asset that is your promissory note, which is your liability.

And what is that $15,000 deposit of funds into an account with your name on it? You can pay out of it and buy the car, because other people and their banks will accept the bank's IOU as payment. So that IOU is as good as money. In fact, it *is* money—*bona fide* US dollars, as recognized by the Fed. That was the deal when the bank was licensed, in a "charter" agreement. As it continues to pass monitoring tests, it continues to have the Fed's permission to issue dollar promises, "monetizing" the United States' full faith and credit.

So when you take out a loan, what you've done is temporarily swap your own promissory notes for Fed promissory notes—your private IOU for public IOUs. As you repay, you're swapping back over time. This is what bank lending is.

It is also what bank "money creation" is. The banks don't "create" money single-handedly; the Fed does that. The Fed "issues" its own promissory notes and their depository equivalent, by "accommodating" payments drawn on such deposits via the payments system, which the Fed conveniently administers. But the

Fed does this without deciding who gets what loans. That important decision is left to the banks. We in effect "outsource" it to them, letting private sector entities perform this public function. We let the banks decide whose private promises are "publicly recognized," whose promises shall be counted as money.

But one might still struggle with the idea: *How can a bank lend what it doesn't already have?* The answer is that you don't have it *until* you lend it. For bank lending isn't about having and conveying at all. It's about *issuing and trading*. It's about swapping publicly issued—"vertical"—IOUs for privately issued—"horizontal"—IOUs. It's about *business*, because trading promises *is* its business, the way it profits. It's also the important job society has come to ask of it, a kind of public service.

So, there you have it. Banks are our "gatekeepers." Are your promises credible? We let the banks answer on society's behalf. Through their stamp of approval, in the very act of declaring you creditworthy, new units of public money (dollars) are made from nothing.

A BANK FOR ALL OF US

Modern banking is complex, but ultimately rooted in something simple: converting private promises into public promises. When Ms. Smith or Mr. Jones signs a private promissory note to repay a loan for a car, a home, or a business, a bank's stamp of credibility converts it into a public promissory note that we call money. *Your* promises and *my* promises become *our* promises—legal tender—by a kind of "social contract" mediated by our publicly licensed and supported banking system.

It's worth pausing to ponder the remarkable simplicity of what, basically, we ask those who operate in the tall buildings, stately structures, and aged institutions to do for us. And that is: checking and stamping. Banks check our creditworthiness, then stamp our private promissory notes into public promissory notes (dollars)—that is, into real, spendable money, i.e., legal tender.

That's almost disappointing. How is it that bankers are so well paid just for sizing people up and dropping a stamp to the table? Wouldn't the public *really* be mad about the outsized salaries top bankers take home today if they knew that banks such as Citigroup or Wells Fargo really have only one indispensable job: to "check our credit" and decide whether our promises are credible?

And what if we *already* know that every citizen is worthy of some amount of "credit"? Much as with Mr. Jones or Ms. Smith, maybe we can safely assume that ordinary people will by and large use some basic amount of money given to them productively. For the most part, they'll use it in order to meet their basic needs, or the needs of their families, or they'll spend the money and stimulate economic activity. In that case, why do we need a *second* credit check—by a private bank—on those same basic funds? Isn't that redundant, unnecessary, inefficient? Aren't we thus giving our bankers, in the form of the interest they charge, something for nothing?

We believe the second credit check is unnecessary, at least for some basic level of income. The central bank should do the job instead. The Fed or the Treasury can just give public IOUs, i.e., money, to people directly, crediting our bank accounts on a regular (e.g., monthly) basis. As we noted earlier, the US Congress has already begun authorizing such payments in response to the coronavirus pandemic of 2020. The private banks can continue doing their jobs for credit decisions *above* such basic amounts.

If that sounds exotic, just think a bit more about what the central bank has long been doing already. It *already is* issuing promises to people. It simply does that indirectly, via the private sector banks. They check our credit and stamp units of money into existence with the public's blessing, for the sake of our general prosperity. If the Fed gave us money directly, it would be doing *the very same thing*—only in a more direct, more reliable way. As we'll explain in Chapter 10, the Fed can conduct monetary operations much as it now does, and *more effectively* than it now does, in a more harmonious monetary symphony.

EXPANDING THE CIRCLE OF TRUST

We saw in Chapter 8 that our banking system evolved from a fraught history. Would we choose this end result again if we could start from scratch? It's hard to say. The trouble isn't our current public bank–private bank partnership, per se; it's that the private banks can't be fully trusted to do their parts. And we simply don't have to entrust as much to them as we used to given new credit-checking and money-transfer technologies.

The idea of a public–private partnership does, or at least did, have a compelling rationale, which is worth recalling. For starters, we should want people to be able to secure a loan. People often have very good ideas about how to produce new, useful, even exciting goods and services. They simply don't have money. They don't have sufficient funds to purchase or rent the necessary "inputs," so that they can command the right to use them productively. "It takes money to make money," we often hear. Because people need temporary *claims* over resources, in order to control those resources' disposition and "put them to use." That would have been why, in the auto-loan story we told earlier, Mr. Jones ventured into a bank one afternoon. He stood to earn more money—and therefore, in all likelihood, to "add more value"—by taking the new job he'd been offered. But he only could take the job if he could purchase the car as an "input." And without a bank loan, he wouldn't have that money.

What *did* Jones have? He had his word. And his word was believable, "worthy" of credit. If everybody could see just how creditworthy he was given his sterling smile and good reputation, the automobile dealer might have accepted his promissory note *itself* in payment for the car. That is not quite as ridiculous as it may sound. Oftentimes among friends and family your promise alone *is* enough to secure control over resources. ("Mom, may I borrow the car?" "Yes, son.") But generally, this works only among family and friends. This is the sense in which Hyman Minsky was right when he said anyone can issue a money with the trick being to get it accepted beyond one's circle of trust.

After all, our private circles have boundaries for good reason; knowing who to believe is complicated. Could we really expect everyone from whom you might wish to purchase or rent resources somehow to check your credit score and decide whether to accept your personal promissory notes in payment for what they are selling or renting out? That's a lot of work, when it's even feasible to ask around. To expect it would be unworkable, or at least considerably slow down and limit value-creating transaction activity, the motor of economic growth in all "exchange economies" such as our own.

Society solved this problem long ago. We just *delegate* the task of issuing universally acceptable, "vertical" public promissory notes. We assign that task, first and foremost, to our central bank. It is "central" both because it is the "hub" to which the other banks all connect and because it is the one bank that's there for *all* of us—as citizens—rather than just certain special "clients." The central bank then delegates the job of deciding who gets the government's money. The banks do that, again, by checking and stamping—checking our creditworthiness and stamping units of money into existence.

Why give private banks this job? Because they're supposed to be "closer to the ground" and better able than "bureaucrats in Washington" to make particular credit assessments and lending decisions, prudently and productively. Being more sensitive to the state of the neighborhood or region and to the creditworthiness of people who live in their communities, local officials can better decide who we can prudently allow to "swap" their private notes temporarily for public notes in order to gain command over resources and thus carry out all of that promised productive activity—activity that grows the sum total of wealth.

We agree that private banks do have that useful function, to a large extent—as long as their lending activities are regulated in ways we'll return to later. As we'll see, optimal regulation ensures the "optimal swapping" of private money for public money: not too much, not too little; and only for truly productive, not merely speculative, purposes. With banks doing the checking and stamping, the "horizontal" dimension of promises extends far more widely and in far more directions. That allows more people to gain command over resources to produce further resources, and much more abundantly than if we actually had to be personally acquainted with the people who we might get to accept our personal promises. There's far more transacting than could otherwise ever occur, and so far more productive activity than could otherwise ever occur, in time making us richer overall.

But as much as we need good credit-checking at work "on the ground," a central bank is also needed to oversee all the promises being made in the economy. Like a mechanic that constantly tunes a high-performance engine, a central bank will make steady, daily adjustments to the total amount of spendable claims over resources in circulation. It does that by tracking what stock of resources there already is and guessing how that stock is likely to change when people look poised to use it productively. That's not something any particular private bank can do for us. As we saw in Chapter 8, that was the important lesson of history that led to the Fed's establishment. This is why central banking is the only known way to enlist the power of money in the service of greater economic production and our commonweal.

Think of the whole central public bank–private bank partnership as a useful way to "pool" promises: we convert "his" and "her" promises into "our" promises—promises that can be believed and redeemed anywhere, with anyone, by anyone. Because we often don't know who we can trust, the range of people who will accept a given person's promissory notes as money-like claims over resources is far smaller than the vast population who will accept society's Fed promissory notes for such purposes. Those "vertical" claims against a trusted government will circulate more widely than "horizontal" IOUs within smaller circles of trust. So they're more suitable for use as a *widely* circulating, "basic money," as we called it in Chapter 1. Once we add a "vertical" dimension into the realm of our promising, by a public backing, we enable much more promising across the "horizontal" dimension in our market activities as well. And with more money in our hands and bank accounts, we enable far more productive activity, eventually making us all richer.

The banks, then, are just the crossroads of "vertical" and "horizontal" money. For administering the "big swap" of promises, they charge interest as payment for the service. The interest is, if you will, "privatized seignorage"—their piece of the money creation action. (Recall our discussion of "seignorage" from Chapter 5: the rents that feudal lords—Old French seigniors—enjoyed in virtue of issuing the "coins of their realms," which they could spend as freely as they could lend.)

CHECKING THE BANKERS' FINGERNAILS

It's a sensible arrangement, in theory. Each "partner" does what it can do best. Naturally, we the public will want to be very careful in choosing and then overseeing anyone we permit to distribute public money—much more so than they themselves will be in deciding to whom to lend. Those private bankers, you know, you'd want to look 'em over, up and down, pretty thoroughly. No dirt under the fingernails. No sign of motives that might corrupt their sense of public purpose, such as mindless love of money. You'd ideally employ only the upright types rather than the greedy types—the types who like money but aren't in it *just* for the money. They'd labor in solemn appreciation of their service to the public and take utmost care in being sure to deliver.

It's an amusing thought by today's standards. Ever since the "greed is good" 1980s and '90s, it has been more fashionable for bankers to brazenly ignore their public responsibilities. Along with steady trends toward deregulation and blind "markets know best" deference, the 2008 crisis is the unsurprising result of this thinking.

Still, we, the public, do have ways of screening. That's precisely what our regime of conditional bank-licensure and exacting bank regulation is. We can always deny a bank deposit insurance, or even revoke its charter. Wells Fargo has been heavily disciplined lately for its disservices to society—including outright theft from its customers—under an implicit threat of being booted from the finance franchise.

There is a distinguished history of expecting bankers to rise to their public responsibilities. When President Woodrow Wilson signed the 1913 Federal Reserve Act, with an eye to catching up with Europe (he called its currency system "far better than our own"), he specifically praised J. P. Morgan, the Wall Street banker, for preserving his honor in comparison to the greed and "undefined wickedness" among most bankers of the day. Bankers, he said, should be "statesmen." Even so, what Morgan taught us, ultimately, was that private bankers could not be entrusted with the fate of society.

The crisis of 1893 had brought the United States into what was by that time its deepest depression in history. Suddenly, J. P. Morgan was the last hope. After the booming 1880s, the railroads had been overbuilt and poorly financed, forcing numerous banks into bankruptcy. Unemployment spiked in industrial cities and towns. Farms hit hard times with collapsing prices of cotton and wheat. Banks went broke. Violence broke out in the streets of Ohio, Pennsylvania, and Illinois. The Pullman Strike shut down the nation's transportation system. After a series of ham-handed measures that only made matters worse, President Grover Cleveland finally approached an esteemed private banker, one J. Pierpont Morgan, with a business proposition: a loan to the government of $63 million, along with his assistance in procuring gold and keeping it in the country.

The approach was itself an embarrassment. A sovereign republic and its president, hat in hand, seeking the good graces of one rich man, offering him a sweetheart's bargain. Perhaps it was fortunate that Morgan agreed. President Cleveland was able to buy up enough gold to maintain the gold standard. That brought the start of a slow recovery, as well as a major political realignment and a new president, William McKinley. Even so, counting on one rich man is no way to run an economy.

After the next big crisis, the Panic of 1907, Morgan was called upon for help yet again. In backroom dealings, he helped the main private bankers work out a plan. These dealings worried people. Conspiracy theories do sometimes have an element of truth, after all. (The paranoid style of thought is just highly unreliable about what that element is.) So Morgan was compelled to appear before Congress and asked to assuage fears that he would monopolize money for the bankers' or his own interests. Surely his lending decisions would be based on money and property, right? Morgan dug in: "No, sir: the first thing is character ... A man I do not trust could not get money from me on all the bonds in Christendom." Morgan seemed rather clear: yes indeed, money could be monopolized in private hands much as the oil, steel, and railroads had been. He'd do as he personally saw fit, like it or not.

That defiant testimony seems to have helped many Americans overcome their deep reluctance about anything so menacing-sounding as a "central bank." After all, what was Mr. Morgan himself but a one-man central bank, acting in its own private rather than the public interest? The old republican idea finally held sway: a country could not trust its fate to the good graces and whims of one rich man, or a financial oligarchy of such people. Plus, Morgan was mortal, and when the guy died, then what?

A compromise was reached. In 1913 Woodrow Wilson signed the Federal Reserve Act, which finally established a system of regional banks and centralized committees, a public-private partnership.

TRUST THE BANKERS LESS

The whole history of money and banking is a story of restraint and its lack, trust and abuse—then ultimately collapsed trust. Things are hardly different today. Can we really trust private profiteers to show due restraint when so many banks abuse our trust? If anything, here we aren't paranoid enough. Wells Fargo is only the latest and worst of brazen miscreants. All of the big banks got caught up in the irrational exuberance of the recent boom times. This time, JPMorgan Chase Bank was itself bailed out by the US government in 2008, along with most major US banks, in an ironic twist.

If we shouldn't trust the unstable profiteering of private banks, we do have a sound alternative. Just rely on them less. Insource the now outsourced functions. Use new technological advances that make that easier to do than in times past.

We've learned that an economy runs much better when a central bank is conducting the symphony. And if the trombones are blaring too loudly, overtaking the other instruments, the conductor should tone down their part in the score. Meaning, if our banking system isn't exactly making beautiful music lately, we can simply ask less of the private banks. Our central bank can do more for us, so that we can depend on private bankers less. And we can establish a more direct and efficient way of accomplishing what our system already does: we citizens should transact directly with the central bank. Let's see how this would work.

CHAPTER 10

HOW TO CUT OUT THE MIDDLEMAN

Our central bank, the Fed, is now a bank for banks. It could easily become a bank for all of us. You'd go online to the central bank website, enter a password to open your personal account. Et voila, you've got money! Right there on the screen, an extra $1,000 per month with your name on it. You'd have sure money, based on nothing more, and nothing less, than Federal Reserve promises, made in the full faith and credit of the United States of America.[1]

What you do with the money would be up to you. Maybe you hit a button and transfer funds to your private account at the local credit union, where you keep most of your personal savings. Maybe you'd make payments directly from your Citizen Account at the Fed, using one of the many new device-accessible payment technologies now coming online. You might buy a lamp, or car seat cover, or other things for sale directly with your Fed digital wallet, by an electronic payment. Or you could withdraw cold hard cash at an ATM. The Fed-issued digital dollar would be as good as any dollar—as "golden" as any other Fed promise.

Is this too good to be true? Not really. The Fed already credits the big private banks with large sums at very low interest rates. And proposals for "helicopter money" during slumps come with no interest at all—just free money! As explained in Chapter 2, here's how things currently work: officials open the accounts of Bank of America or Wells Fargo, and mark up numbers over here, mark down numbers over there, on an electronic spread-sheet. And that's pretty much it; the rest of the process is nothing more than various ways of doing the bookkeeping. So there's no technological reason why Fed officials can't open an account on the central bank's books for every citizen and type in, say, $1,000 or even $2,000 per month into all of our personal accounts (or run a program that does this automatically). It could also provide free banking services to all businesses, not just privileged bank-ing and other big financial firms, in this way. That would mean rather less overhead for small businesses.

So why shouldn't every citizen and authorized business or resi-dent have a "Citizen Account" or a "Resident Account" at the Fed with his or her name on it? An account would be opened auto-matically for citizens on their dates of birth or naturalization, and upon request by others. The government could run any and all federal payments, including procurement payments, Social Secu-rity "checks," or tax refunds, through those accounts. But then, in addition to current payments, the Fed could regularly credit a guaranteed income. (We could also pay for "baby bonds," or proceeds from sovereign wealth funds or national investments, in the same way.)

Call it one's "birthright" for being a citizen or authorized resi-dent of the richest country in human history.

Earlier we suggested that every citizen is worthy of a little credit. This would allow people of lesser means to spend extra money into the economy, stimulating consumer demand, com-pany sales, hiring, and investment. Which is good for everyone.

The state of Alaska pays a dividend on oil resources to every Alaskan. It is a very popular program, unsurprisingly. American political figures regularly celebrate the promise of shared pros-perity. But talk is cheap. Why shouldn't the central bank give sure money to everyone—a "Prosperity Dividend," say, analogous to

Alaska's or Norway's petroleum dividend? Think of it as a small down payment on that old shared-prosperity promise, a token of good faith to keep politicians honest.

THE DIRECT ROUTE

Is this too idealistic, too looney, or just too Alaskan? Not really. The Fed's whole purpose is to increase the "purchasing power" of citizens up to the point that this "power" threatens to become inflationary. It just does that by an indirect route, via the publicly licensed private sector banks that stand between you and it—our bank, our "central" bank, owned by the citizenry itself.

As we explained in Chapter 9, the Fed (very cheaply) lends to the banks, which are then supposed to lend to us, thereby creating money for us to spend for productive purposes. But if the Fed can achieve the same end as well or better by a more direct route, shouldn't it? In the past, when communications technologies were more primitive, "middleman" banks might have made good network sense. But from time to time we should ask: Do they still make as much sense, when technology can make the link between us and our central bank more direct? Aren't they a wasteful relic of a more primitive, more technologically backward past? Capitalists loathe inefficiency. So surely all of them would favor a more direct, more effective way of getting the same job done. (Or could it be that it's not efficiency that they care about after all?)

We rely on private banks as much as we do, as we've suggested already, partly because private banks are thought to be good at checking credit. They didn't do so well with that during the "subprime" lending boom in the lead-up to 2008—they barely checked. And while direct central-bank-to-citizen banking would have been difficult in the nineteenth century, when communications networks across our continent-sized country were primitive, this doesn't explain why we still rely on private banks as heavily as we do now.

That has a more political explanation. In the days when J. P.

Morgan personally backed the US financial system in handshake deals made in a cigar smoke–filled backroom, Wall Street bankers could demand a sweetheart deal just to go along with the Federal Reserve's establishment (a deal that eventually included ownership stakes in the Fed's regional banks, seats on those regional banks' boards, and claims on income generated in a self-financing system).

What began in political expediency became the unquestioned order of things.

Despite reform after reform, which changed the way the Fed works, the central bank has yet to bank directly with each citizen. Originally, the Fed didn't even set interest rates that we now hear so much about. And if it turns out that, after over a hundred years of experience, the private banks are not doing certain jobs very effectively, the Fed can perfectly well bring those jobs "in-house." As we'll see, our central bank can operate more effectively and more equitably by "cutting out the middleman" and issuing dollars through Citizen Accounts.

"PUSHING ON A STRING"

When the Fed now lends cheap money to the banks, they are supposed to pass the money on in cheap loans to us. But they don't necessarily pass the money on. They're trying to make money (for their shareholders), and whether to lend, or not, is a business decision. Simply having more money on their books, by itself, won't lead them to immediately take on additional credit risk—not until there's a good opportunity for profit. And often there looks to be more profit in betting on speculative derivatives and commodity markets than in lending to you or us. What's more, during a slump people need money, as does the economy as a whole. But the banks are understandably reluctant to take on more debt. Too much private debt is what brought on the crash and the slump in the first place. Getting the banks to lend and people to borrow and spend is accordingly said to be like "pushing on a string" in these circumstances: when pressure is applied, the thing bulges, getting fatter, instead of being efficiently moved forward.

The string really went noodle-like during the crisis aftermath of 2008 to 2012. The Fed and Treasury hoped to "pump liquidity into the system" so that banks could keep lending despite the 2008 "credit crunch." Many banks simply hoarded the additional money, hoping to ride out the storm and come out ahead.[2] Others speculated with the extra funds, on price swings in secondary markets that do little or nothing for consumers. And anyway why would the banks ramp up lending to consumers without a commitment from the federal authorities to forgive their debts or otherwise prop up consumer spending? Millions of people were left "underwater" in the crisis aftermath, owing more than they owned. And a lot of them weren't especially keen to borrow even more, especially not during a protracted slump, when they may or may not have had a job.[3]

Yet most Americans really could use some extra money—especially now, during the coronavirus pandemic and its aftermath. They're likely to spend any new income they receive on employment-enhancing consumer goods and services. If the billions of dollars spent on quantitative easing after 2008 were given to people directly, hoarding would never have been a problem. The money would have been spent immediately, creating conditions in which the banks would find it profitable to lend again. No more effective "pump priming" could be imagined. The same is true today. In 2020 the U.S. sent out $1200 checks to many, but that was only a start. The millions upon millions of Americans now just getting by are prone to spend any new income, not hoard it. That makes them a much more reliable partner for stimulating the economy than derivatives, speculators, and banker fat cats. We don't have to "push on a string" with private banks. We can give people money and "pull on the string"—moving things along in the intended direction. Which is to say, we can make banking work more efficiently for us.

"SOCIALISM FOR THE RICH"

Some 40 million people in the United States are now "unbanked." Yet more are "underbanked," with only limited or intermittent access to banking and payment services. Though usually poor, they spend 10 percent of their incomes on financial transactions that the "banked" needn't bother with—typically in "payday lender" fees and interest charges. If a Citizen Account were established in every citizen's name, many millions of these people would immediately have easy, free access to the banking system. They'd no longer be preyed upon by "fringe finance" firms that exist solely to exploit their disadvantages.

And what if noncitizens want in on the action? What about small businesses and other nonbank firms who may wish to bank with the central bank? If there is enough interest, the Fed can offer "Resident Accounts" to these persons. They'd be like Citizen Accounts for most intents and purposes, but opened only upon request, rather than automatically upon birth or attainment of citizenship. The accounts might close out more frequently, for instance, when a business turns out to be short-lived. Resident aliens might be granted temporary use as well, especially when they have trouble establishing an account at a private bank.

It is one thing to offer Resident Accounts as banking services, and quite another for the Fed to offer free money. So they may or may not receive the basic income payments and "helicopter money" drops that flow to Citizen Accounts, depending on whether policy makers decide they have good public reasons for having them. Were officials to decide that they do—e.g., for the sake of stoking purchasing activity—we could also decide that the payments could be made only for special purposes, agreed upon as a condition of receipt. One might have to agree to spend the money on real goods and services rather than simply speculate, for instance (since that wouldn't sustainably stimulate the economy).

At the moment, the big banks enjoy a "public option" with

respect to banking that ordinary citizens have never been offered. And as it happens, the option comes with lavish handouts from the government as well. The government issues Treasurys—a safe asset with a certain interest payment—as part of its monetary operations. Dealer banks and other institutions are happy to take the easy, sure money for the "service" of simply not doing something else with the funds.

Indeed, as noted in Chapter 2, simply for parking funds at the central bank, the banks are now paid interest (so-called "interest on reserves," or IOR). But while the banks "earn" a premium on their accounts with the Fed, they pass only a fraction of it on to people like us who hold deposits with them; ordinary bank deposits pay a much lower rate of interest. So the banks receive a gratuitous "rent" payment just because we need transaction accounts for ordinary purchases.

If we had no choice but to give handouts to the rich, for lack of any real alternative, we could write it off as a "cost of doing business" in the service of larger social purposes. So it goes, occasionally. But we actually do have an alternative, which is not only feasible, but both more effective and more equitable. We don't need to privilege the big financial firms with a free "public bank option." Not anymore, anyway. The option can be extended to everyone, by giving everyone a Citizen or Resident Account. Instead of the Fed paying interest on private-bank reserve accounts, it can pay interest on our personal Citizen Accounts, putting money directly in our pockets.

"LEANING AGAINST THE WIND"

The private banks, for their part, would still lend as they now do, doing what they do best. If you worry about the United States veering uncontrollably toward "socialism," rest assured, we'd still have good ol' financial capitalism, with fat cat bankers getting filthy, greedily rich. A public bank, the Fed, has long been the foundation of American capitalism. Making it a bank for everyone would simply make sure everyone—literally all of us—gets a bigger, fairer slice of the capitalist pie.

The Fed, for its part, would do pretty much what it does now to manage the overall supply of money. It would simply run normal operations through our Citizen Accounts instead of solely through big-bank reserve accounts.[4] Each Citizen Account would pay its holder a rate of interest, just as Fed reserve accounts do now. The Fed would then raise or lower the rate in order to influence how much we all save or spend. Like any good central bank, it would "lean against the wind," smoothing out the ups and downs of the cycle of private business.

During a bubble or boom years, the Fed would raise the rate in order to make saving more attractive than spending. The overall level of credit and spending would drop until things "cool off." During a bust or recession, the rate would be lowered, so that spending is more appealing than saving, until things "heat up." (The rate could even be lowered to "negative" rates or their functional equivalent, if more spending is really necessary. That's what "helicopter money" is—it's just that there's presently no helicopter for us, only for the banks.)

In times of acute distress, such as a pandemic, the Fed could adopt unusual measures just as it has in the past. When it took extraordinary measures of "quantitative easing" between 2009 and 2016, the banks got virtually free "helicopter money."[5] But if the Fed is going to drop free extra money on the economy, it should do "QE for the people" directly to our Citizen Accounts.[6] Then Main Street would be sure to benefit, with Wall Street profiting as benefits "trickle up."

If inflation ever looms, the Fed can take even sharper measures. Inflation rose quickly once the United States began spending big during World War Two. The Fed took the right steps and held prices stable. We'll dig through the Fed's toolbox in Chapter 12. For now, let's identify one new tool that would become available. If raising interest rates is not doing enough to encourage people to save instead of spend, the Fed could place a "hold" on Citizen Account funds above some threshold. The funds would still be there in our personal accounts, accruing interest as promised. We'd be assured it would become available again, soon enough. But we'd know we're all saving a bit more, temporarily, in order to hold inflation to a healthy level—a cause we could all, in principle, support. And we'd know we had lots of pent-up spending power to unleash once things slowed—precisely when more spending is needed. In effect, we would be "smoothening" the "business cycle," which is precisely what monetary policy is for.

Relying less on private banks would also reduce the public's exposure to large institutions that spend or dispense credit with abandon. "Rogue banking" was an especially big problem when the Fed itself, under Alan Greenspan's leadership, lost all sight of its role in ensuring "quality control" of the loans and "investments" being made. That in turn fueled volatility in the financial markets, created housing and other asset price bubbles, and then precipitated a catastrophic bust. And that's on top of a gross misallocation of the nation's credit, toward speculative rather than productive uses in the larger economy.[7] This was outrageous, even grotesque. But it is much less likely to occur if credit is being evenly distributed among ordinary people who spend to live, rather than only to megaspeculators who spend only to gamble.

Capitalists can rest assured, people will still accumulate private wealth, and use private financial services, just as they do now. One could choose to forgo the "public option," or even "opt out" of receiving a basic income grant. What we'd no longer have is indefinitely extended, monetized, public full faith and credit flowing or gushing toward artfully inflated secondary and tertiary markets. That is what our present arrangement allows and, too often, encourages. Instead, public full faith and credit will run only toward primary markets and only to those further markets—like those for home mortgage, higher education, small business, and public utility loans—that really legitimately require government support.[8]

Private investors could be expected to speculate less and invest more in primary markets for consumers, in part thanks to greater confidence in public investment. Meanwhile, speculative markets, where public credit-money flows are now far larger than any real need for liquidity or hedging could ever justify, will become private affairs. For that reason, those markets will shrink and pose much lower risks to the larger economy. They'll be there for high rollers, but the high rollers will no longer be rolling over us.

MONEY'S PAST IS CRYPTO'S FUTURE

Cutting out the middleman can work fine with existing financial technology.[9] Our current system processes millions upon millions of payments every day, quickly and efficiently. We could make do with it. But we'd do even better to run the whole thing on a Citizens' Ledger managed by the Fed.

Many central banks are already upgrading their payment systems. Singapore, for example, has been ahead of the curve in using distributed ledger technology ("DLT"), which distributes the same ledger around so many computers. Sweden for its part is poised to issue a new e-krona, a bona fide central bank digital currency—or "CBDC." Many other countries are following suit, or seriously considering the advantages.[10] The Fed could likewise run a "crypto-dollar" or "Fed coin." Indeed this seems all but inevitable.

So while we're doing our upgrades, we may as well do what is anyway right: pay every citizen a guaranteed income.

Cryptocurrency is not as new as it may seem. The story of America's paper and plastic money is a preview of the story we'll soon see unfold for crypto-money. If you think about the evolution of money along the lines we've already sketched in Chapter 8, we should expect "crypto-assets" to eventually be brought under government management. If the Fed does establish a "crypto-dollar," it probably would have happened anyway—yet another reason to make sure we do what is right.

As we told the story of the dollar in Chapter 8, the era of "wildcat" banking gave way to national standards in 1862 and 1863, which finally brought full central banking in 1913. Digital money is now in its own "wildcat" era. Crypto-coins are essentially digital wildcat banknotes. The parallels are striking. There is a bewildering array of different crypto-coins, all privately issued. Some seem more or less reputable. Others . . . well, not so much. And their values fluctuate wildly, both relative to what they can purchase and relative to one another. Yet again, history repeating itself.

Nothing with a wildly unstable value can function for long as a money. So something will have to change before digital currency could expect a future. But given money's past, crypto's future seems obvious. It's ripe for standardization and then centralization—as happened late in the nineteenth and early in the twentieth centuries, as wildcat banknotes gave way to Treasury-issued greenbacks, then Fed-managed Federal Reserve notes.

Unlike during the late nineteenth and early twentieth centuries, however, there is no reason these last two stages can't come together, at the same time, where digital currency is concerned. It took fifty years for our nation to appreciate that it needed not only a standardized, stable currency like the greenback, but a fully elastic currency like the Federal Reserve note, managed by a central bank. That's why the Federal Reserve Act came fifty years later than the national bank, currency, and legal tender acts. Now that we're familiar with those necessities, we could expect accelerated learning and move to adopt both simultaneously.

The Fed, like other central banks worldwide, is now looking to upgrade the national payments architecture. Distributed ledger or some similar digital technology looks particularly promising in that capacity. So it's a fair bet that, soon enough, payments systems worldwide will be built on distributed ledgers or something very much like them. The United States will be late to the party as always. But we'll get there soon.[11]

When that happens, the dollar will go digital. The Fed will issue "Federal Reserve Coins" and their keystroke equivalents, much like the "Federal Reserve Notes" it issues now. In this new world, the present horde of "wildcat coin" offerings will be driven out of the marketplace, just as "wildcat notes" were driven out of use after the national banking and legal tender acts nationalized the dollar in the early to mid-1860s. They'll fade out to the margins, being used by criminals for illicit transactions until the outlaws are rounded up.

Money's past is always and everywhere money's prologue. What changes is only the technical base upon which our money systems are founded. Insofar as the state of the art now is digital technology, money itself will go digital. But it will still be stable and elastic, if it is money. And that means it will be sovereign— it will be our public money. So long, then, bitcoin, and so long, ether. And welcome to America, new Digital Dollar.

CHAPTER 11

KEEPING SCORE IN THE DIGITAL AGE (AND BEYOND)

"Money is just a way of keeping score." So said the Texas oil tycoon H. L. Hunt, who was reputed to be the richest man in the world by his death in 1974. He probably wasn't thinking of monetary metaphysics in the way that we are, but he makes an astute point: money is a device of scorekeeping.

Think of a scoreboard at a baseball game. Money is like the hanging cards or flashing bulbs. The numbers are constantly adjusted, so that everyone can stay on the same page about the score—in runs, balls, strikes, and outs. And, just so, as our bank accounts are simultaneously credited and debited as we make payments to each other, it's as if the banking system were running a huge scoreboard, this time with millions of players whose scores are continually adjusted, around the clock, all over the world. The banks, who do the accounting, are our scorekeepers.

The idea of a national "crypto-dollar" in the United States may sound, well, cryptic. Is it a strange, possibly dangerous suggestion, or somehow contrary to the proper order of things? One might think so. So it may help to pause, step back, and put this in philo-sophical perspective. All it means is that the central bank would take over certain basic scorekeeping duties, tracking accounts on a public ledger through the "distributed ledger" technology that undergirds all cryptocurrencies. That way we'd all see more plainly what's now going on behind the scenes. We'd "pull back the curtain" on the private banks with transparency befitting a democracy. No more "Oz," only "Us."

THE PUBLIC'S LEDGER

When we think of money, we tend to think of cash, coin, or currency—especially coins and bills with interesting inscriptions. But really, coins and paper were always just scorekeeping devices, substitutes for ledgers once societies grew too large, given the technologies then available, for all credits and debits to be tracked on one literal "book." Money was always about "debt scorekeeping," either in account books or on "tally sticks" or, later, clay tablets, even going back to Mesopotamia, as our history of money in Chapter 5 suggested. If memory couldn't be trusted, some public medium was necessary. Circulating paper or coinage may have been the most useful payments technologies in certain times and places, but those days are for the most part now over. Now we have electronic banking, which is clearer about the original nature of money than coins and paper ever were. Accounting, i.e., debt scorekeeping, was always where the money is.

It's confusing that we've had so many scorekeeping devices. One can see why we fixate on the devices that we can touch, and grab, and clench; they seem less abstract and ethereal. But what ties all the various public representations of money together, over through the ages? The answer is: *authorization*. The coins or slips of paper have certain markings; debit cards have certain embedded chips or magnetic strips; keystrokes are made by certain authorized persons at authorized keyboards in authorized offices. These are the signs of proper provenance: a promise has been duly authorized, and any promise made without such authorization is punished severely as "counterfeiting." Accordingly, most countries now have "monetary authorities" in the form of central banks like our Federal Reserve, which determine what qualifies as money.

In the sibling "favor economy" we described in Chapter 7, the authorizing was implicit. That's often how things work in small-ish, intimate groups. People spontaneously trust and rely on each other. They take on and fulfill obligations to one another, keeping track of who owes what to whom, informally, by memory alone. It's only when practices of giving and receiving grow larger and less intimate that we cease to be able to trust our memories alone for an honest reckoning. That's when the public authorities must intervene and formalize what is or is not legal tender.

As we told the story of the siblings trading favors, they opted for a sort of intrafamily public ledger in the kitchen area. They could have issued a "currency," printing up paper bits, to represent chore-points and pay them to one another directly. Or their parents could have handed out chits to acknowledge when particular chores were completed. A "bathroom-clean" chit might come to be worth one "vacuuming-done" chit, rather as a five-dollar bill is worth five one-dollar bills in the broader American economy. We left such currencies out of our model for a reason: They weren't essential to our story. They aren't necessary when a ledger will do, and often don't work well as money in any case. In nineteenth-century America, as you may recall from Chapter 9, the motley notes in circulation were so lacking in uniform value that "the dollar" wasn't up to the task of a good, proper money. The dollar became money par excellence only after the United States established national standards and then a central bank, the Federal Reserve. America finally caught up with the demands of a large, interstate economy.

In small groups, people can keep score among themselves. In large economies, the job must be delegated to a third party. We often overlook this outside scorekeeper's role; we're too focused on the "cash changing hands." But as the cash itself is usually withdrawn from and deposited into "accounts," the circulating cash was never really where the action was. What really counted were the changing "account balances" behind the scenes. Now that we pay mostly with plastic, phones, etc., that behind-the-scenes truth is coming once again into the foreground. We are relearning, in other words, what Aaron, Bob, and Catherine knew all along in our "favor economy" story.

We've now entered an era in which ledger technology can be used among large populations as easily as it was in that small sibling economy of favors. The way we pay each other today already works like the paperless credits and debits that flow among Aaron, Bob, and Catherine in our story. And if or when a new public ledger is established, distributed across various computers, we'll simply have a clearer understanding of what we are already doing. We'll see more plainly what's going on "behind the curtain."

In a democracy, it is crucial that all participants understand their governing institutions—how they work, their founding purposes, how decisions are made within them. There should be no *Wizard of Oz* curtain to pull back, no noble lies, no useful budget superstitions. Money and banking are no exception. But our current system is hardly transparent. If the Fed issues a "crypto-dollar" on a public ledger, relying less on the private banking system, we'd have a public scoreboard all can see.

Rest assured, that wouldn't change things fundamentally. It would only change the way we record, verify, and account for our obligations. Money would still be what it always has been: debt scorekeeping, a way of keeping track of what we owe each other. This would simply represent a more democratic, *public* ledger, a scoreboard people can all see, in a banking system we can all comprehend.

GIVE ME LIBERTY!

Of course, as important as "transparency" is, *liberty* is surely just as important. And the new age of surveillance often threatens our personal liberties. But would a new big public ledger only further violate our privacy and freedom?

During Mao Tse-tung's rule as Chairman of the People's Republic of China during the 1950s, people wore "Mao-pins," or

"Mao-badges," carrying a Communist slogan. This showed loyalty to the chairman and boosted one's social standing. The pins were awarded for good behavior and began to circulate widely, almost like a money. Eventually one could even buy loyalty—or at least the pin-shaped symbol of it—on black markets. The pins were a way of keeping score, a marker of where one stood in the eyes of society.

Nowadays China is running a more radical "social credit index" that scores people for good or bad behavior of multiple kinds. Give blood, volunteer, and keep the right company and you get points and discounted internet services, expedited car rentals, and access to business-class air or train travel. Go about your business with no regard for social credit, and you will lose points. Your life on what is in effect a public blacklist grows much, much harder. Millions of locals have already been deemed "untrustworthy" and blocked from booking flights and train tickets. A new system, to be rolled out in 2020, aims to make things even more onerous. As one former official explained, the hope is to make "discredited people become bankrupt."[1]

At one level, China's system of social control is similar to the American financial sector's FICO-score system for credit assessment. Through a system established in 1956 (right around the time "Mao-pins" had currency), people are assigned "credit scores" based on factors such as the timeliness of their payments, credit use, length of credit history, savings balances, and types of debt. But this isn't just a way of deciding who is likely to repay a loan; it's a device for controlling how we live. We know we may eventually need a loan to buy a car for a job or a home as an investment or abode, so we run our lives around keeping a high score—perhaps noting a high score as a badge of pride, or feeling ashamed when the score drops. The Chinese version is a bit more intrusive and more oppressive of basic freedoms. But the differences are largely a matter of degree.

In our system, which is dominated by three private companies (Experian, Exquifax, and TransUnion), Americans have no control other than the lax regulatory laws we give those compa- nies. They to a large extent run our lives. The scoring can be arbi- trary, subject to fraud and "hacking," and difficult to appeal. A weak score makes it more difficult to get a job, buy a car or house, rent an apartment, or receive a line of credit. For people with low scores—who tend to be poorer—auto insurance companies are even demanding higher premiums, despite the fact that there is no connection at all between one's payment history and one's driving record or chance of getting into an accident.

China's money system and social credit indexes were simply imposed upon the population. The American ways of scorekeep- ing were at least nominally chosen by democratic means. The dol- lar and our monetary authority, the Fed, also have an ultimately democratic origin—the Constitutional Convention of 1787 and then the Congress—as we've seen. But then, one might worry: Were the Fed to manage a central, public ledger, would that take us too far in China's direction? If government officials could look directly into our Fed bank accounts, how different is that from Chinese surveillance and punishment of those deemed "untrust- worthy"? If individual liberty must be protected, is not private banking a first line of defense?

Actually, no, it isn't. The chief threat to our liberties is the pri- vate banks themselves. Public banking would offer us a real alter- native and help keep them accountable.

The Fed could easily run a crypto-dollar while respecting our privacy. For starters, Citizen Accounts would only be a "public option," which one could choose not to use. Anyone, at any time, could still hold a private bank account as well—so no loss of lib- erty there. A public ledger of the flow of transactions wouldn't even need to have our personal names attached. A Citizen Account under a person's name might be veiled from the pry- ing eyes of government officials—except by a court order. A judge can *already* demand to see one's private bank records, with cause. Even the famously secretive Swiss banks have been pried open for law enforcement purposes in recent years.

Here Sweden's Riksbank's e-krona system offers a particularly attractive model. Transactions up to a certain kronor amount are cryptographically anonymized as a matter of course, in order to replicate the anonymity of cash transactions. In effect, that's a digital-currency rendition of current American bank transaction reporting laws, which require that banks report to regulators only such individual transactions as exceed threshold dollar amounts.

Public sector financial regulators are not the primary threat to financial privacy. The primary threat is the private sector financial firms, all of which stand to make a massive profit from collecting your payment and other financial data, "harvesting" it, and selling it to marketing firms. So powerful is this temptation that most financial privacy law has to be directed not against the democratically accountable Fed or other financial regulators, but against the profit-motivated private sector firms that those regulators regulate.

And as more and more transactions migrate from anonymous cash to all manner of web-traceable modes of payment, the danger of private sector invasions of financial privacy grows even larger. In that case, what's needed is a partial move from banking with private sector firms, which must constantly seek out new ways of squeezing profits from people, to banking with the Fed. The Fed not only doesn't but legally *can't* seek and retain profits. Entrusting the Fed with more of our data is a move toward *more* financial privacy, not less.

As if that weren't enough to assuage—and reverse—your privacy fears, note that legal tender laws would still be confined to *market* relationships, in which we produce or exchange things. They wouldn't apply to the whole of life, or even most of it, in the way credit scores, private sector "data harvesting" and China's "social credit" system do. If people do use dollars as a measure of noncommercial value—in choosing a marriage partner, for instance—that, for better or for worse, is a matter of personal liberty.

To many libertarians, the issue is more fundamental. The Fed is already "too much government," so of course *any* new risks of intrusion would be intolerable. The more radical libertarians barely accept *any* state at all—even one with a democratic government. For those who feel queasy about Rousseau's modern democratic vision, the "natural liberties" and "limited government" of John Locke are far easier on the stomach.[2]

If Rousseau was all-in for democracy, it's true that personal liberty doesn't much figure into his story. That was a real flaw in his thinking. But history had no problem blending insights from Locke and Rousseau into what we now call *liberal democracy*. Democracies the world over now give pride of place to personal liberty, secure property, privacy, and the like. And that wasn't just a pragmatic mash-up. John Rawls, the great political philosopher of the twentieth century, showed that liberty can be paramount within a social contract theory much like Rousseau's. Liberty and equality can go hand in hand.[3]

Today we face grave invasions into our privacy, of an almost Orwellian nature. But "limited government" is not the solution. It's part of the problem. The threat comes primarily from *within* the free market for our data—a market in which, again, huge oligopolistic companies see ways to profit by harvesting our data as giant agribusinesses harvest pigs. Amazon, Facebook, Twitter, and Google now routinely gather our data and either use it or sell it for profit. Banks and other financial institutions are keen to get in on the action. Some of them are buying up "fintech" firms in hopes of sidestepping what few bank-secrecy and financial-privacy laws we already have.

So, yes indeed, the champions of liberty have much work to do—for starters, by *reining in those free market trends*. Here a Fed-issued "crypto-dollar," run on a Citizens' Ledger, would only help *safeguard* our privacy. If we hold accounts at the Fed, no private bank would ever have access to our financial information without our permission. We'd be freer from their behind-the-scenes profiteering.

And because people could always abandon their private

accounts for central banking, the private banks might even take notice. They might feel compelled to *deliver* on their now broken promises to secure our data. Nothing like a little competition to keep them honest. We'd be less subject to the winds of technology, with more control over the trends in privacy protection.

THE CITIZEN'S SCORE

But to return to our original worry: Wouldn't a Fed "crypto-dollar" still be weird, sort of unnatural, or out of order? Not really. Seen in larger perspective, it wouldn't be peculiar at all. The job of the private banker is less special than those stately structures and well-dressed officials might suggest.

"Accounting" and "banking" may sound technical to nonfinanciers, but we know them better than we might think. They're of a piece with all the scorekeeping we do in the home, among friends, in the neighborhood, city, or country, in the community of nations, and, in some religions, in the very relationship God bears to humanity. In more than one language the word for "sin," "wrong," or "guilt" is also used for "obligation" or "debt." In almost every relationship, we each "keep score" in the "books" we keep on where things stand between us. We "settle scores," perhaps after a haggle or quarrel over bookkeeping discrepancies. And now we have a digital "score" in the eyes of others, in social media followers and "likes," and can always hope to earn a few extra "points." If you thought you'd *never* work a job so tedious as accounting, well, think again: if you have a social life at all, you're already doing it.

In our culture, one surefire way to get ahead in "points" is acquiring money: every dollar is a point in your favor. (And just wait until you hit a billion points, when you score a bonus-points bonanza, acquiring the vaunted title "billionaire.") Among all the finer goods of life, such as beauty, skill, artistic attainment, friendship, common decency, service to others, and communion with nature, our culture scores people by their bank account and asset figures. Money thus taps into a basic human motive. Not greed or venality, per se, but our fierce need to feel seen and valued. As Rousseau put it, we love ourselves according to how we rank ourselves in the eyes of others—which is to say, by how we score ourselves, or guess how others will score us. And while money can easily corrupt us, it can also serve as proof of everyone's equal standing before each other and society.[4]

But then, who will be the trusted scorekeeper? Who will best do the job? As we've seen, private banks do some of their score-keeping duties reasonably well. For other duties, not so much. But then scorekeeping jobs aren't fixed for all eternity; there's no reason not to have our public bank assume some of them as new technology makes them ever easier to handle. We granted them the power to promote good public purposes in the first place. So we can take some power back when it serves those purposes.

Indeed public institutions are already a public referee of sorts, declaring that all citizens are recognized as equals, at least in certain civic and political matters. Which is to say, either rank is inappropriate, or everyone has the same rank—if you will, being tied for first place. And wouldn't a bold signal of our equal standing coming from the heart of our monetary system—in guaranteed income for every citizen—help to draw forth our better, more cooperative nature and re-establish good faith? Would it not clarify the "score," in a way that is visible to everyone?

Some fine words about our equal dignity are a good start. Better to "put our money where our mouth is." A bit of sure money is of course nice to have, especially for those of lesser means; with extra and more secure money, working people could feel they are getting a fairer shake. But to really reassure people of their equal standing before society, a guaranteed income, paid by the Fed on a public Citizens' Ledger, would send an unmistakable message. It would reaffirm every citizen's basic equality in the larger cooperative nexus by which any of us have anything.

PART IV

A MORE TRUSTWORTHY FINANCE

We've now said what money is, what banks are, and what they do for us. We've admittedly postponed some of the real-world complications of the idea of simply giving people money until now. The paranoid style of money politics is most influential when otherwise sensible people are made to worry. And, one might ask, *shouldn't* we worry? Why be so sure the inflation or debt scares really *can* be answered? Isn't there *something* to them, something potentially terrifying? If we don't worry, are we blithely flirting with disaster?! Would we find out only after it's too late?!

But worry not, we now lay such concerns to rest. We start with the single most important worry: inflation. Can the central bank really manage a lot of new money spent into the economy? We then say why we needn't worry about public debt, and why we *should* worry about bad governance.

CHAPTER 12

TOO MANY PROMISES?

If money is a promise as we have been saying, and if our government can issue money "without limit," doesn't this raise the dark specter of inflation? The very thought of "hyperinflation" seems to strike terror into the hearts of some people. So little would have to be different, it seems; officials hit the keys too hard, a "fat finger" clipping too many extra zeros and things go south, fast. Once you pass a certain threshold, inflation accelerates and spirals out of control. And we don't even know where that "trigger point" is! Better, then, to "play it safe."

Indeed, inflation fears can be enough to get the sane to lurch for the old identification of money with scarce metal objects. Even if that identification was a "noble lie" or disciplining device, it might at least prevent "runaway inflation" of the kind that devastated Weimar Germany, Zimbabwe, and Venezuela in the last one hundred years. If we don't use that device any longer, surely we need something like it, don't we?

The answer is yes, inflation matters, but, no, we don't need to trick ourselves into having discipline—and even gold was never the secret of inflation management. We most certainly cannot allow "hyperinflation"; we do need reliable devices to ensure we neither underpromise nor overpromise. So we turn, in other words, to the heady topic of inflation (and deflation) management—the job of our central bank, the Federal Reserve.

THE SUBLIME POSSIBILITY OF SUDDEN, VIOLENT DEATH

Fine-tuning monetary policy is a lot like being a responsible driver. Let's say you are driving along one of the many interstate highways that traverses the United States—a remarkable infrastructural achievement that, over the course of the 1950s, at once helped avoid the danger of deflation that loomed after the Second World War and laid the foundation for one of the greatest advances in productivity that the United States ever enjoyed. If you drive along this interstate at the intended rate, as all those around you are doing, all will go smoothly unless there's some flaw in your car or some bump or bottleneck in the road ahead, or some oncoming vehicle that's left its lane, that you don't see . . . "in time."

The fact that there *could* be such a flaw, bump, or bottleneck probably doesn't keep you from driving. After all, you "could" be hit by lightning the very moment you set foot out the door on the top-floor balcony of your apartment. That doesn't lead you to become a recluse. It simply leads you to take what we call "reasonable precautions." You check the weather before going out, or perhaps shelter in your basement if—and only if—you learn that a nasty storm's imminent.

While driving along on a curvy mountain road, you *could* veer off a cliff to your death. If you were *just over there*, only ten feet away, the car would plummet into the canyon and river below. Likewise with oncoming traffic—were someone heading opposite your direction to lose control of the wheel for only a second or two, and drift only ten feet or so to the left . . . boom, lights out!

Perhaps you ponder these sublime possibilities in your driving daydreams. Curious, how little the world would have to change for me to face sudden, violent death. *Just ten feet over there. It would all be over.* Yet even that "possibility" doesn't lead you to stop the car and hug the roadside cliff or the interstate shoulder. Not when both hands are planted firmly on the steering wheel, you know how to drive a car, and the brakes are well maintained. You just have your car "safety inspected" each year. You "check the tires" before taking a long car trip. And while driving you "keep your eyes on the road," as the saying goes, watching ahead for signs of trouble. You can drive *very* safely—enough so to soundly entrust your life to a car, even just for the sake of a nice drive to see snow.

Suppose you are driving and do see such signs of trouble. The cars ahead seem to be backed up. Brake lights appear to be flashing. You see a squad car and ambulance lights, and hear sirens. In this case your reaction will depend upon how far ahead the danger appears to loom.

If trouble still is quite distant, the first thing you'll do is step less heavily on the accelerator, possibly removing your foot altogether. If after doing that you still seem to be drawing upon the slower cars too rapidly, you might downshift if driving a truck, or move your foot straight to the brake pedal if driving a car with automatic transmission. You'll then steadily up the pressure on that brake pedal. Not pressing too hard (which can cause a crash of its own—a "rear-ender"). But not pressing too softly, either. You'll try to brake Goldilocks-style—"just right."

And of course, if you only spot the danger late in the game and you're nearly upon it, you may have to "slam on the brakes," perhaps even pull the emergency brake.

The one thing you will not do, unless you are the unusually morbid type, is to cease and foreswear driving or riding altogether, resolving thenceforth just to walk everywhere. Nor will you resolve never to drive more than ten miles per hour on the highway forevermore, which would be just as dangerous as speeding. The signage on highways that states maximum *and minimum* rates of speed do after all perform a key safety function.

Money can "move too fast"—being issued or "turned over" at too high or too low a "velocity," to use Irving Fisher's evocative term. There are many ways to accelerate or decelerate at varying rates, depending on what lies ahead. And there are multiple means of "looking ahead." Some as simple as peering forward, others as sophisticated as radar, to ascertain both *what* lies ahead and *how far* ahead.

Is anyone "at the wheel" when it comes to money? Yes indeed; again, that is the Fed's very job—"stable prices," as the statutory mandate puts it. Like any central bank, the Fed has ample tools for steering the Goldilocks course between deflation and unhealthy inflation, accelerating and decelerating the supply of money in circulation depending on what lies ahead. It's easy to appreciate what those reliable tools might be, as well as what they already are, if you grasp what inflation and deflation are. So let's start there.

THE GOLDEN MEAN

Promises and money bring both inflationary and deflationary dangers. Just consider promising and planning in your own life, as we suggested in Chapter 3. If you make too many promises too quickly, they can outrun your ability to live up to them. People will begin "discounting" them. They'll no longer "buy" you as much in the form of making commitments with and to you as they once did. On the other hand, if you make too few promises, too infrequently, you'll share much less of your life with others. You'll accomplish less (your employment contract, after all, is a promise), as your life becomes poorer.

Too much money is too many promises, while too little money is too few promises. But how much is too much, and how little is too little? Well, think of the car again. "Too fast" is understood largely by reference to what lies ahead. "Too little" is understood largely by reference to what is behind and now gaining. What both of these have in common is their *relational* character—relational to the traffic ahead and the traffic behind.

In the monetary realm, what matters is money's relation to what money buys. What is an inflated dollar? Simply a dollar that's issued in excess of our capacity to produce or supply goods and services that those dollars can purchase in goods and services. Hence the nice colloquial definition, "too much money chasing too few goods."

On the flip side, "deflation" is the problem of too little money chasing too many goods. This is a problem because, in a market economy like our own "price signals" are supposed to tell people what and how much to produce and thus how many to hire and how much to pay. Thus falling prices lead to production slowdowns, and thus layoffs and wage cuts.

Keep the relational nature of inflation and deflation in mind. It helps us see very clearly how to craft Goldilocks monetary policy and achieve the proverbial "golden mean"—though gold ain't got nuthin' to do with it.

The key is to *modulate* the promise supply—that is, the money supply. The Fed carefully measures past, present, and expected prices each day, ensuring there's never too much or too little money out there. And because we are talking relations here, it measures both the money supply *and* the likely goods and service supply in so doing. It does that in as detailed and up-to-date a manner as possible, day to day, hour by hour, given the best data available—just as in driving you look ahead and check your speedometer often (we hope).

Monetary and fiscal authorities have many ways of doing this job—lots of eyes, radar, levers, and pedals, so to speak. Even computers to analyze what they see and make forecasts in light of it. Some of these tools and methods will be familiar to you. Others might not. So let's go through the most important ones.

ABSORBING THE MONEY

We'll begin with the familiar. The first thing to note is that fiscal and monetary policies that improve productivity won't tend to be inflationary at all. The rough definition of "inflation" we mentioned above—"too much money chasing too few goods"—

tells you something right away: there are different ways to manage inflation. Is there too much money? Or are there too few goods? You can limit the amount of money in circulation. Or you can *increase* the amount of goods. Is "capacity" underutilized, meaning that more goods and services could easily be produced and supplied than is happening now? Then issuing more money isn't inflationary; properly targeted, it merely jump-starts production.

So when productivity is boosted, the only danger is *deflation*, not inflation. And that happens only if the monetary benefits of productivity growth don't flow to people who spend the extra money. When the benefits flow widely, to people who do spend the money, the money is out there chasing goods, encouraging the production of yet more goods—more wealth.

Think of it this way: the right policies produce the means of money absorption itself—more goods and services, more real wealth—in tandem with the money issuance that finances those improvements. There is no precise analogue to this in driving, but there would be if, in some science fiction future, there were an accelerator which, when you pressed down on it, not only increased your speed but also laid clear new roadway ahead of you. Much public spending is actually like that. We call it "investment."

Investment in infrastructures, education, and research and development, for example, are all classic cases of productivity-enhancing expenditures. They are "real" investments. Like the interstate highway system itself, they boost the production of real goods and the supply of valued services. In so doing they bring into existence the very things needed to absorb the new expenditures. They thereby both add to our real wealth and prevent excess "paper" wealth—that is, inflation.

Public finance, done right as public investment, has always been like this. Take it for a useful public axiom: any time we find inflation in one or more sectors of our economy—as in the mortgage and other financial markets of recent decades, for example— we have proof positive that putative "investment" is not being managed productively, but merely speculatively. *That* is when things tend to go south. The problem isn't the extra money being spent, as such, it is where the money is flowing.

REMOVING THE MONEY

Staying with the familiar monetary tools a bit longer, taxes and bond sales, recognizable to most of us, have long been employed to absorb "excess money" during times of high growth. This is precisely what they are for.

As we explained in Chapter 2, because money is issued by citizenries rather than citizens, sovereign taxes and bond sales, which are also public acts, are never about "raising more money." They are about "lowering money aggregates," so that there's not too much money out there in private bank accounts relative to the stock of goods and services that money buys.

This, by the way, is why people sometimes complain that public bond issuance can "crowd out" private sector investment, or that taxes can "squelch growth." It is also why tax cuts or bond buy-backs are often said to be "stimulative." Under the right conditions, these observations can be correct. But everything depends on the *conditions*—just as whether it makes sense to brake or accelerate while driving depends on the *traffic* conditions.

TARGETED TAXES

Turning to something a bit less familiar, we should note that such tools as bond issuance and taxation can be targeted at specific sources of inflation or deflation. A financial transaction tax, such as that favored by the Nobel laureate James Tobin and many economists and lawmakers since, would help prevent *financial market* inflation—i.e., asset price "bubbles"—of the sort that have plagued us in recent years. A "value-added tax," or "VAT," on particular items that become objects of speculation—tulips in seventeenth-century Amsterdam, for example—would work in much the same way.

Same goes in bond issuance. The US Treasury already offers a variety of different such instruments, classified by time-to-maturity and yield. The classification offers our government the option of soaking up money from different sectors of society, from those seeking short-term yield to those seeking longer-term yield. Here the "sales" are swaps of unspendable instruments for spendable, liquid instruments—dollars, a.k.a. "legal tender." The New York Fed trading desk already fine-tunes the money supply in this way—in "open market operations"—every working day. It plans these operations on a daily basis, using reams of data and forecasts of likely purchases of goods and services. It is the equivalent of advanced radar at the front of your car on the highway.

MANAGING PRIVATE BANKS

Turning now to even less familiar policy instruments, we should note that much of financial regulation can and should be deployed to *prevent* both deflation and inflation—what we've been calling "modulation."

As we explained in Chapter 9, banks generate money by lending, as do other financial institutions—especially those in the so-called "shadow banking" sector.[1] This is the sense in which credit is money, or "credit-money." That means the regulations we impose on how far banks can extend credit are essentially regulations on their ability to create money.[2] So, when signs of trouble appear, we can also just require banks to raise more equity capital per dollar's worth of credit than they extend. Likewise, we can limit what kinds of lending or investing they can do, narrowing what can go in their portfolios, and they won't generate as much money.

Banking lawyers and financial regulators call these things "capital" (or "leverage") and "portfolio" regulation, respectively. We initially developed them to protect individual institutions and their depositors or investors against excessive lending and associated bankruptcy risk. But we now use them also to modulate credit aggregates economy-wide. It's called "macroprudential regulation."[3] Its rediscovery after the crash of 2008 is one of the signal achievements of the postcrisis era. For our purposes, it is a powerful anti-inflationary as well as anti-deflationary tool, all thanks, again, to money's relation to promise, i.e., credit.

HIKE INTEREST RATES

Another money-modulatory tool, more familiar to some than to others, is simple interest-rate regulation. Banks and other financial institutions often borrow from one another, and they "benchmark" the rates by reference either to what the Fed itself charges—"the Fed funds rate"—domestically, or to what global megabanks do—the "London interbank offer rate," or "LIBOR"—internationally. This means that the Fed at home and the Fed in collaboration with other central banks globally can move borrowing costs everywhere simply by changing those benchmarks. This is essentially what the late US Fed chairman Paul Volcker did when he raised interest rates in the early 1980s as inflation appeared (to some) to be looming in the United States.

Some people worried that Volcker's inflation "cure" was worse than the "disease." The problem is that interest rates operate economy-wide—they're a very blunt instrument. They can risk squelching activity in healthy and unhealthy markets alike—amputating a whole leg, so to speak, in response to an ingrown toenail. For this reason it's generally best to use steep interest-rate hikes as a last resort, and to start with more targeted strategies like those mentioned above and further elaborated below to avoid having to use them. After all, to return to our driving analogy, if you downshift or apply the brakes gently sooner you won't have to "slam on the brakes" later and risk causing more injury.

COLLARS FOR KEY PRICES

If our existing tools are not enough, there are yet others we could use, but haven't yet. They are like additional levers or pedals that might in the future be added to your car—tools that make your car fly over an unexpected obstacle, or suddenly buffer itself with quickly inflated or soft rubber bumpers. One such tool would be for the New York Fed trading desk (or some other authority) to buy or sell not only Treasury securities of varying maturities and yields, as they do now, but also other financial instruments in order to target specific prices of broad economic significance, such as housing, fuel, or food, when they grow too low or too high.

During the Fed's experiments with "quantitative easing" (QE), for example, commodity prices ended up rising in ways that harmed lower-income Americans. One of us—Bob—worked at the New York Fed at the time and proposed that it "short" commodities in its open market operations. That would put downward pressure on their prices.[4] The Fed didn't follow that suggestion at the time. But it did do something similar a year and a half later: it committed through QEIII to buy $85 billion in mortgage-related assets each month until a "floor" was established beneath still-falling house prices. The Fed quickly resumed those purchases as the 2020 pandemic erupted. It could do much more of this in the future, in as narrowly targeted a manner as necessary, if ever inflation or deflation emerges in particular markets. And an authority with a balance sheet of the Fed's size can influence prices quite massively.

So instead of thinking of "inflation" in prices across a whole economy, think of prices moving upward or downward in various different sectors—commodities, real estate, medical services, wages, and so forth.[5] Each gets tracked by the abundance of data available to the Fed, day in and day out. Not every price needs to be tracked; just the systemically significant ones, that pose a real risk of crisis or particularly big disruption of people's lives. The Fed can target a broad "collar" on the prices in each, with a "floor" and a "ceiling" for their daily, weekly, or monthly movements. It can then keep the prices within that spectrum by intervening in the market, buying or selling, much in the way it *already* buys and sells Treasurys in the open market. It performs this task each and every day in the name of one price admitted by all to be critical to the whole system—the cost of borrowing money, that is, interest.

How, more precisely, does the Fed do that? Each business day, Fed officials prepare something of a Treasurys "shopping list," which other officials follow after sitting down at their computer terminals. They then just type in the numbers and make the purchases. What we are suggesting is no different, except they buy in the market from a longer, more diverse shopping list. Guided by the wealth of data flowing into the central bank from all manner of sources, the Fed can simply watch and track the key prices, nudging them up or down as needed.

In doing that, it can rely less on abstract models based on unobservable quantities and theoretical constructs like "rational expectations."[6] It should aspire to be less like high theoretical physics and more like laboratory science. It can observe what is happening and react in real time, keeping prices rising only at a desired, "safe," and productive level.

CITIZEN ACCOUNTS

A final way we might combat inflation or deflation is with the revolutionary new citizen-focused public banking plan we pitched in Chapter 10. Instead of just offering "reserve accounts" to privileged banks as it does now, the Fed can set up interest-bearing Citizen Accounts for all citizens. In opening those accounts, we'd gain a powerful tool for money modulation. During "deflations" like the one that befell us after 2008, for example, the Fed could drop debt-free "helicopter money" into those Citizen Accounts, rather than giving it to banks in the hope that they'll lend (which they mainly didn't). Were inflation ever to emerge, the Fed can simply raise interest rates on those accounts, encouraging people to save more and spend less.

And in a serious pinch, the Fed can temporarily impound some portion of the funds or planned deposits into those accounts. Not to worry: The money is still there, ready and waiting. The deposits can keep flowing and grow with high interest, rather like a bank CD does. The funds can't be spent, but only temporarily. J. M. Keynes proposed equivalent "rationing" measures in the U.K. when spending on the Second World War threatened serious wage-price inflation. That worked. But if proper foresight is exercised and less extreme tools used right, this kind of situation would likely only occur in a true national emergency such as war. The other tools we've described would prevent any need for it. It would be much as with your car's emergency brake. If all goes well with the other methods of deceleration, you won't have to use it. But it's there, for precaution's sake.

THE PUBLIC'S GUARANTEE

Despite all these tools at the Fed's disposal, a nervous public may worry. Will Fed officials "hit the brakes" when we need them to? If the central bank is behind the monetary "wheel," how can the public as a "passenger" be reassured?

The Fed already cares about maintaining public trust. So it should provide a public anti-inflation guarantee. How? It can simply precommit, announcing what it plans to do ahead of time. It would set its growth targets, along with the measures it plans to take to achieve them, perhaps indicating its degree of confidence in green, yellow, and red "lights." As things go according to plan, the Fed helping us to understand along the way, we can all keep up "confidence."

So, for example, say the plan is to spend 10 trillion new dollars over the next five years on green energy investment. Sounds like *a lot* of new money. Should we worry? Quite the contrary. We can be *certain*, for all practical purposes, this won't cause excessive inflation. Start with $2 trillion during the first year, check the dials, steady as she goes. Two trillion more the next year, check the engine lights, all systems go. Two trillion more, still no problem. Two more, then three more, in the same careful manner, and voila, $10 trillion spent. As expected, there was no inflationary consequence, in part for skillful inflation-tool use.

Were there any suggestion of excessive inflation as the data comes in, the Fed could have done open market operations in the inflated sector, keeping prices within the promised band. If there was a more general problem, it could raise interest rates on Citizen Accounts, to discourage spending. If there are "red flags" ahead, it can simply put a hold or temporary "impound" on some portion of the new funds being deposited in those Citizen Accounts. If worse came to worst, it could hike private-bank interest rates, as Volker did. But that highly disruptive measure would be an absolute last resort.

WHY THINGS GO WRONG

Taking the Fed's deep toolbox into account, it is easy to see why the United States has not suffered inflation in goods and services markets now for many decades. It's also easy to see why it *has* suffered hyperinflation—that is, "bubbles"—in the financial markets in particular. The bugbears that "inflation hawks" always raise— again, Weimar, Zimbabwe, and Venezuela—actually have much more in common with US mortgage and financial markets than with goods and services markets generally. Let's first describe the American situation, then turn to the others.

In US mortgage and financial markets, we did see inflation, even during the so-called "Great Moderation" of thirty years' low "consumer price index" ("CPI") inflation. That increase was deliberately sought by public officials, specifically Fed chairman Alan Greenspan, who was first appointed by President Ronald Reagan in 1987, then reappointed by both Bushes and President Clinton, serving until 2006. Greenspan saw that wage and salary incomes in the United States were stagnating from the mid-1970s onward, threatening long-term stagnation in consumer demand and thus growth and employment. So he engineered a housing bubble, using very low interest rates. The idea was to generate a

"wealth effect" among homeowners and encourage more consumer spending. Getting people to buy washing machines and
cars and expensive dinners seems also to have been the goal of
ultralight regulation of newfangled mortgage-finance and con-
sumer-debt products, along with refusal to use new Fed authority
to regulate mortgages.

Greenspan overestimated the productivity growth brought
by new communications technologies. And he underestimated
the significance of the fact that these gains were no longer being
shared with ordinary people. It was a "let them eat debt" policy package. It generated enormous inflationary pressure in the
housing, consumer debt, and associated sectors of the American
economy.

Worse still, Greenspan didn't see the macroeconomic importance of financial regulation. Surprisingly, he and other economists tended to think inflation and hyperinflation would occur
only in consumer goods markets, not also in financial markets.
(And this notwithstanding the fact that the Fed's statutory mandate speaks of "price stability," generally, not "*consumer* goods
price stability.") But hyperinflation *did* strike the housing and
financial markets, the bubbles and busts of the 1990s and early
2000s being the awful result.

This episode wasn't so different from historic inflations in
other countries. Weimar Germany deliberately inflated its currency, just as Greenspan deliberately inflated housing. It did this
in order to lighten the burden of the draconian "reparations" debt
placed on it by the victorious allies at Versailles after the First
World War. Keynes warned at the time that this would bring on
catastrophe and renewed war, and, alas, it did.

The inflation deliberately courted by Weimar grew "out of
hand" just as US housing and related asset prices did in the early
2000s. German companies had relied on American lenders. They
had to, given Weimar's austerity policies meant to choke off the
inflation. But that meant that the Wall Street crash of 1929 crashed
Weimar's economy too. And thus an obscure man with a funny

mustache, who had run often for German office and been laughed off from 1920 to 1932, suddenly grew popular on the strength of his anti-Wall Street "I told you sos".

Zimbabwe's and Venezuela's stories are similar. Here, too, monetary expansion was pursued deliberately. No serious effort was made to enhance productivity in ways that could generate the means of absorbing the money. In both cases "productivity growth" was pursued mainly in the form of resource extraction— with at most one or two resources. The extracted resources were sold mainly to foreigners. Foreign money thus poured into both countries. That boosted their money supplies further, but without being directed toward the right places—that is, productivity-developing places. The extra money wasn't finding industries that might domestically generate more goods and services that locals could buy with new income and thus "absorb" the new money.

That wasn't inevitable. Both countries could have imported goods and services from abroad, in order to reduce the inflationary pressure (much as cheap Chinese imports do here in America). But, understandably, the authorities were reluctant to become too dependent on imports. That's a fine strategy if there's a plan to develop domestic production. (Our own politicians would do well to remember that right now!) But neither Zimbabwe nor Venezuela had developed such plans in detail. Neither did they have much experience with sophisticated forms of financial regulation—which even the United States, with Mr. Greenspan at the helm, professed skepticism about. The result was inflationary pressure, which these governments proved no better at controlling than did Mr. Greenspan with housing and related asset prices in the run-up to 2008.

None of this has anything to do with money's decoupling from gold or other precious metals. People who point to Weimar, Zimbabwe, and Venezuela and then say we ought to "return to the gold standard" seem to have two things in common. The first is that they are themselves invested in gold, meaning that they'll become rich if you follow their advice and buy gold. The second is that while they talk of oil or tulips, hence twentieth-century Venezuela or seventeenth-century Holland, they never discuss sixteenth-century Spain.

Spain experienced enormous inflation in that era precisely because it found huge deposits of gold and silver in its new Western Hemisphere colonies and then shipped the stuff back home. The resultant "supply shock" tanked the prices of those metals in relation to other things. And since those metals were then counted as money, Spain now had far too much money chasing far too few goods—i.e., inflation—just as Venezuela did four hundred years later. And so it was passed up by other nations that focused on serious economic development and the financing thereof—nations like Britain.

THE NUMBERS AIN'T LYIN'

If you're somehow still worried about inflation in America, let's look at some hard data.

Billions of dollars in tax cuts flowed into the economy during the 1980s Reagan years. There was no upward effect on consumer price inflation (excluding financial price inflation, which did rise). Paul Volcker, who put the kibosh on 1970s "stagflation," was the last Fed chair to see CPI inflation. Since then, during the George W. Bush years, tax cuts and war spending flowed like mighty waters. Still no inflation. The Trump tax cuts of December 2017 pumped yet more trillions—at least two of them—into the economy. Still no inflation—not in consumer goods and services markets. What we do see, up till the "exogenous shock" of the coronavirus pandemic of 2020, is yet more inflation in Wall Street financial markets.

In fact, no "developed" economy has seen significant CPI inflation for some forty years now. Why think "this time (or place) is different"? Indeed, since 2012, the Fed has been officially (and unofficially even longer) trying to hit a 2 percent inflation target from below, and barely managed to hit it only in a few quarters over many, many years. Clearly the Fed "can't get it up"—even while trying, very hard. (Has it lost its potent "essence," much as General Ripper feared?) Why is it trying so hard? Because it understands that deflation is as bad as or worse than inflation. The Fed's impotence in increasing the money supply outside of the financial sector has been by far our biggest economic policy problem ever since the day Reagan took office. So why think things will suddenly grow very scary, even should it have to at some point tamp prices *down* a bit?

Or if you're a "trust the markets" type, well, then you *can* trust the markets. Take it from investors themselves—people who follow the numbers, betting their own money, for their line of work. For years now our Treasury Department has issued "inflation-protected" securities (often called "TIPS") along with the traditional Treasury securities we noted earlier. The "spread" between prices of the former and prices of the latter is effectively a measure of what economists call "inflation expectations": if investors are willing to pay substantially more for inflation-protected than for ordinary Treasurys, then those investors must have substantial inflation fears; otherwise not. The current spread is effectively zero—and has been for well over a decade.

If investment professionals, whose very jobs and whose profits depend on their getting things right, see no reason to purchase even cheap "inflation insurance" in the form of TIPS, why should *we* wish to "purchase" such insurance in the form of inaction, while both our republic's economy and its social and political fabric continue to unravel around us? Isn't that a bit like refusing to drive, for fear of an unexpected car accident, even with a spouse giving birth or a parent suffering cardiac arrest in the back seat?

In fact, if only to preserve the fabric of society, we believe the Fed should allow more inflation so that more people who want it can find work. Which is to say, it should "flip" its traditional inflation-unemployment target. Its current 2–4 target (2 percent inflation, 4 percent unemployment) would become its reciprocal, a 4–2 target (4 percent inflation, 2 percent unemployment). Why?

Because the current 2 percent inflation target is overcautious. We never reach it even while really trying! So just raise the target and let people work and begin to earn more. Targeting a 4 percent inflation rate, with a lot more spending in the aggregate, might just get us there.

Smart people used to think an unemployment rate as low as 5 percent was pushing things: inflation would be just around the corner. But since we've seen unemployment well *below 4 percent* for a long while with no inflationary trend at all, it seems clear that those smart people were wrong. Far more people can have jobs. Current Fed chair Jerome Powell has been saying as much in the last couple of years, and he's clearly right. Going forward, 4–2, not 2–4, should be the Fed's "dual mandate" mantra.

CHAPTER 13

TOO MUCH DEBT?

You may have seen those "national debt clocks" posted in major cities such as New York or San Francisco. As of time of writing, in fall 2019, one of them reads:

OUR NATIONAL DEBT
$22,780,590,701,324
YOUR *family share* $69,074

So that's around 22-plus TRILLION DOLLARS, and the number is flying upward, moving too quickly to easily make out an exact figure.

This is meant to be a SCARY number. The rising national debt, we are meant to believe, is a SERIOUS, ONGOING, and EVER-WORSENING problem, which we'd do something about if our "leaders" had the courage to make HARD CHOICES. Many families will feel especially worried to learn that they own, as their "family share," a rather large (presumably per capita) total of $69,074. And where in the world will they or their children or their grandchildren, after paying for college and maybe buying an apartment, come up with that kind of money?! Be afraid, very afraid.

But let's relabel the sign a little. We'll keep the exact same numbers, and simply alter the letters, creating a big, beautiful sign that reads like this:

OUR PRIVATE WEALTH
$22,780,590,701,324
YOUR family share $69,074

Wow! Amazing! That's a *huge* number! And look how fast our assets are *flying* upward! We're stinking *rich*, and getting richer every second! Richest nation in human history, doggone it, and, ho boy, *my* family share is looking solid as well. All those folks who make at or below the median $50,000 or so income per year and spend everything, with little or nothing left to save in a bank account, will be *very* pleased to learn of this wealth! Little Johnny *can* go to college and even buy an apartment eventually. Or maybe the family can stop renting and put a down payment on a small, nice house. But, wait . . . if that kind of money isn't sitting around in a car or house or bank account already, *why the hell aren't we seeing our share of the money?*

The second sign seems to reverse things dramatically. And yet it is as correct as the first. They are *exactly equivalent*. The "national debt" just *is* one and the same number as "private wealth." The two numbers are *exactly the same*, dollar for dollar, to the penny. (At least if you leave out dollar-denominated assets held by foreigners, especially governments such as China—a matter we'll get back to.)

This isn't true by some strange "fuzzy math" or esoteric financial model. It's a rudimentary fact about US money, which we've noted already: every dollar or Treasury denominated in dollars is, of necessity, at once a government liability *and* an asset for the party who holds it. This is true simply by definition, just as a thing with a right side must have a left side, and as a promise brings an obligation *to* someone (the promisee) at the same time that it raises an obligation *from* someone (the promissor). Financiers call this "double-entry bookkeeping," a matter of so many "accounting identities." But it's basically what you learned in seventh or eighth grade, where it was called algebra.

Many people have the following jumbled picture: There are lots of dollar assets, like currency or bank deposits. There are also lots of public liabilities out there, like government Treasury debt. But these two items are just thrown into the economic hopper separately, maybe with some complicated connection that economists have theories about but must disagree over. But the connection is not complicated. The liabilities and assets aren't just accidently related; they travel together *of necessity*, as a matter of basic accounting. Meaning, *nothing counts* as a dollar liability unless there is also someone out there who holds the corresponding dollar asset. From there, all it takes is simple algebra to prove—with mathematical certainty—that public debts and private (or foreign) assets are exactly equivalent. The very same number. Down to the penny.

But if both ways of labelling the "national debt clock" numbers are perfectly correct, only the one very scary sign actually is posted all over cities and the internet. Is this not blatantly confusing, perhaps deliberately so? Yup. Should we suspect paranoia at work— and perhaps even a Plot to Scare America by well-funded parties with a Secret Agenda (such as cutting Granny's welfare checks— which is often what's meant by making "the hard choices")?

Perhaps, but not exactly. The folks who pay good money to keep these signs running are indeed very well funded and otherwise sophisticated. But many do believe the original message out of a misguided concern for the public interest. They are "patriots," if you will, who could learn a little accounting. Presumably former president Barack Obama also meant well when he called lack of concern for the rising national debt "unpatriotic," in a moment of confusion. (He was a constitutional lawyer, after all, not an accountant.)

How could so many of us be so confused, so very afraid of nothing? The answer, probably, is just that most of us haven't had the chance to appreciate a pretty elementary fact about what a dollar is. So just to reiterate the point: Every dollar—whether in cash, bank deposits, or "borrowed back" in Treasurys—is a government liability *and at the very same time* a private or foreign asset. The national debt *is* the private wealth of the nation (albeit shared with some other nations).

As we noted in Chapter 2, a sovereign government—if it issues its own money and borrows only or mainly in that money without a fixed exchange rate—cannot be forced into default, involuntarily. It can keep "writing checks" against its present and future members, forever. It has always done so, and should never stop.

Does that turn public debt into a big Ponzi scheme? No, it doesn't—not of itself, anyway. We have every reason to expect that the private schemes of Bernie Madoff and other criminals will end in default, eventually. That's why they're illegal. The US union, by comparison, is a different and unusual sort of entity. At its very founding, it's presumed to exist *in perpetuity*, with each generation creating obligations for the next. There's no final day of reckoning—no Judgment Day, when all balances due must be repaid.

And what connects the present to the future? Promises and money, including in the contracts or "constitutions" that make for enduring societies. They are what make social relations "continuous" across time. What is a promise, after all, but a commitment formed now to do something later? Money, a kind of shared communal promise, is what quite literally constitutes every generation of Americans into one great web of social relations known as the United States, persisting over centuries.

HOW TO KEEP CONTROL

If the impossibility of going broke sounds too philosophical, history bears it out. The United States has never defaulted on its debts, not even once. That shouldn't be surprising. No government in the whole history of the world that issues its own money and borrows only or mainly in it, without a fixed exchange rate to gold or some other money, has defaulted on debts denominated in its own money, *ever*. Not even once.

Not that world history isn't littered with "sovereign debt defaults" and a trail of consequent human misery. Take only a cursory glance at Carmen Reinhart and Kenneth Rogoff's tome *This Time Is Different*. One can feel queasy. Just the thought of all the pain, the years of suffering the aftermath, can get one hankering for "sound money," based on gold, or something seemingly *unbreakably solid* and *utterly trustworthy*, like God, or, you know, if not God then the mystical metaphysical bedrock of civilization and all things good and holy, if there is such a thing.

But as with any morass of data, like that in the Reinhart and Rogoff book, the trick is to hear the signal through the noise. And in the great horror show of public debt crashes through history, there is a clear pattern: the government in default, in every single case, either did not issue its own money, or did not borrow only or mainly in its own money, or "pegged" its money at some rate of exchange to something outside of itself, like gold or a foreign currency. That is the only way to default—to promise, directly or indirectly, to pay what you don't yourself issue.

This is a remarkable and all-important fact about sovereign debt, though for some reason it doesn't stop paranoid commentators from shouting from the rooftops about the United States' going the way of Weimar Germany, Zimbabwe, Greece, or today's Venezuela as discussed in the last chapter. It's an easy scare tactic—for a quick op-ed or tweet. And, rest assured, otherwise smart people are not above using scare tactics, especially when they aren't necessarily paying attention to detail.

The United States is not at all in the same situation as, for example, Greece. Since Greece joined the euro, it relinquished sovereign control over its money, and so can indeed fall into default in euros. The euro for it is what gold was for us before FDR ended the domestic gold standard and Nixon ended the global gold standard. It can't simply issue new euros to make interest payments on its debts (not without the European Central Bank's blessing, at any rate). Not any more than most countries could simply "make" gold back when gold was a money (notwithstanding a whole profession of so-called "alchemists"). And so, right there, the United States is not in the same leaky boat as Greece.

The grand lesson of history is not that governments can easily go broke, try as they might to stay afloat—in which case rigorous adherence to a strict "balanced budget" would be the only prudent course. The lesson, rather, is that careful governments aware of the perils before them should strive to attain "monetary sovereignty," giving them full control over their money and their debts.[1] Then they *can't* default, except voluntarily, and shouldn't worry about sovereign debt default. They can focus on bigger problems, or just spend an easier day relaxing at the beach.

Plenty of countries already have this sort of control over their money and debts, at least to some approximation—including the United States, England, Japan, Australia, Canada, Switzerland, Singapore, and China, for example. Officials in these countries don't always realize the power in their hands, or know how to wield it effectively. Many other governments, including many developing countries, could attain "monetary sovereignty" as well. South Africa, for example, is now discussing how to do just that.

Still, most countries today do not enjoy "monetary sovereignty," though to the extent possible, every country should seek control of its money and public debts.

The eurozone countries entirely abandoned control over their moneys in adopting the euro. In the wake of the 2008 crisis and eurozone mess, that now seems to have been a huge mistake. What now? Here are three good options, from easy to hard.

First, the easiest option: the European Central Bank ("ECB"), which runs euro policy for the whole group, can more freely issue euros to governments as needed. It's done that once, already, in a limited way. In order to keep Greece in the union, it in effect promised to back its bonds in the secondary market, making Greek bonds a sure thing. The rules would have to change to do that regularly. But in principle, the ECB can simply promise to buy any eurozone government's sovereign bonds on the open market. Greece, Italy, Portugal and Spain would in effect have the power to create euros as needed, giving each of them far more control over their fortunes.

Second, a less easy option: the euro might be broken into southern and northern zones. A euro-north and a euro-south would be managed in parallel by the ECB on separate balance sheets. Perhaps what we've learned is that the southern countries are just too different from the northern ones for a common money to make a lot of sense. Thus we could group the similar economies together and break up the euro accordingly.[2]

Finally, the hardest option, which might not be possible now but could become possible later: add a fiscal transfer union to the monetary union. Which is to say, transfer funds between the eurozone countries, so they can manage their deficits and surpluses in an orderly manner. That's what we do in America among the states. Have you ever noticed that Mississippi's economy is much different than California's, or that New York's is different from Arkansas's? Yet we all share the dollar. How is that possible? Why aren't Mississippi and Arkansas always in debt like, say, Greece, with New York and California always in surplus like Germany? The answer is: because they share fiscal along with monetary union.

This can look like a bad deal for some of us. For every dollar a New Yorker or Californian pays in federal taxes, he or she gets roughly 50 cents back in federal program expenditure. And for each buck a Mississippian or Arkansan pays in, he or she gets about *two dollars* back. In effect, our union recycles money from surplus places to deficit places, no strings attached. The eurozone transfers as well, but there are strings attached: Greeks grow indebted to Germans—they borrow from Germans rather than having unconditional money just sent to them from Germans, as Mississippians and Arkansans receive from Californians and New Yorkers. And that's why there's trouble in euroland.

Of course, fiscal transfer unions aren't easy. For one thing, their members have to feel a sense of "one nation" with one another, in order to tolerate the unconditional transfers like family members do. For another thing, they have to *keep* feeling that way, even when the "one-way street" character of the transfers foments resentment by dependents toward their successful benefactors or by benefactors toward their seemingly "ingrate" dependents. The United States' fiscal union was hard fought and hard won, and even today it feels tenuous sometimes—especially when pundits, who either know nothing about, or actively lie about, fiscal and monetary matters, cynically whip up emotions for ratings and advertising revenue.

But in the final analysis, Americans still seem to identify more as Americans than as Oklahomans or Oregonians, and that makes our fiscal and monetary union still "work." Europe, it seems, is not there yet, so it might have to partly decouple until it can reunite much more deeply—that is, fiscally rather than just monetarily. In seeking monetary union without fiscal union, it might be trying—and failing—to occupy a not-quite-existent middle ground.

To some this might sound disappointing. The single-currency union came with much cosmopolitan fanfare about unifying Europe. Okay, but would moving to *two* euros that work better for everyone be any sort of defeat—especially if billed as temporary until fuller union is possible? Call it learning, in this case the hard way. Call it *saving* the union, if you like, by taking a partial and temporary "time-out." There'd be plenty of "unity" left, and much less stress and hardship—especially for the good people of Greece, Italy, Portugal, and Spain.

Developing countries present their own delicate circumstances. So as not to be presumptuous, let us just say: each country is different and requires its own special diagnosis.[3] In francophone Africa, for instance, a swathe of countries maintain a currency union like the euro, the CFA franc. The CFA franc was originally pegged to the French franc. After France adopted the euro, the CFA franc became effectively tied to the euro as well.

This is a bad arrangement—probably worse than the euro itself—and thus might be simply broken up. Each country should simply issue its own money, borrow in that money, and run an independent central bank, with the aid and support of the international community. Then in time each country might gradually integrate fiscally and monetarily in tandem, as Europe should have done in the first place, and as America did long ago with the help of a rare statesman who knew public finance as did few others in his day—Alexander Hamilton.

Actually, it would be a huge help if developing countries were simply to borrow mainly in their own moneys.[4] At the moment, many of them borrow and so repay in dollars, in order to woo investors and bondholders, by protecting them against exchange-rate risk. But then the country itself carries the risk if its exchange rate against the dollar goes south. Just so, the "tiger" economies of Asia crashed in the Asian financial crisis twenty-three years ago. So, instead of allowing that to happen, investors and bondholders should be asked to step right up and place their bets denominated in the local money. There's always risk, of course. And if the idea is to reduce the risks and attract foreign lending and investment, better to make the country's economy itself into a good bet. What form that takes varies from country to country, with no promises of an easy "silver bullet" policy fix.[5]

WHAT MADE AMERICA GREAT

If all this makes public debt sound like a bad or at least risky thing, it's actually a good, even *great* thing—Hamilton called it "a national blessing." It is nothing less than the foundation of the wealth and prosperity Americans say they're all about. As much as anything, it explains how the country itself developed its fabulous wealth.

America has steadily run a public deficit since its founding, running a surplus only twice. If you think about it, this makes perfect sense. Dollar bills, after all, are Fed promissory notes— they are circulating public liabilities, debt instruments. No public debts would mean no circulating instruments—that is, no money.

What do you reckon that'd do to the volume of transactions, the market exchanges that prompt production and hence employment in the first place? Treasury securities are like dollar bills in this sense—along with the dollar, they are the other form of circulating public liability, issued by the Treasury just as the dollar is issued by the Fed. All that differs is that they pay out (very low!) interest. And with the Fed now paying banks interest on their dollar reserves held with the Fed, even that difference is disappearing. No wonder that Treasurys, which at over $22 trillion constitute by far the biggest financial market in the world, are used in payments—that is, as money—in the financial markets.

Only once in recent decades, near the end of President Bill Clinton's years in office, has the United States "balanced its budget" and thus not issued more Treasury securities than it redeemed. What happened is instructive: the markets and "market watchers," not to mention the Fed and the Treasury Department themselves, freaked out. Why? Because "balancing the budget" and "paying down the national debt" means that the safest of "safe assets" dry up, even as the national and global financial markets depend on them. And it isn't just "snowflake" financiers. Pension and retiree funds rely on Treasurys as well. Indeed, all financial professionals use them to "benchmark" the values of all other tradable assets. They play the role of a "risk-free asset" in all of the trading formulae—from the capital asset pricing model ("CAPM") to the arbitrage pricing model ("APM")—that guide trading in all of the world's financial markets.

So when Bill Clinton "balanced the budget"—hoping to prove that his fellow Democrats were not those unsavory "tax-and-spend liberals" of Republican talking points, but indeed "fiscally responsible"—the government went into the black but the private sector, businesses, and households went into the red (way, way, way into the red). The markets rightly panicked. This was terribly dangerous, a tinderbox waiting to alight. Since business and households don't issue dollars themselves, they, unlike the United States, *can* go broke.

Many citizens did just that during the 2008 financial conflagration. So, you know, another decade, another well-meaning president—this time Obama rather than Clinton—who failed to note a crucial truth about the dollar: Every dollar in public debt is an asset in someone else's pocket or bank account, i.e., someone's *wealth*. And every surplus on the government books means that families and business are, taken all together, at heightened risk of going bust.

Clinton the very clever "triangulator" let himself get boxed in by the deficit scolds. Liberals like him had to prove their fiscal "responsibility" on their own spending priorities in a way Ronald Reagan the great "deficit spender" never did. But surely the real responsibility of a president and ruling party is to be a worthy trustee of America's past and future. It is to be a trustee who carries the noblest features of our past, which make us who we most fundamentally are, *into* the future.

In that case, literally going for broke in the private sector through a public sector "balanced budget" was and always is a colossal error. America would never have become the richest country in human history had it behaved like this for long. And it will never find widespread prosperity again unless it learns to get comfortable with, or even come to love, public debt, deployed properly.

What is "proper deployment"? Here an analogy to private sector situations might help—at least if interpreted carefully. Ask yourself what you have borrowed money to do in the past, and what others, including businesses, borrow money to do now. Chances are that most of your debt, if you have or have had it, was incurred seeking higher education or a home or a car. All of these are usually productive investments—they afford means of making you more productive and higher earning, of owning a valuable asset that gradually rises in value over time, or both. That means that they afford means of quickly paying the debt itself and thus clearing the books to borrow again and make other investments. The same goes for private sector businesses, which borrow in order to produce and to prosper more, which when done right liquidates debt itself. These are full analogues of the noninflationary "productivity-improving" expenditures discussed above in Chapter 12.

Things are similar in the case of government Treasury issuance, with just one twist. When the government invests, it does so not with "borrowed" funds as you do; again, it unlike you *issues* the money that does the "funding." The Treasury issuance is thus not for borrowing, but for "recapturing" just enough money to prevent inflation. But note what this means: it means productive public investment, which yields more goods and services to absorb the spent money, requires less Treasury issuance than would unproductive investment.

That's not because unproductive investment yields less return with which to "pay down the debt"—which *would* be your personal worry since you do not issue money. It is because unproductive investment is more *inflationary* and thus requires more "absorption" of "excess money" in the form of Treasury securities. So the public must invest carefully just as you must, but it must do so for a different reason. You must do so in order to earn enough to "liquidate" your debt. The government must do so in order not to have to "*de*liquidate" the money supply by issuing more "debt" to tamp down inflation by soaking up excess money that isn't absorbed by goods and services when investment isn't productive.

So we are back to inflation as the sole constraint on public spending. Just as with dollars in Chapter 12, so now with Treasurys here in Chapter 13, the thing about public issuances— currency or bonds—isn't the danger of bankruptcy. It is the danger of imbalance between public liabilities and what those liabilities purchase. Too much of the former relative to the latter and you have inflation. Too little of the former in relation to the latter—which happens *either* when the government spends too little or when it "issues" too little—and you have deflation. Goldilocks strikes again!

Alexander Hamilton understood this. In this sense the new American republic was uncommonly blessed. In early America, the problem was always too *little* money, not too much money. A shortage of precious metals when money was tied to those metals meant a shortage of money itself. And since money was needed for market exchange and to incentivize production, the dearth of money in circulation meant our economy couldn't grow. So Americans innovated new forms of money. More available items, such as tobacco or shells, were recognized in settling accounts, in paying exchange debts and fulfilling obligations. Even when provincial governors sympathetic to the British Crown's priorities resisted, some early municipalities recognized shells in payment of local taxes, to ensure there would be enough money in circulation. The native inhabitants of our continent who created these special shells were taxed as tribute, in effect being forced to produce them for the larger community—being turned into something of a "mint" at gunpoint.

Eventually the colonial settlers and then founders took more innovative steps: they converted to paper currency more quickly than European nations, precisely because gold and silver shortages necessitated it. Hamilton's bank, which we mentioned in Chapter 8, issued tradable bonds—forerunners to today's Treasury securities—both to fund investment and to disseminate a new monetary medium all across the fledgling United States, which eventually made the new nation into an industrial powerhouse. It was the South's hostility to any central bank, its success in taking Hamilton's bank and its successor down, and the gold standard that, if anything, limited issuance of money and public debt. But that finally brought a wave of deflationary crises, as we've explained, leading us ultimately to embrace the Hamiltonian fiscal and monetary arrangements that we have today.

If two-hundred-plus years of history is any guide, we really should worry more about having "too little money" and too little public debt, or at least too little of it flowing in the right (productive!) directions, than too much. Public debt is exactly how America marshaled its abundant resources and became rich from the start, and how it can grow even richer in the future.

WHEN DEFICITS MATTER

But surely at some point we can have too much debt, right? Isn't some *percentage* of debt to, say, what we produce (gross domestic production, or "GDP") just too high?

We'd respond to that question by asking: What do you mean by "too much" or "too high"? Often people just mean that, when you see the figure in the newspaper, you feel surprised, even shocked, because, *wow*, doesn't that number *just seem rather large*? Like 200 percent or even 240 percent debt to GDP, as in Japan. That's pretty large, right, as in *big*?

But without any point of reference, this thought is basically meaningless. The number means little in itself. There simply is no "right size" for deficits, no special debt-to-GDP ratio that a country should aim to stay below or to hit, that is independent of that which money and debt are both for—productive activity and associated wealth generation. The size of public debt is, in other words, just a proxy for *something else* that really does matter, something we already do worry plenty about, more so than we should. Which is to say: the relation between spending and producing, i.e., the Scylla and Charybdis of inflation and deflation. And as we explained in Chapter 12, with new tools, central banks and fiscal authorities can reliably manage both.

Even with no inflation problem in the cards, there is still one last cause for concern. Once we've created as much money as we productively can, at the limit of "full employment," the question remains: Is the money going to the right places? Are public debts allocated in the most efficient, productive, and equitable way? Or is the debt we accrue going to waste, or even counterproductive, because the assets are better directed elsewhere? This is the public allocation question noted above. It is like the private sector question: Should you issue promissory notes to banks—i.e., borrow— in order to buy and consume lots of cigarettes and potato chips? Wouldn't it be better to procure a reliable car or education?

This is what should be at stake in our Sturm und Drang about public debt: efficiency and allocation, equity and distribution. Do we really need another aircraft carrier? Do the rich, who are maxed out on consumption and hence use their surplus to generate hyperinflations ("bubbles") in financial markets, need yet another tax cut? Might new investment in infrastructure or education or green energy, say, be a better use for the money and "debt" that we issue? *Yes.* Productive spending is smart spending—and is both counter-inflationary and counter-deflationary spending. It is Goldilocks spending rather than gold spending.

So, when it comes to deficits as such, worry not. But let us take them as an opportunity to ask pointed questions about whether or not the money being left in the economy is doing the good it can and should do for us. Think, in other words, of "opportunity costs," not just of costs.

CHAPTER 14

CAN PROMISES BE TRUSTED AGAIN? ASSHOLE-PROOF GOVERNANCE

So public spending is good. Great even. But can we really trust legislators, prone as they are said to be to "spend like drunken sailors," to resist the siren song of spending for the wrong reasons?

The proper asshole politicians certainly can't be trusted; they should simply be removed, or, better, kept far away from power in the first place.[1] Yet one wouldn't have to be a cynic to suspect any politician of looking mainly at the very short run, the polls and the upcoming election. We see it all the time, with legislators promising "belt tightening" often while spending on the sly— all too often for campaign contributors. The economy should be managed for the medium and longer run. But if Ulysses tied his hands to the mast in order to resist the siren's song of sexual bliss, can we expect our less heroic "leaders" to control their lust to keep power, once elected?

We've seen a traditional answer: "balanced budget" religion. Get people to believe that every dollar spent must be matched with a dollar in tax revenue or borrowing, at least eventually. As we argued in Chapters 2 and 13, that noble lie has become downright pernicious, an ignoble threat to democracy itself. It has kept us from fulfilling our economic promises, eroded trust in our institutions, and allowed demagogues and authoritarians to capitalize on broken promises and distrust. It is, in a big way, what gave us the explosive political-asshole problem we're in.

Ideally, we'd have a well-run legislature. We could expect it to do much more to adjust spending levels as needed, to keep the economy at prosperous full employment while itself managing inflation and deflation.[2] Elected officials would keep their hands steadily on what twentieth-century economist Abba Lerner called the "economic steering wheel." They'd make necessary adjustments, in a timely fashion, instead of acting as though there is no wheel to turn, or as though turning it would be dictatorship.[3] On the other hand, given the legislature we have and can hope for, realistically, we can't expect ultraskilled driving over the longer run. We are too likely to fall into the sort of crisis that spawns demagogues, once again.

Fortunately, there is a decent solution to that problem already: put an "independent" central bank in charge of certain delicate monetary tasks in the short run, holding it accountable for its decisions in the medium run. Which is to say, insulate it from the winds of electoral politics, much as we do with our courts (which is why we no longer have "justice" by lynch mobs). As we saw in Chapter 12, a new and improved Fed can give us guaranteed money directly *and* reliably manage the risks of deflation and inflation. Then we really *can* be confident that a promise of shared prosperity will be faithfully kept, season after season, from one generation to the next.

Still, since good governance isn't exactly in fashion lately, one might honestly wonder whether old-time monetary religion is better than anything we can hope for. Even central bank "independence" is being corrupted, it seems. In a series of mean 2018 tweets (and maybe more hectoring behind the scenes), President Donald Trump took to browbeating his own appointed Fed chairman, Jerome Powell. The hope was to spur Powell to lower interest rates and juice the economy, just in time for Trump's reelection campaign. Because, you know, good growth numbers are a great political talking point and influence voter sentiment. To many, the Fed looks as though it capitulated, bowing to political pressure, lowering interest rates again notwithstanding historically low unemployment numbers.[4]

Public criticism *can* be a very good thing. International law runs in large measure on "naming and shaming." When governments are "jawboned" for their poor human rights records, there's a better chance they'll improve them, if only to spare the country further embarrassment. But this works subtly and over time, when the public display calls up a legitimate, healthy norm or principle. Much of "democratic" governance works simply by exchange of relevant, public reasons for a decision in good faith, often outside of legislatures.[5] So when criticism invokes a norm that thoughtful people will defend on principle, with considered, weighty reasons, especially when it has gained a significant consensus, officials may know they don't really have an answer. They may feel ashamed and embarrassed for being on the wrong side of it. They'll resist shameless bullshitting, except as a last resort.

When Trump criticized Powell, it was by a dictator's threat, the sort intended to single out and scare a man into submission. He "needed a favor," and made little effort to give good, relevant reasons for it. When asked to explain, Trump says "I do like low interest rates," dodging the real question: "And *why,* pray tell, is that good for the country, aside from what's good for you politically?" Journalists, knowing they'll get a runaround, may not bother to press. Plausible public justification is beside the point.

Let's hope all the bluster never really mattered, that the Fed didn't capitulate so much as it made its own informed decision. Still, even the *attempt* to badger and hassle a Fed chairman violated a crucial principle: that central bank officials must be allowed to make their own best decision about monetary policy, unmolested by the pressures of short-term electoral politics. Trump's attacks upon Powell echoed his slanders of judges ("so-called judge," for instance) made after court decisions that he didn't like.

Despite Trump's overreach, we have a pretty good system for the Fed's "political independence" in place already—hardly perfect, but sound in important respects. That independence means three things, mainly. First, appointment power: the executive selects the Fed chairperson, but on fixed, five-year terms that don't align with the political calendar. If Powell had to worry about not being reappointed by Trump—a man known for his vindictiveness—that might cloud or corrupt his judgment about what's best for the country.

Second, congressional oversight: the Congress can and does demand a public justification for the decisions central bankers have made, albeit after the fact. Beforehand, a subtle pressure is exerted. The Fed chairperson knows that, in time, he or she will have to answer for his or her judgment calls in a public forum.

Third, professional incentives: if central bankers aren't immediately beholden to elected officials, they are subject to peer pressure and the practical and scientific expectations of other central bankers, who hold each other accountable for best monetary practice as it evolves and improves. These "craft norms" still matter in central banking. They haven't been displaced by ephemeral political or social media fads, thank goodness.

DEMOCRATIC ACCOUNTABILITY

None of this should be confused with other ways central bankers have been shielded from accountability. Not so long ago, central banking was shrouded in secrecy: "independence" meant independence from nearly all public scrutiny. After the 1929 stock market crash, Deputy Governor of the Bank of England Sir Ernest Musgrave Harvey was interrogated before the Macmillan Committee, which was charged with investigating what happened. Here's how the discussion went:[6]

Committee member John Maynard Keynes: [I]s it a practice of the Bank of England never to explain [. . .] the reasons for its policy?
Harvey: It is a dangerous thing to start to give reasons.

Keynes: Or to defend it against criticism?
Harvey: [. . .] As regards defense against criticism, I am afraid, though the Committee may not all agree, we do not admit there is need for defense; to defend ourselves is somewhat akin to a lady starting to defend her virtue.

In reply, committee member Keynes made what must have at that point sounded like a new, rather "democratic" argument:

Keynes: Does not the policy of secrecy as to its intentions deprive the Bank of what I might call the collective wisdom of the community? These questions are very difficult and very novel. They require a great deal of co-operative thinking by all people who are competent to contribute to the common stock. Does not the policy of secrecy of the Bank mean that no one outside the Bank can express an opinion which is founded on sound information?

This sounds like common sense to us now—an early invocation of the "hive mind" or "wisdom of crowds" idea. Yet another sign of progress. Central bankers do require discretion on key issues, in order to make quick decisions for careful, scientific reasons. That requires *insulation* from political *pressure*, but not complete *isolation* from *contrary thinking*, as we've come to understand.[7]

Even so, public accountability has not matured enough. For the latter half of the twentieth century, "independence" was often thought to mean blind faith in allegedly value-free, technocratic expertise. Never you mind, ordinary citizens; don't bother your pretty little heads about complicated matters. Just accept the mystery of money and sleep soundly. Let the Fed chairman's techno-jargon be your lullaby, as rising asset prices bring sweet dreams of "new paradigms" and a bright, happy future. The technocratic priests of monetary policy—the ones exalted as "maestros" in the headlines—know best, whatever the seemingly adverse consequences for financial stability, employment, wages, or declining trust in democracy.

That mythology fell apart after the 2008 crisis. Greenspan was called "the maestro" during the 1990s when he *seemed* to be skillfully conducting the economic symphony. Once it was clear he was mainly sitting on his hands, operating with blind faith in individual investor prudence and its collective sufficiency, the image of value-free orchestration quickly flew out the window. Cheered on by the economics profession, central bankers had fallen into "groupthink" for their lack of diversity. They were too insensitive to the basic "political" values they were entrusted with. And how could they not be held accountable for such a profound misjudgment? After allowing such a wantonly destructive conflagration, how could they not be held to account for what serves the real needs of society?[8]

Chairman Greenspan was called to explain himself before Congress in 2008, where he admitted a "flaw" in his thinking (though he later recanted). Again, a sign of progress. After Chairman Bernanke—who served from 2006 to 2014—took unorthodox measures that led to recovery, he also had to explain them publicly, this time under withering scrutiny in the financial media. The central bank didn't do much that it should have.[9] But sustained public argument about just that was a very good thing. Keynes was right: central bank policies are best discussed in open sunlight, with the help of general educated opinion and important public values. Which means *not* leaving things to a cabal of elites, not without vigilant public scrutiny by an informed populace.

ROOM FOR IMPROVEMENT

An *informed* populace? About money and public finance? The very idea may raise eyebrows or prompt a chuckle. There's not just the usual ignorance or indifference, in this case about complicated matters. Along with honest differences in opinion, the purveyors of noble lies and superstitions are still out there sow-ing confusion. But if better decisions can sometimes be made in secrecy (or under cover of bad or vague slogans), surely their real justification should eventually educate the public. That helps clear the political air for better decisions in the future. In a democracy, the answer is not monetary superstition, but better decisions *and* a better-informed public, with the help, hopefully, of cooperative financial media. As we noted in the Preface, that's why we wrote this book. Once we "pull back the curtain" on how things work already, we can see fresh possibilities for our future.

The image of the "all-knowing Fed" always required banking to be shrouded in *Wizard of Oz* optics—which is to say, propagandistic smoke and mirrors, or, if you will, bullshit. This has no place in the sound management of a democracy's money. So the Fed might do better at admitting and explaining its mistakes.

Central bankers do invest a great deal of time and effort into learning already. Despite their reputation for stodgy conservativism, they're often quite good at figuring out their mistakes and finding better methods—far more so than academic economists wedded to grand entrenched models and half-baked philosophical visions. The central banking community should celebrate their openness to learning and share the results with the public more forthrightly; they are, after all, like academics in their insulation, but also like the private sector in their responsibility for economic developments "on the ground." (Hence Bernanke's quip that "there are no atheists in foxholes and no ideologues in financial crises."[10]) Were central banks to establish a reputation for being especially skilled at learning on the fly, that itself would engender confidence in them and trust in their expert testimony. This is far better, over time, than cultivating an image of infallibility that explodes after the next crisis.

As for its internal learning process, central banks can do even better by cultivating greater diversity. As noted earlier, after the 2008 crisis, the New York Fed worried about "groupthink" and brought in out-of-the-box, "heterodox" thinkers. The introduction of a more diverse set of ideas and methods can significantly improve a learning process, which is often about exploring neglected possibilities.[11]

A more diverse set of people, with different backgrounds and experiences, can ensure that a full range of important values are spoken for. The appointment of Janet Yellen as Fed chairperson in 2015 was an important first step toward gender diversity—as was the appointment of consumer finance expert Sarah Bloom Raskin to the Fed Board of Governors in 2010. Much more can be done to include people from different socioeconomic backgrounds, who are often more attuned to issues "on the ground" than those with the usual elite educations. Yet another way to ensure a full range of important public values are thoughtfully considered.

Some bankers will worry that many values, important as they are, are simply beyond the Fed's legal mandate or professional expertise. It is often thought that the central bank, concerned as it is with "monetary policy," must steer clear of "fiscal" policy and "distribution," which is the job of the legislature. This is wrong about the Fed's mandated goals: employment and price stability. Those are both goals written into its enabling legislation, and the trade-off between them, especially, is a value judgment, indeed, a "distributive" one. To prioritize stable prices over full employment, thus allowing millions of willing workers to go without jobs, as the Fed has since the 1980s, is "distribution" par excellence—far more so than many "fiscal" decisions made over in the legislature. Add to this the tight correlation between inequality and financial market fragility, and you see at once that setting aside distribution is as conceptually impossible as is "squaring the circle."[12]

Central bankers will rightly wonder where the limits to their discretion lie. But of course any institution must interpret its own mandate with careful decisions about what it might, or might not, cover. We think the Fed should take on a much more "distributive" role. That would stretch the current mandate pretty far. But that's mainly to say the Fed's job should be broadened in new legislation—the very legislation that authorizes the new tools we described in Chapter 12. And if the old guard is very wary of having an expressly "distributive" mandate, just hand some of the jobs to a Fed offshoot, which works in coordination with the Fed by its own explicit, value-infused mandate.

PLAYING "WHACK-A-MOLE"

Of course, even if the central bank makes sound decisions, the larger financial markets may be chock-full of assholes. All sorts of misbehavior, fueled by convenient rationalizations, helped drive the United States and the world off of a cliff in 2008. Many still grouse that private bankers were not only bailed out, but never really punished for their sins. Even outright lawbreakers were never prosecuted.

And of course, even in normal times, the Fed's orchestration of any sort of symphony requires a minimum of cooperation, even among all the greedy moneymaking. And in a "greed is good" culture—where moneymaking is a mark of virtue and the mere mention of regulation can send bankers into a fit of entitled rage, for feeling unappreciated—isn't the Fed rather constrained?[13] Is it not forced to do the bidding of asshole capitalists, rather than somehow reining in financial market assholery?

If the Fed is not all-knowing, it certainly isn't omnipotent, either. In a public-private partnership, it depends on financial markets, much as any symphony conductor depends on its musicians. But financial regulators *can* rein in bad behavior, so that financial markets actually achieve their intended purpose, for the benefit of everyone.

For starters, there is conventional financial regulation. Whatever the merits of criminal punishment, regulators can and should prosecute "bad banks." Wells Fargo, for example, in effect stole from its own customers on a huge scale.[14] Fines for misbehavior are not so effective, and likely to be seen as "the cost of business" rather than a deterrent. The bad press from fines might be a better deterrent—though then the fines need to be eye-popping enough to make news.

Far more effective is the threat of charter revocation.[15] The sword of Damocles dangling over their heads, private bankers know they're at risk of being ejected from the finance franchise. We the public entrust banks with awesome powers of creating money—bona fide US dollars from nothing. So we have the right to remove our blessing, forcing uncooperative bankers to find another line of business. The threat of ejection does need to be credible. The sword should be dropped occasionally (we could start with Wells Fargo). Let the bankers know we, the public, mean it.

New regulation can also go a long way toward fixing larger, systemic problems. We can end "too big to fail" institutions, fully segregate banking from speculation, and impose other "macro-prudential" measures. As for how to separate banking from speculation, the Fed Citizen and Resident Accounts that we outlined in Chapter 10 would move many ordinary deposits off of private sector bank balance sheets to the Fed's balance sheet. That would segregate depository functions from speculative activity right off the bat—more so than the 1933 Glass-Steagall Act, which had the same purpose, ever did. With respect to macroprudential regulation, in turn, the direct Fed "collaring" of sensitive market prices described in Chapter 12 would do that far better than anything done yet. For the rest, the tools fleshed out since 2009 should suffice.[16]

Regulation is hardly ever perfect. Firms often quickly exploit the slightest loopholes or ambiguities, often with considerable cunning and creativity. Cynics say this makes regulation pointless. The rules will never be fully kept, so why bother?

But rules can and often should be blunt. They should be free of exceptions, vague terms, and nuance. They may seem crude taken by themselves. And yes, they'll be easy to criticize in the op-ed pages. One can always point to some seemingly legitimate thing you couldn't do under them, and, *you see*, yet another un-

American government intrusion into financial liberty, whatever the public benefit!

In practice, though, blunt rules are more difficult to cheat. There are fewer loopholes to exploit. Everyone may have greater assurance that cheating is being kept on the margins. And if the rules do then gain a good measure of compliance—curbing or isolating unproductive speculation, for instance—they've served their point of advancing the public interest.

As for the regulator, the job isn't just to enforce this or that rule. It is to play "whack-a-mole," persistently, in the face of new avoidance or arbitrage strategies. When firms come up with a clever new tactic, the job is to learn and adapt. The regulators can't always stay one step ahead. But that, after all, is also the game of "cops and robbers," which is to say, law enforcement for public benefit.

THE FALSE CHOICE: REGULATION VS. FREE MARKETS

To many, it is either "government rules" *or* the "free market." We are led to assume we have to choose one or the other. Are you a "capitalist," who favors the free market, or a "New Deal liberal" or "socialist," who favors top-down regulation? Choose your side!

But really, there is only *one* game in town—"market-state balance," with more weight for one or the other in the balance. One of our main messages in this book is this: we are not forced to choose between "regulation" and "markets." This is because the central bank can shape market behavior *as a market actor*—not just as a cop that makes sure the market plays fair.

As we've noted many times now, the Fed already buys and sells assets in "open market operations." These transactions are mediated by "dealer banks," so the parties buying or selling often don't know they are transacting with the central bank. And yet, because the sums changing hands are very large—the Fed essentially operates like another "whale" in the market—they shape prices and market incentives through their actions.

The Fed can do just the same thing in a much more robust way. If, left to their own devices, rapaciously greedy and shortsighted speculators are prone to drive the economy into crisis, the Fed can monitor the situation and preempt financial and other price "bubbles." It can save the bankers and speculators from themselves, and save the rest of us from their disaster in the making.

The Fed would also be a direct actor in our proposed "public banking option." The Fed can keystroke money directly into our Citizen Accounts. Then we can bank from those accounts, saving and spending dollars. As we've explained, we then wouldn't be forced to do business with private banks. Nor would our deposits, as Fed liabilities, any longer be paired with speculative assets, since the Fed doesn't deal in those for a profit. In both our joint and our several capacities, we'd all have a safe option.

Through its actions, the Fed can help keep the private banks honest. The public bank can in effect set a benchmark for services and privacy *without* direct regulation. Then, the private banks will have to offer comparable services or privacy just to compete in the marketplace. And what's wrong with a little competition? We citizens would see greater liberty, for being free to pursue public banking, private banking, or some measure of both, as we each see fit.

PART V

A MORE PROMISING ECONOMY

So a new social compact is both possible and necessary. We *have* the money, because we have promises, along with reliable ways of managing them. But what should a renewed social bargain promise? At very least, it should promise a more prosperous future—for each of our lives *and* for the environment we live in.

CHAPTER 15

FOUR PROMISES: INCOME, WORK, WEALTH, AND LEISURE

Wealthy investors have diverse portfolios of valuable assets. For all the market ups and downs, the numbers they read about in the morning news usually suggest continuing good fortune in at least four key areas: increased income (which they may not even need), work that is meaningful, accrued wealth, and plenty of interesting leisure. One can certainly understand why the wealthy could feel rather pleased with this whole capitalist democratic republic arrangement.

But promises and hope aren't just for them. Every citizen of our union, the very people who make wealth in such abundance possible, should also have his or her own "portfolio" of promises, in this case public promises for each of those four areas of life.

For income: each of us could receive a guaranteed income or the means of earning one, in the form of a basic income grant, a job guarantee, or both. Everyone's incomes would become more secure. Which is not only great in itself. It would also raise wages across the economy. Private firms would have to compete for workers by offering better salaries and benefits. Workers would get the pay raise they've had coming, but haven't seen, for almost fifty years.

For work: guaranteed work could be more flexible, or even part-time. This would encourage private employers also to reduce hours and increase flexibility, as some have begun to do already. It would help reduce the pay gap between men and women. The time we do spend working would be more focused, efficient, vigorous, and enjoyable.

For wealth: workers can be given a greater share of capital via capital grants and other measures. Every child could be given a certain tidy sum, to be released to his or her discretion at age eighteen. It could be used to buy more education, learn a trade, or start a business, and maybe, just maybe, launch more of us into the entrepreneurial class.

And finally for leisure: with more secure incomes and shorter or more flexible work hours, each of us could enjoy a more meaningful life in time away from work—whether in service to others, political engagement, skillful pursuits, or just a more relaxed attunement to each other and to nature.

Something a lot like these promises were once the "American Dream." In the decades after the great war, with that fabled rising tide of prosperity and the new, shorter workweek, people felt that a bright future lay ahead and was already beginning. It didn't exactly keep happening, not for most people, alas. But this doesn't mean that it can't happen now, better late than never.

We hope you can see by now, dear reader, that we really can "pay for" all this. Every American really *can* enjoy an updated and upgraded "American Dream," refashioned for the twenty-first century. We have the money; it is financially possible, entirely feasible, if only we are bold enough to choose it.

Finance isn't political philosophy. What we *can* do and what we *should* do are different questions. But if we really can finance better lives for us all, why not go for it?! Why not actually keep America's best promises—because they were promises, and for all the good reasons we made them in the first place? Why not do a little justice and show the world that the United States' image of itself as both morally and financially rich is not a delusion, but a *prediction*, our future reality?!

THE FIRST PROMISE: GUARANTEED INCOME

The idea of paying a "basic income" to people is often thought to be laughably "utopian." There's no "free lunch" in capitalist America, right? To others, a modest basic income payment is woefully insufficient, no more than a last-ditch effort by Silicon Valley moguls to save capitalism from itself—or themselves from the desperately starving masses.

There's plenty of news, lately, about experiments with basic income payments, in countries like Finland and cities like Stockton, California. One might suspect that giving people money is the way of the future, especially if you think ahead a bit. Robots or AI are "coming for our jobs." What are vast number of truckers going to do when trucks are fully automated? Install solar panels? And anyway isn't it already harder than ever to find good work?[17] But what's less often appreciated it is that "free money" is the way of the present. The "free lunch" is being served up already, just in scrawny portions.

One country in particular is way behind its industrialized peers in allowing yawning inequality, known for its ardor for "free markets" and hostility to lazy, no-good, free-loving freeloaders, who would rather surf all day off of Malibu than hold down even a part-time job. And yet it's been passing out free money for decades. For almost five decades now, it has been guaranteeing people's income from work up to a certain level. If your yearly income comes in below a certain level, you get free money back from the government in the form of a check or electronic credit, no questions asked. The country in question is not one of those "socialist" northern European experiments where people report being very happy. No, it is the one and the only U. S. of A., that rugged pioneer in the cause of giving people free money.

If you happen to live in the state of Alaska—which, mind you, trends conservative and Republican—you receive $2,072 per year as of 2015. And that's on top of any free money you get from the federal government, no questions asked. The US federal government has been doling out cash, free and clear, since 1975, in the form of the earned income tax credit ("EITC"), which was ramped up in the 1990s.

At first the brainchild of libertarian economists F. A. Hayek and Milton Friedman and called a "negative income tax," the national tax benefit was championed by Republican president Richard Nixon, and enacted under his successor President Gerald Ford as the slightly different EITC. The credit worked wonders in its intended purpose of reducing poverty. Rates of extreme, as distinguished from ordinary, poverty fell dramatically over subsequent years. Even now the EITC maintains bipartisan support, more so than perhaps any social insurance program.

Here generations of *both* right- and left-wing thinkers can claim a modest victory. Proponents on the right such as Hayek, Friedman, Charles Murray, and others, and proponents on the left such as Thomas Paine, Martin Luther King Jr., and many others, have found themselves on the same winning team. Which is rather remarkable given how divided and tribalistic American politics seems to have become of late. It is a stunning victory for the right/left idea of giving people "free stuff," or rather cash to buy stuff, no strings attached.

Sure, an EITC payment ain't much, not by any stretch. The American commitment to free-market discipline turns out to mean that you *do* get free stuff, just not *a lot* of it, unless you're already rich—in which case the freebies keep coming. If you're poor, you don't have to make very much in a given year before you no longer qualify for the free money. Then you are on your own (until you're very rich). And anyway you do have to work. If you don't work, other benefits may be available, but they can be difficult to get, with years-long waiting lists.

But still, all this means there should be no serious question about whether paying a guaranteed income is *feasible*. The idea of an income guarantee, of one sort, isn't "utopian," it's already here. So if there's a question to ponder now, it is only *what form* passing out free money should take, not whether to do it in the first place. Envelopes? Helicopter drops?

Some worry that if we raised the payouts, the poorer folks now working three jobs will suddenly stay home all day getting drunk or high on the couch—as opposed to cutting back to just *two* jobs, in order to spend more time with the family. Because you see, unless they're threatened with destitution, they'll be slothful and undeserving and should spend time at some "bullshit job," away from the family.[18]

Realistically, with a bit more steady money some folks would cut back on low-paid work. But recent experiments show that, on average, people continue to work about as much, but report being less stressed. Those being better paid for full-time work could sup on the American Dream of weekends off and restful two-week vacations. And wasn't that supposed to be a major part of the Dream?

That postwar promise of a forty-hour workweek has all but vanished. Americans now tend to work *more* than forty hours per week on average, working longer for the same money, in effect taking a per-hour pay cut. They vacation on average only one week per year, despite the official promise of two weeks per year off—and despite Europeans enjoying over *four* weeks off. They aren't benefiting from the promises made some fifty years ago— and that was *before* the subsequent increases in national wealth, surges in technology, and booms in worker productivity. Those trends sound great, except that, during the same period, wages have flatlined. After almost a half century without a real pay increase, one can understand why people would doubt whether the glowing promise of shared prosperity will ever be kept.

Here any good accountant would ask: Okay, fine; what would make up the difference, given what's owed in arrears? Well, for starters, we could pay people a basic income, say, a guaranteed $1,000 or $2,000 per month. It's a little late by now, of course— a half century amounts to many people's entire working lives. Many people who labored their whole adult lives under America's

promises now live in poverty on nothing more than Social Security, and they can't go back to work at this late date. But the extra
money from a basic income grant would most definitely help with
medical and caretaking bills. As the proverb goes, the best time
to plant a tree is fifty years ago. The second-best time is . . . today,
before the *next* fifty years slip away.

One can already hear the pundits barging in to say, "Sounds
nice, but how are you going to pay for that?" What they mean, in
particular, is whose *taxes* are going to pay for that. Democratic
presidential candidate Andrew Yang was asked that question
throughout his 2020 campaign. He stumped for a basic income
grant, pitched as a dividend drawn from the enormous gains generated by life in a capitalist society. And his answer: new taxes to
offset the cost of a basic income grant. Disappointingly, this buys
into the old "balanced budget" myths and the trap of thinking
that taxes have to pay for any nice stuff. But then—you know how
the retort goes—taxes you can't raise, so nice stuff you can't have.
Better to forget about "free money," you lazy loafer, and keep
looking for better work.

It's true that even if taxes *had* to pay for a basic income grant—
which they don't—there would be plenty of decent options. One
could tax "consumption," as with Europe's sales tax (a VAT), a
well-tested way of raising vast revenue sums. Or you could tax
Wall Street speculation, as Nobel laureate economist James Tobin
proposed. We definitely don't need to raise taxes on incomes,
which Americans seem to sort of dislike. We *can* "pay for" a basic
income the same way we already pay for all our aircraft carriers
and wars: just decide to do it, spend the money into existence, and
allow the central bank to manage any inflation risks.

The Federal Reserve does that well already—too well, in fact.
And it can manage inflation even more reliably with a few new
policy tweaks. As we explained in Chapter 12, the central bank
really can hold inflation to a healthy level even with large new
spending outlays. There is simply no technical reason why the
central bank can't be allowed to simply pay people money directly,

each and every month. Any risk of inflation or deflation can be handled by adjusting interest rates on our Citizen Accounts, and, if necessary, imposing temporary freezes ("impounds," while we all collect interest).

So, a guaranteed income really *can* be arranged, if we decide it's a good idea. The question is not technical feasibility, but whether it's a good idea—i.e., the right, just, best way forward. Why would we do such a wild and crazy thing, you ask? Lots of reasons. For starters, a guaranteed income would give hardworking Americans suffering from fifty years of wage stagnation a bit of a break. That would help make up for five decades of broken promises of shared prosperity. Good people would be less stressed, have better opportunity and more freedom, and feel like they are getting a fairer shake. And maybe, just maybe, they'd spend more time with the kids, at home or in splendid days at the lake or the beach. More people who work constantly could get a little taste of the good life, just like the rich. Because we're all supposedly equals in a shared republic.

THE SECOND PROMISE: WORK

Proponents of modern monetary theory, and many before them—including Coretta Scott King, Hyman Minsky, and Sadie Alexander[19]—have long argued that every man and woman willing to work should be guaranteed a job at a decent wage. The unemployed, here defined as people looking for work, are often already in the public sector—collecting unemployment or other social benefits, i.e., more free money, no strings attached. And so, it is argued, if they're *already* in on the public dole, why not have them work! What self-respecting American would complain about that?

So if climate change is a problem, we, through our government, can arrange for people to be trained in solar panel installation, or call-center support for people confused about their solar panel options. Even the surfers down at the beach, given all their knowledge of riptides and the like, can lend a hand with lifeguarding duties and get paid for it. There's plenty of work to be done, as long as people are looking for work, and there's no reason at all why those people can't be given work, if only as a "transitional job" before returning to private sector employment where the better money is. Unemployment, the idea goes, is an unnecessary evil, which we should end by simply instituting a new job guarantee program, perhaps as part of a Green New Deal.

We agree. Except many MMT advocates take this to mean that we therefore *shouldn't* have a basic income grant. To them it is one or the other—a job guarantee, *or* a basic income grant; we can't have both. But why can't we have both? Why shouldn't the beleaguered working person have both a bit of guaranteed money and a job if he or she wants it, so as to "top up" his or her income to a reasonable (albeit relatively low) level?

The MMTers won't say we can't afford it, for lack of tax revenue. They're with us on that point: taxes do not "pay for" public spending, in the way ordinarily assumed. What some do say, however, is that a basic income would be inflationary. If people are more comfortable at home and out of work, firms will have to offer higher wages to attract them into the workforce. And as the firms compete with each other for those folks, wages will be pushed ever higher. Which means the average working person will have a lot more money to spend, and then spend it, causing rising prices and an unhealthy level of inflation.

To them, the job guarantee, on the other hand, is *not* inflationary—at least as long as the guaranteed wage is low enough so as not to draw people out of the private sector. It's high enough to get people to work, but *low enough* not to bid up the wages offered by private firms. So there's no inflation risk. You pull people off the couch, but still give them reason to take a private sector job, for the still higher pay.

We're on board with a job guarantee. It's a good idea. Why shouldn't everyone willing to work for a decent wage be able to? Why should your ability to earn an adequate living depend upon some rich person's willingness to hire you, just as a medieval peasant's ability to eat turned on a landlord's willingness to bring her on as a sharecropper? What's more American than producing goods or services for others at a humble wage—good 'ol American self-sacrifice! What we can't quite see is why that *precludes* paying a basic income grant as well.

It only *seems* like a dilemma when you haven't quite appreciated the power in central banking and, if necessary, countercyclical fiscal policy as a supplement. The Fed really can manage any inflationary trends, at least with the new tools we described in Chapter 12. A basic income payment wouldn't cause unhealthy inflation if we got central banking and fiscal policy right (and, again, in our current deflationary environment, we're a long way off from an inflation problem).

So, if people are willing to work, let's ensure that they can, by all means. Put people to work in the service of the public good! Create jobs! But whether or not a given person can or would work a conventional job at this particular juncture in life, given their children, or their schooling, or the injury, or a creative project, let's also make sure they have enough money to live. It's no sweat on our part, after all. We just order the central bank to keystroke a bit of money into bank accounts—$1,000 per month, at very least.

THE THIRD PROMISE: WEALTH

Life need not and ought not be a treadmill. You ought to be able to accumulate, to grow and store up, a "nest egg" as well—for your kids, your retirement, your next new business, or whatever. That, too, is part of the American Dream—an aspect of our small-*r* republican heritage that many Americans seem to have forgotten. In the pre-imperial Roman ideal that our "founders" intended to replicate, a polity's citizens would own their own bases of sustenance—small farms for agriculturalists, tools for craftspeople, and so on. Economically self-sufficient people, the thought ran, made ideal republican citizens. They were not sufficiently desperate to be bribable. And they all owned a piece of that "common-weal"—that common wealth—that was the republic's as a whole.

This was the idea behind talk of "sturdy yeomanry" by Thomas Jefferson and others. It suffused Abraham Lincoln's great speeches about American labor owning its own tools and workplaces. And it is why the early American republic did so well both politically and economically—at least if you were a white man, the only people then allowed to own property and other productive assets. But it's a grave error to think this was all private action. It was *public* action to *enable* private action. Just look at countless federal policies from the founding on down to the present—including, for instance, the land reforms and Northwest Ordinance of the late eighteenth century, the Homestead and Morrill Land-Grant College Acts of the 1860s and after, and home and higher education finance policy from the New Deal era until the 1980s.

It is time to restore this essential feature of the American republican ideal. It is well documented that returns to capital have been greater than returns to labor for centuries—this is what Thomas Piketty's 2014 blockbuster book *Capital in the Twenty-First Century* was all about. It is also well documented that homes in the United States, at least until privatization despoiled our home finance programs beginning in the 1990s, have long been one of the two best possible investments that middle-class citizens can make. The other, also until late in the game, has been "human capital"—higher education—whose finance till the late 1980s was publicly facilitated just as home finance was.

How could we make good on that ideal at this point? In the case of homes and higher education, it's very easy: simply restore the pre-privatization status quo, which worked wonders. But we can go further—*much* further. The thing about "homesteads" in the nineteenth and early twentieth centuries is that they were much more than just homes. They were means of earning a livelihood, back when the US economy was still largely agricultural and there really were millions of "small family farms." But we're not farmers anymore; most of us must earn our livelihoods in nonagricultural sectors. So, in order to be a republic in the classical sense, we need to find means of "capital homesteading" much as we used to have means of farm homesteading.

How? Well, higher ed and vocational ed are one way to help. But businesses need more than human capital to "start up" and grow. So why don't we make that available too? We have, after all, a Small Business Administration ("SBA") established during the New Deal. We have all manner of government procurement contracting, aimed at encouraging new businesses formed by historically wronged groups, including members of ethnic and racial minorities. Why not, then, adapt these plans also to give a leg up to worker co-ops and other kinds of employee-owned firms?

Our tax code already helps here by giving write-offs to employee stock ownership plans ("ESOP"). We can do more than just forgo tax collecting—we can *directly finance*. We do this already with industries tied to "defense" and to "national security." Why not do likewise for firms that make owners of all of us, as millions of farms used to do? "From farms to firms" . . . that should be our new mantra where public encouragement to private enterprise is concerned.

An owning citizenry is a stable and responsible citizenry—that's a lesson of history, both here and abroad, in past times and present times. It is also a prosperous and far less unequal citizenry, hence a less vulnerable and volatile citizenry. Rome lost its republic and got Caesar, who appealed to newly landless and desperate mobs of plebeians, when it forgot about the economic foundations of political republics. It is hardly controversial to suggest that America's seeing a bit of neo-Caesarism today—and for the very same reasons. America must renew the productive contract that Lincoln suggested—a contract by which a worker begins as an apprentice and then graduates to ownership of the tools she uses and the firms for which she toils.

This is not hard to do. Today firms are dominated by people born into money who hire people not born into money. That trend stems from the same myth we've dispelled above—the myth that money-capital is inherently scarce and supplied only by rich individuals. Toss out that myth and you open the door to concerted public action—to capitalize worker-owned firms, and to reward even private investment. But we can do that through inexpensive debt rather than equity financing, of worker-owned firms. Even capital-owned firms can be made more worker-controlled, by either requiring or publicly financially rewarding labor "codetermination" on corporate boards, as is done in Germany and elsewhere in Europe.

It's ironic that we've fallen behind Europe here, since our republic is actually founded on the "yeoman republic" ideal. But falling behind needn't mean staying behind. The tools we've laid out are the best means of restoring America to its former republican glory as a society of owning, cooperating producers. Only such societies' members are truly free. And only free citizens in this sense can build—and "keep," as Ben Franklin would say— free republics.

THE FOURTH PROMISE: LEISURE

But life isn't *just* about working and producing. Life is also about living. We take the forty-hour workweek for granted. But what was first established in the 1940s was a major achievement of the labor movement. As valuable as work is, no one should be expected to work every waking hour, in reasonable fear of getting fired and becoming unemployed and poor. So even the capitalists gradually signed on to a social bargain: we can't be expected to give up all of our limited time in life. But much has changed since the 1940s, and there's no reason to assume the leisure-work bargain struck then would work for the ages. With more secure incomes and shorter or more flexible work hours, each of us could enjoy a more meaningful life in time away from work. Or if you must value leisure in terms of money, think of the extra time for the same wages as equivalent to a per-hour pay increase that allows you to cut back the hours.

A shorter workweek is entirely feasible. The lazy Germans work only thirty-five hours per week. Recently a German union bargained that down to twenty-eight hours. Sweden moved to a thirty-hour workweek on grounds of efficiency. People are just as productive overall working six hours per day, for wasting less time. Why shouldn't they have the two extra hours free with the same pay? Switzerland lets people choose how much they work, without loss of benefits, provided sufficient notice—which is great for parenting, family, education, and travel. Even in the belly of the beast of American capitalism, at Amazon.com—which isn't exactly known for kid-glove treatment of its workers—many workers are being offered part-time flexible-hours jobs, many of which can be done from home.

Some self-styled "conservatives" think rest and leisure is about laziness or vegetative states—many while opining from reclining positions in Cayman while being massaged. Our forebears had a much different understanding of leisure's point. In "recreation," they took the "creation" piece quite seriously, emphasizing that work and play in nondesperate settings was the wellspring of most cultural attainment and advance. Think of how many remarkable discoveries and inventions we benefit by now, which would never have been found had their discoverers or inventors been living hand to mouth. Electricity, radium, lightbulbs are discovered and harnessed by kite-flying Ben Franklins, experimenting Marie Curies, tinkering Tom Edisons, not desperate Oliver Twists or people working three jobs to make ends meet.

The promises we propose would recover our ability to play, learn, and build, along with the other terms of our venerable social contract. We'd reclaim the time we need to form families, communities, clubs, and other "affective groups" in what Alexis de Tocqueville, that perceptive observer of the unique new polity that we were developing within decades of seizing our freedom, called "civil society."

Civil society is the wellspring of any healthy and effervescent, not stagnant and retrograde, culture. Science, the arts, even sociability itself all derive from it. So, therefore, do politics and productive arrangements and practices—that is, "the economy." Desperately poor people scrambling to make ends meet lack time to take part in, and hence to constitute, civil society. At best they can eke out a few minutes on ghostly substitutes such as social media, where people may do little more than laugh over cat pictures and yell at each other. This isn't a civil society of embodied beings working together, being together, gently forging a common destiny. It's often more like a virtual hell of conflict, disconnection, grievance, and alienation. To recover leisure, then, isn't to recover more couch time or tweet time. It is to render those dubious therapies less tempting and less necessary, precisely by giving us all once again adequate space to create rather than spectate.[20]

PROMISES RENEWED, CONTRACT RESTORED: MONEY RECLAIMED

And that's it. Simple, right? Restore to ourselves what our great middle class used to have—income, work, wealth, and leisure—and we restore both ourselves and our once-great republic. All we need do is restore twenty-first century renditions of these basic goods that we had through much of the nineteenth and twentieth centuries—while ensuring this time that all of us, not merely the white masculine us, have these birthrights. To do this we need do little more than retake the one thing we've needlessly thrown away: we need only take back our money.

CHAPTER 16

FROM GREEN MONEY TO A GREEN NEW DEAL

Any good investor who keeps an eye on the value of his or her "portfolio" will worry about the larger environment, which influences how its assets are likely to perform. Just so, if we are to offer a new "portfolio" of promises for each citizen, for income, work, wealth, and leisure, we should worry about our larger environment—both *economic* and *natural*.

Economic, because if the promises are to keep their value, the central bank will have to limit the economy's mood swings in new ways. This will aid our personal freedom, which depends on predictability. And it will help reduce inequality, which partly results from instability.

But natural, too, since economic activity has to happen somewhere or other. And the changes afoot in our natural environment, in the steady warming of our planet, shape every aspect of our lives, including our money and prosperity.

We've seen by now that we *have the money* for bold action, if we can summon the courage to use it. We've described a new approach to public finance that's more consonant with our republic's money. It is far more empowering of us as the citizens who "own" our republic and the money we issue. But that can't mean only that each of us benefit, personally—not while the world is burning, or at least dramatically warming, even right now as we write. And we can indeed adopt policies that keep a good measure of stability in our climate—policies that can also, while we're at it, modernize and revitalize every corner of our economy.

We refer, of course, to the Green New Deal—easily the most far-reaching and transformative American policy initiative since its namesake, the original New Deal, of eighty-plus years ago. The Green New Deal (or "GND") is aimed at addressing two urgent and deeply interconnected exigencies simultaneously.[1] On the one hand, climate science tells us that we have no more than a decade to begin reversing the buildup of carbon in earth's atmosphere before reaching a "tipping point," after which carbon buildup and attendant global warming will become all but irreversible. On the other hand, forty-plus years of deliberate deindustrialization and misguided—because monetarily mistaken!—public austerity have brought us to the point that our manufacturing capacities and public infrastructures are by far the most backward and dirty, and the least employment-providing and efficient, of all the "advanced" economies on the planet.

FALLING BEHIND

To see this, just travel most anywhere in the "developed" world, and many parts of the "developing" world as well. Take China, for example. Though still developing and thus still emitting much carbon through some older coal-fired and petroleum-fueled plants and vehicles, it also has thousands of state-of-the art manufacturing plants, and *scores of thousands* of miles of sleek and efficient, high-speed rail connecting its cities. We for our part have run-down plants and Amtrak. Fly into the airports in Beijing, Shanghai, or even smaller cities like Wuhan and you see models of cleanliness and smooth functioning. Fly into LaGuardia or LAX, by contrast, and, well, you'll marvel that "this is America." And so it goes in connection with pretty much any basic infrastructure you can name.

China also is quickly positioning itself to be the leading user, manufacturer, and exporter of advanced robotics, 5G telecommunications technology, electric automobiles, and countless other "next-gen" products and technologies. Through its "Belt and Road" initiative, it is rapidly becoming the engine of modernization throughout Asia and beyond. Here's an especially galling example: China has been forced to handle and improve Greek ports, which Europe, still befuddled by its own monetary backwardness and attendant austerity politics, evidently hasn't seen fit to deal with. Not only is a foreigner handling a critical domestic infrastructure, there's now a fine beachhead for more Chinese import penetration of Europe through what Winston Churchill might have called its "soft underbelly."

Meanwhile American politicians continue to push for broadening use of "beautiful, clean [carcinogenic] coal" and "fracking" for more fossil fuel. This happens even amidst stories of massive spills from even new oil pipelines, fracking-associated cancer epidemics, and lead-poisoned Flint drinking water or flammable Ohio tap water. American industry continues to shrink as a portion of its economy. And job quality continues its decades-long deterioration.

Or take solar panels. No example better illustrates the irony of our present plight. You may have seen solar panels appearing here and there on the roofs of business facilities and even some residences. What you might not know is that (a) China is now by far the world's largest producer, consumer, and exporter of these panels, despite the fact that (b) Americans invented and *used* to be the principal producers, consumers, and exporters of them.

What happened? The answer is that China made a policy of nurturing the growth to maturity of this "infant industry" and quickly surpassed us. It made big promises at the front end, when coordinated assistance is necessary. Changes to entire infrastructures do need to be coordinated. It's financially impossible for most individuals to convert individually when background conditions like power lines, generating and recharging or refueling stations, and the like, which only public authority can change, remain as they have been for decades.

The United States, for its part, did virtually nothing, thanks largely to misguided faux-libertarian politicians—who've evidently forgot about the orthodox economists' concept of the "collective action problem." And so now we buy from a rival what we invented and once produced. We're not only "throwing away money" to an economic competitor. We're also retarding the pace of our own conversion to clean renewable energy.

And of course the paranoid style in politics still works its mischief in order to keep us from reaching our ecological goals. Behold Senator John Barrasso, Republican senator from Wyoming, screaming about ice cream on the floor of Congress: "There's another victim of the Green New Deal—it's ice cream! Livestock will be banned. Say goodbye to dairy, to beef, to family farms, to ranches. American favorites like cheeseburgers and milkshakes would become a thing of the past." *Strangelove*'s lunatic general Jack Ripper couldn't have said it better himself ("Ice cream, Mandrake, children's ice cream"). Never mind that a big new investment push would never require the measures Barrasso fears. The whole point is to secure a more stable ecology that would allow generations of future kids to learn and play and enjoy things like ice cream, instead of running for their lives.

A NEW GOLDEN AGE

A concerted national mobilization to convert our economy to green energy use is not only needed to preserve life itself, it will also jump-start our whole economy into a future of unparalleled productivity and wealth.

Just think of all the high-paying manufacturing and construction jobs that will bring back.

Think of the immense boost to cost-effectiveness it will bring to our modes of production and consumption alike.

Think of how these productivity improvements will enable absorption of the very money we issue to get the job done.

And think, finally, of how our quality of life will leap forward, with no more poisonous air or drinking water, no more filthy "industrial zones," no more continual waiting and stressing at airports, train stations, and subway platforms, and no more insanity-inducing pileups or bottlenecks on our roads, bridges, and highways.

Once again a republic of producers—producing by living, working, and playing—we'll enjoy functional spaces in harmony with, rather than destroying, our life-giving planet and sun.

This is what the Green New Deal promises. It comes with multiple project areas—from overhauling energy, transportation, and communications grids; through retrofitting public and private sector residences, factories, and places of business and commerce; all the way to environmental mitigation and new tech development. Taken all together, the investments will bring a transformation such as the nation has not seen since the original New Deal and the Second World War mobilization of the 1930s and 1940s.[2]

We'll also begin the long process of redressing and reversing the nation's long decline into extreme, anti-republican inequality, in income and wealth. We'll do that precisely by multiplying the nation's existing wealth manyfold from the bottom up, starting with manufacturing and construction work and proceeding from the environmentally hardest-hit places (not coincidentally also the poorest—think Flint, Michigan) and working outward from there. The Green New Deal promises, in short, a new "Golden Age" of a republic whose "gold" is its promises and the work they enable—that is, its money.

HOW WE CAN PAY FOR IT

Here money ingénues of the austerian type—meaning, the folk who effectively gave Greek ports and the American economy to carbon and China—will of course raise the old "how do you pay for it," "what about debt," and "what about inflation" bugbears. By now, we've said why we can and should learn to stop worrying on all of those counts. The foregoing chapters all show how, far from being deep-debt inducing or inflationary, the GND can raise and multiply productivity and growth. They show how the financing can be handled: a major push in public spending that jump-starts and coordinates private spending and producing.

Here we should draw out one point that's only implicit in the foregoing chapters. As we've noted before, by accounting convention, assets are offset by liabilities on balance sheets, and vice versa. Bank deposits, in turn, are bank liabilities. (The bank "owes" you the money in your account—indeed "on demand" in the typical "demand deposit" accounts.) But note what this means in connection with the Fed Citizen Accounts we discussed earlier: your Citizen Account deposits will be Fed liabilities. The Fed will want assets that correspond to those liabilities (just as it now holds assets corresponding to bank reserve accounts held with it, which of course also are Fed liabilities). And what better assets for this purpose than, not only securities held through the "collar" facility we described earlier, but also securities associated with Green New Deal investments?

This can occur via multiple channels. One is direct investment—the Fed can simply purchase, directly, financial instruments used in the financing of GND projects. This it can do whether the securities are private sector, public sector, or hybrid "public-private partnership" issuances. The sheer variety of such instruments, moreover, in light of the great breadth of the national GND project itself, will make for excellent portfolio diversification.[3]

Another channel will be through bank lending itself. Insofar as depositors switch over to Fed Citizen Accounts from private sector bank accounts, banks will require new kinds of liability to "fund" their investments if they wish to continue operating as banks. The obvious source to which to turn is Fed "discount window" lending, whereby the Fed itself becomes, so to speak, a "depositor" in the private sector banks. If the Fed boosts its (already high) discount window lending to make up for lost depositor funds on the part of the banks, it can *condition* this lending quite readily. That is one basis for our earlier observation that Citizen Accounts will fulfill the old Glass-Steagall aim of separating banking from speculation more effectively even than did Glass-Steagall itself. But now we can see the Citizen Account infrastructure will allow even more: it will enable direct Fed influence on what in bank parlance is called "portfolio shaping"—in essence, oversight over what banks invest in.[4]

As a private-sector bank depositor, you might very much wish you could do that, either alone or in concert with other depositors. But of course you can't—you are too "small," and your fellow depositors too scattered, to do that alone or together. Megadepositors like Google or Microsoft, by contrast, often are *quite* influential over the banking institutions they work with. They call the shots that you can't. But our own central bank, the Fed, *is* a mega-megadepositor. As discount window lender, it can call shots like nobody's business (nobody's business but *our*, the public's, business). And so it's easy to envisage a discount window policy whereby the Fed makes its discount window lending ride at least partly on how "green" the portfolios assembled by would-be borrowing banks are. Et voila, yet another channel through which the Fed—our bank—can help shape GND financing without intrusive micromanaging.

Our hope is to convey how nicely the reunderstanding of money we've undertaken throughout this book fits with paying for the most ambitious policy initiative of the century, which is already congressionally proposed (as a Green New Deal Resolution). The two are almost made for each other. The green of the Green New Deal, on the one hand, and the green of the "greenbacks"—the dollar—on the other hand, are effectively one and the same color. And the green is as good as gold—nay, far better. It is the precious green brick road from our present to our sole viable future.

WHAT REPUBLICANISM USED TO MEAN— AND WHAT IT MUST MEAN AGAIN

"Republicanism," like "democracy," is one of those words that we hear and utter so often that we sometimes grow numb to it. We forget its rich meanings and historical resonances, lose track of its significance, and lose sight of how sacred—and vulnerable—this political, social, and economic ideal actually is. Our founders weren't unaware of this. Nor were our most distinguished leaders that followed them in subsequent decades.[1]

There is a reason our Pledge of Allegiance speaks of a republic. There is a reason the new political party that Abraham Lincoln helped found called itself "Republican." And there is a reason the "guarantee clause" of our Constitution charges our federal government with the responsibility to guarantee each of our states "a republican form of government."

The American founders thought of themselves as establishing an updated, continent-spanning rendition of the old pre-imperial Roman republic. The word "republic," they were quite well aware, derives from the Latin "res publica"—that is, "a thing of the public." The republic, in other words, is the thing of its citizens. It is *their* thing—the thing that belongs to them all, the thing through which they act together to solve common problems, including the problem of safeguarding the enjoyment of the more private things that belong to each rather than all.

This thing is *our* thing. It is our republic. And since a republic's money is its money, its money is our money as well. The dollar is ours—ours to do with as we must to preserve and to nourish our republic. We are trustees of our money just as we are trustees of our republic—of the United States itself.

What is our task as trustees? What responsibilities does our role incur to us? What must we *do* with our money? Here too, as we have suggested, our task is to use it to preserve and to strengthen our republic itself. This entails much more than you might realize. As we noted before, a republic is only possible where its citizens are independent. And "independence" doesn't mean simply that "the government" doesn't have you in chains. "*The* government" doesn't exist in a republic—only *our* government does. There is no "our" that includes all unless all are free—free of material want, free of the necessity of desperately clawing out an existence, free of oppression by *one another*.[2]

All of these "free *ofs*" are entailed by a single "free *to*"—the freedom to take active part in the life and decisions of the republic itself. The freedom, in other words, to participate fully with one another in addressing common challenges and concerns, and in pursuing shared national goals. This requires more than mere freedom from literal handcuffs and jail cells. It requires what the founders knew to be *material*, not just legal freedom. It requires freedom from fear, freedom from want, freedom from desperation and distraction—and freedom from abject dependence on others who "own everything" as prerequisite to "earning a living."

Abraham Lincoln understood this more clearly than perhaps any American leader after the founders. While campaigning against legal slavery in the American South during the 1850s and '60s, he campaigned also against what he called the "wage slavery" that was by that time emerging and spreading in the North. People with nothing to sell but their labor, he warned, are like slaves who are rented instead of being owned. Such people could not, he inveighed, be republican citizens in the true sense of the word. For one thing, they would be working too desperately and too long in the factories whose owners rented them to be able to pay attention to public affairs or take part in public decisions. For another thing, they would be so dependent on their employers that they could never afford to think differently—or vote differently—from those employers.

The only way to carry the republican ideal into the newly emerging industrial age, Lincoln concluded, was to develop a republican economics that didn't presuppose or depend on a primarily agrarian economy like early America's and pre-imperial ancient Rome's. What was needed, in other words, were arrangements under which working people could own their own industrial capital just as small farmers owned their own land and agricultural capital (plows, horses, barns, etc.).

It is noteworthy, against this backdrop, that among the first and most lasting things Lincoln and Congress did in the early 1860s—even as civil war raged!—was not only to sponsor and pass the homestead and land-grant acts, but also to retake, for the public, the republic's money. The currency, banking, and legal tender acts of that period gave us our first truly national currency—suggestively called the "greenback"—and our first nationwide network of nationally chartered banks. That system remains with us to this day. You see it each time you notice the "N.A." following a bank name like "Chase" or "Wells Fargo." (The "N.A." means "national (banking) association.") And you hear it whenever someone invokes the name our national bank chartering authority and regulator, whose name—OCC—stands suggestively for Office of the Comptroller (i.e., controller) of the Currency.

But this banking system we still live with, installed to protect republican ideals some 160 years ago, is no longer compatible, in its present form, with the republican ideal. The banks and the dollars they issue work not for yeomen and self-employed labor as they originally did, but for megafirms owned by few that rent many much as plantations once owned many. To retake our working lives, playing lives, and political lives we must retake our banks and our money.

This is essentially what we've been showing how to do over the previous chapters. Making our Fed—established only fifty years after the Lincoln reforms noted above—truly our Fed, a bank of the citizenry rather than of the banks, is the first crucial step. Mandating that it manage our money—our republic's money—in the name of us all, in ways that preserve not only price stability, but also what we'd call *republican* stability, is the second such step. That means enabling us all, each and every one, to be not only legally, but materially free and thus able to build both individual private lives and a complementary shared public life worth living.

We've tried to show how. Now let us get on with doing it.

MAKING GLOBAL FINANCE SAFE FOR DOMESTIC AUTONOMY

Imagine a world in which no country can go broke, except by its own stupidity. It's a world in which wise and good rulers have the means to "pay for" what their respective countries need to become decent, just societies, at least eventually. They simply pay in their own sovereign money. Sure, the people will have to argue about what is decent and just and vote. That may or may not go well, alas. But finance, for its part, would not be a problem. What's technologically possible would be financially possible. The question for the people of every country would be simply what sort of society to have.

It's a utopian thought at the moment, but not as far off from reality as it might at first seem. We noted earlier in the book that "monetary sovereigns" can't go broke involuntarily. In Chapter 13 (note 2), we defined full *monetary sovereignty* this way. A government:

1. issues its own money, in a chosen unit of account;
2. imposes a tax liability in that unit, which ensures its "currency" (by the fear of prison);
3. borrows only or mainly in its own money;
4. has a "floating" rather than a fixed exchange rate (or a "dirty float," with occasional intervention that limits an

upper or lower bound on rates of exchange with other
moneys);

5. has limited trade dependence in essential goods such
   as food or energy sources, in order to mitigate foreign
   exchange and inflation risk; and

6. has reasonably effective, noncorrupt institutions for inflation management, via an "independent" central bank,
   or appropriate legislative planning, where it is politically
   feasible.

As we noted earlier, many countries already meet these conditions to a reasonable approximation. The closer a government
gets, the more control it enjoys over its finances and its destiny.
As we suggested earlier, in the countries that plainly aren't "monetary sovereigns" at the moment, they might adopt reforms that
get them ever closer—perhaps with assistance from the international community. That would be well worth it. For when full
monetary sovereignty is attained, a government *can't* be forced to
default on its public debts. And what public wouldn't want that?
Why shouldn't every government that can have it, get it, at least
eventually?

It follows that "balanced budgets" are not necessary to avoid
bankruptcy. The seeming need for them—stemming from a false
analogy with personal or corporate finance—can be cast away as
superstition, as we explained earlier in the book. Still, there is a
small grain of truth in the religion of the "balanced budget," and
it requires us to say a bit more about "imbalance" in international
finance.

We in our different countries are of course all sharing a rather
small planet, and now are pretty connected by a global economy.
So not every government can happily run "deficit spending" in
the service of optimizing their own national economic output.
For what may be nationally prudent for one country, for a time,
may soon bring crisis, for other countries and perhaps for the
world. Just that happened in 2008, when banks and households

in the United States went belly-up, taking the world economy off of a cliff.

How did that happen? Due to that most boring and most profoundly important weave in the fabric of civilization: accounting. From an accounting point of view, when the world is taken as a whole, all assets and liabilities must sum to zero. A public deficit has to be matched with a surplus somewhere else in the book-keeping, so the two in effect "cancel each other out" on different sides of the balance sheet.

A proper accounting carves out "sectors" and the "sectoral balances" between them, especially between (a) public and private sectors in each country and (b) each country's relation to the rest of the world.[1] This is helpful; you can spot trouble if you track the flow of assets and liabilities interact across countries and their sectors. Given trade and each country's fiscal position, you're looking at constant flowing changes across countries and between their respective public and private balance sheets.

This gets complicated, fast, and thank goodness accounting types are willing keep careful track of who owes who what and how much. For even if monetary sovereigns can't default on their public debts, except by their own stupid choice, those debts may often correspond to excessive *surpluses* in other countries. When those are *public* surpluses, especially, that can make for dangerous outlays of *private* debt, among people that can easily go broke.

Just so, the Chinese "dollar glut" arguably explains why the United States ran such high private debt levels during the run up to 2008. China was (and still is) running a large public *surplus* with respect to the United States. That put the United States in an unsustainable position, given how it otherwise handled (i.e., mishandled) things. The country wound up with dangerously high *private* debt buildups, by homeowners and banks. Those private entities are *not* monetary sovereigns—they *use* the government's money, rather than issue money themselves. So they *can* go belly-up, and of course did in spectacular fashion.

So while public debt is a wonderful thing, it has to be managed properly worldwide. But if we're talking about decisions being made across almost two hundred countries, what good management is needed? The answer is: nothing less than a trusty system of international financial cooperation.

A good, working global financial system would do at least the following six "jobs":

1. facilitate currency conversion for cross-border trade;
2. provide or issue the "global" currency into which national moneys are converted (ideally avoiding the "n+1" problem, where n is the number of national moneys);
3. provide emergency liquidity as needed, on a global scale;
4. administer and oversee the global payments system;
5. oversee and regulate financial stability, including long-run current account balances, globally accounted for, whilst providing "adjustments" to one money relative to another, mitigating long-run surpluses; and
6. fund global/international investment (for development, social insurance support, climate-change mitigation, among other priorities), where domestic investment falls short.

These "jobs" can be done in different ways. We might have a more centralized or more formal system aimed at a given objective. Or we could decentralize or run things informally in hopes that the same objectives will be achieved that way. We've already got a pretty okay framework of institutions that pick up different bits of the jobs listed. Our existing "nonsystem system" includes the world's various central banks, the International Monetary Fund, the World Bank, and the Bank of International Settlements, among other players.

These agencies already coordinate in various formal and informal ways. Their cooperation expanded in the wake of the 2008 crisis when central banks established currency "swap lines." It is usually said that today most currencies are "freely convertible" without government intrusion, their values being set daily by the foreign-exchange market. In practice, central banks often intervene, in effect shaping those rates. What they're doing, together, is setting an upper or lower bound on one currency's rate of exchange for another (a "dirty float"). That helps them manage longer-run current account balances and prevent unstable "imbalances" ahead of time, a very good thing.

The Fed looms large in these informal arrangements. It already functions as something like a global central bank. Which may be fine if it can prove itself a reliable steward of its global monetary responsibilities. The trouble is that all central banks tend to be nationally minded and work under parochial mandates. A Fed-centric "system" may be too ad hoc, or too open to arbitrary policies, based on considerations of global political power or of "damage potential" to the world economy rather than to the needs of a given domestic public. For those reasons, one might make a case for new agreements that limit volatility and spreads in exchange rates (e.g., with further new currency "swap lines" and more formal procedures for their negotiation, at very least).

Perhaps we need nothing less than a return to J. M. Keynes's original International Clearing Union (ICU) plan—the one that got watered down at the Bretton Woods negotiations, when our current system was established.[2] But maybe establishing what is in effect a new world currency for the orderly management of trade flows won't be possible for a while. Even so, as we suggested in Chapter 6, we should "dethrone the dollar" with a much-expanded use of the Special Drawing Right, or SDR. It is, again, real international money. But it could be used much more widely and effectively.[3]

Even that may be politically unlikely at the moment. Yet it is entirely feasible in a technical sense. The financial architecture established today represents a radical improvement over prior history. Nothing was remotely as effective or even well established during the years between the two great wars, when trade wars and currency competition set the stage for the Second World War. The new measures we need are mainly attunements within today's system. They are small changes within an order that marks a vast and radical improvement over what the world had only a century ago.

THE PLAGUE

As this book goes to press, both the U.S. and the wider world have entered into a crisis that already has dwarfed that of 2008–09 in magnitude, and is on course to surpass even the Great Depression. We refer to the Covid-19 pandemic that has already taken hundreds of thousands of lives worldwide and, especially in the U.S., shows little sign of abating. In a way we would never have hoped, the messages of this book are now more relevant than they were even when we first began writing.

Like the plagues of old, the Covid pandemic is a public health crisis in the first instance. But it has quickly become a monetary, economic, political, and indeed "existential" crisis as well. It has struck at the heart of our promise-issuing res publica itself. What renders an economy *our* economy—like what renders a res publica *our* republic—is the coordinated, shared agency that we conduct *together*, in order to maintain an environment that allows *each* of us to create, produce, and materially flourish. A viral pandemic, by making it perilous to *be* together, strikes at the very core of that *we*.

Think of the evocative terms we've heard so much lately: "social distancing," "self-isolation," and "sheltering in place" are all about *limiting* interaction with colleagues and fellow citizens who must act together to produce and to govern. No wonder economies worldwide are shriveling and polities worldwide are fragmenting. Apart from the "knowledge economy," our productive economy shrinks when we can't work or shop in proximity to each other. And apart from "virtual" deliberation and mail-in voting, the *res publica* shrinks when we can't assemble in town halls or queue up at polling stations.

Productive activity has plummeted as people stay home, "sheltering in place," and businesses furlough employees. Political activity has become rife with confusion, panic, and mutual suspicion, being pushed from social *life* to social *media*—where all of our worst "tribal" tendencies flourish. This is what's truly so awful about all of those numbers you're reading about—negative growth rates, spiking unemployment and bankruptcy rates, and the like. And it's why so much political speech has become angry and painful—all at a time when police violence against our fellow citizens, especially those of color, seems to have grown out of control.

What we *haven't* lost amidst all of this is our same promise-making, promise-keeping, and hence money-issuing capacity. So what to do now? *Use* it! Use it to *address* and *reverse* the current crisis. Three measures in particular strike us as necessary.

For starters, we have to further boost household purchasing power while people are out of work. The one-time $1200 stimulus checks sent out in U.S. this spring, along with increased unemployment benefits for low-income folks, are helpful but not up to the task. Something like the universal basic income we proposed in the book must be put into place quickly, even if temporarily. That means we simply can't wait for the big Fed reforms that we've also proposed in the book, which will require months if not years to implement. But, fortunately, there is much we can do quickly.

Remember those "greenbacks" we mentioned in the book— the Treasury dollars we used during the fifty years prior to the establishment of our own central bank, the Fed? Well, the Treasury can issue those dollars again, now *in digital form*, via digital accounts with the Treasury. You may be surprised to hear that such digital accounts *already exist*. But they do. Just Google the name "TreasuryDirect."[1] Go ahead, we'll wait …

Every citizen and legally recognized business in America can *already* open an online account with the U.S. Treasury. It takes about ten minutes.[2] At present these accounts allow only for "vertical" transacting in Treasury securities between account holders and our nation's fiscal authority. You need a bank account with Federal Reserve Notes or their electronic equivalent to buy or sell Treasury securities from or to the Treasury. But we could easily tweak those digital accounts, creating a new, spendable Digital Dollar.

How? Just officially count some new Treasury instrument as legal tender—just as the greenback was declared legal tender during the Civil War.[3] Then we all just use our TreasuryDirect accounts as bank accounts! We'll need to add P2P "horizontal" connectivity to these accounts alongside their present vertical connectivity. But that step can be done quickly with existing technology. Then anybody could use his or her account to transact with anybody else! Aaron could pay Bob and Bob could pay Aaron, simply by electronically instructing Treasury to credit and debit each other's accounts. We could authorize those payments via our phones or other devices, a simple app, or debit cards.

That way we'd quickly have freely available, publicly provided digital banking and payment services for all. The relief payments which too many have been waiting too long to receive—we just make them immediately available to our TreasuryDirect accounts. That'd be far better than the out-of-date system we have now. At the moment, those who don't have full private bank accounts—presently the poorest 25% of our population[4]—must either forgo relief payments entirely or receive them by potentially virus-carrying paper checks in the mail, which they then have to cash, for large fees, at payday lending firms where they stand in line and risk catching or spreading coronavirus.

This plan is already being considered by members of Congress.

One of us—Bob—has drawn up a "Digital Greenbacks" plan, which includes a "Treasury Dollar Act."[5] It is so simple it requires only three pages to lay out! Meanwhile US DigitalService, an executive agency charged with precisely the task of technically upgrading federal facilities, has averred that it could convert TreasuryDirect accounts into fully functional P2P connectivity within only weeks.[6] And if we worry about freaking out banks or mucking up Fed monetary policy, it is easy enough to limit the amounts in TreasuryDirect wallets to no more than two or three thousand dollars, say. Later we can migrate the whole system over to the Fed—just as we did with the original paper Greenback in 1913, fifty years after inception.[7]

So much for the "demand side" of our economy. What about the "supply side"? Here again we can just speed up the sorts of investments we note in the book. Congress and the Fed have laudably acted to afford temporary relief to businesses. But note what they haven't done: thus far, no serious measures whatever have been taken to ramp up production of the testing, contact tracing, and personal protective equipment (PPE) we need to arrest the pandemic. That is absolutely essential for us to commence working together again without risking our lives and the lives of our loved ones. This is a spectacular waste of months of social distancing. The whole idea from the get-go was to create (literal) "breathing space" so that we could ramp up that essential production. We stayed home and stayed away and crippled the economy, but then didn't do what was necessary for its recovery. And now we're in an even bigger mess.[8]

What to do now? Well, the First and Second World Wars, not to mention the Spanish Flu pandemic of 1918–19 and the Great Depression of the 1930s, confronted America with similar "existential" threats. And we can now use the power of money, much as we did then. In 1917 we instituted a War Industries Board (WIB) and War Finance Corporation (WFC), first to coordinate and finance World War I mobilization and then to address the "Spanish Flu" pandemic that followed—a pandemic that killed six times as many Americans (almost twenty times more per capita) as the Covid pandemic has thus far.[9] In the 1930s we instituted a Reconstruction Finance Corporation (RFC) patterned after the WFC in order to address the Great Depression. We then supplemented it with a War Production Board (WPB) to handle the World War II mobilization.[10] These entities were means of institutionalizing national collective agency to address what amounted to national collective action and coordination problems—problems that sub-national states, cities, firms and citizens by definition can't handle on their own.

How could the federal government step up again? Just establish a National Infrastructure Council, comprising the heads of the Fed, the Treasury, and all cabinet-level executive agencies in the country. That council could then plan and coordinate the nationwide production of all essential equipment—tests, vaccines, other medicines, hospital beds, respiratory ventilators, and PPE.[11] We could have everything we need to address the pandemic comprehensively and resume productive activity over the remainder of its duration.

As things currently stand, there is no indication that our republic's chief executive is aware of the WIB, WFC, RFC and WPB precedents. Still more worrisome, there's little sign that he understands or even cares about the enormous collective action challenges we face, which require our federal institutions to address. Indeed the man in question shows every sign of being precisely that kind of "imbecile" (Hamilton's word) that Hamilton had in mind when insisting, in the late 18th century, on both the new constitution and the new fiscal and monetary capacities we've described in the book. Happily, the descendant of Hamilton's Bank of the U.S.—our Fed—does not suffer this cognitive debility. So there is hope.

The Fed has already stepped up to the plate, reviving and expanding facilities used to manage the 2008–09 crisis. One is entirely novel, though not yet in its optimal state. The Fed's new "Main Street Lending" and "Municipal Liquidity Facilities" aim to replace at least some of what is lacking in current White House's meager or counter-productive response efforts.[12] The former aim to tide over small businesses—which are both most vulnerable and our most employing productive units—until the Covid crisis is fully contained. The latter aims to *fund* as federal agencies those state and city instrumentalities that are now in effect *filling in*, as best they can, for absent federal agencies.

Since state and cities lack the authority to issue our national currency, they can't simply issue money to pay for pandemic response efforts. Their own promissory struments are not legal tender. So what the Fed has now offered to do is to "monetize" those instruments—typically called "municipal bonds," or "munis." That way, they in effect become able to spend dollars into existence as fully-fledged federal agencies. This is, if you will, Community QE—an adaptation of 2008–09 style QE to the needs of our de facto pandemic "first responders."[13]

Community QE is as welcome as it is unprecedented. Yet for the Fed's MLF plan to operate as intended, eligibility requirements remain too stringent, and borrowing costs remain too high.[14] Moreover, both it and the Main Street lending facilities are being administered out of just one regional Federal Reserve Bank, in New York.[15] But the New York Fed's shoestring staff, brilliant and earnest as it is, is just too small in number and too northeast-focused to know how best to aid Hank's Tractor Repair in Billings, Montana, Sophie's Salon in Watts, California, or the municipal government of Kailua-Kona, Hawaii. We need, then, to "Spread the Fed."[16]

Happily, one of us—Bob—still retains friends and colleagues at the Fed, and has worked extensively with state and city governments in the past to implement his eminent domain plan for "underwater" mortgage loans during the last crisis.[17] So he's been able to bring state and city leaders into (of course, Zoom Room) discussions about how to make MLF work as it ought. He's also organized a petition effort by state treasurers nationwide to convince the Fed to optimize its new facilities in the ways mentioned.[18] That leaves but one task still to accomplish: getting more of the Federal Reserve Banks involved.

As we've noted in the book, the original purpose envisioned for the Fed was not only to issue and modulate our republic's supply of circulating promises—our money. It was also to facilitate ongoing inclusive and sustainable productive development nationwide. That is why we *have* a national system of Regional Federal Reserve Banks in addition to the Federal Reserve Board. It is why our Fed is, well, *federated*. Why not, then, use this feature? Just re-distribute administration of the Main Street Lending and Municipal Liquidity Facilities over all of the Federal Reserve Banks across the country (along with some new ones out west). And then *continue* to use those banks as instrumentalities of regional development finance nationwide. Which is to say, again, "Spread the Fed!"[19]

The subtitle of this book is "learning to love the Federal Reserve." Wouldn't a Fed that works everywhere, not just the northeast, be more lovable? We think it would—and that it must. As awful as it is to re-live the plagues of old, we are delighted to see the Fed quickly take steps in the directions we recommended in the book. But a new, more lovable Fed isn't just for emergencies. Or at least it is equally necessary for the many *other* crises, both political and ecological, we now face. Hence our discussion in the book of the Green New Deal.

Yet the paranoid debt scolds are already out howling about how we must "go back" to "normal" after the current pandemic subsides. We hate to be bearers of bad news: but there is no going back; this *is* the new normal. And, thank goodness, we can not only hope the Fed will be there for us. We can democratically ensure that it is.

ACKNOWLEDGMENTS

We've incurred many debts in order to produce this book—our personal currencies would have very wide circulations! For starters, we'd like to thank our editor at Melville House, Ryan Harrington, for his careful eye and patient forbearing with us, and our agents Melissa Chinchllo and Donald Lamm, for their wise counsel and unflagging support. We also thank documentary producer John Walker, who, while trying to make a film that isn't about money, put up with our incessant talking about money, public finance, and philosophy, which led to this book. While those debts are shared, we'd also like here to pay our further individual debts to colleagues, students, friends and family, for many stimulating discussions and much encouragement, separately.

Though not all of those named will agree with every point made in the book, and though he is cringing at the thought that he might be momentarily forgetting some folk who are *not* named here, Bob would like to thank Tobias Adrian, Hilary Allen, Dan Alpert, David Andolfatto, Marshall Auerback, Colleen Baker, Christian Barry, Andres Bérnal, Kaushik Basu, Sarah Bloom Raskin, Mark Blyth, Mike Campbell, Michael Casey, Saikat Chakrabarti, Frank Chapparo, Jon Dever, Christine Desan, Katia Dmitrieva, Zack Exley, Rana Foroohar, Matt Forstater, Robert Frank, Richard Freeman, Jamie Galbraith, June Grasso, David Grewal, Anshul Gupta, Sean Hagan, Emma Jordan, Fadhel Kaboub, Izabella Kaminska, Ravi Kanbur, Steve Keen, Steph Kelton, Ron Kim, Nomiki Konst, Roy Kreitner, Michael Kumhof, Rosa Lastra, Sandra Lee, Tammy Lothian, Marc Lavoie, Nick Lyons, Jeff Madrick, Mariana Mazzucato, Jamie McAndrews, Perry Mehrling, Paul McCulley, Thorvald Grung Mo, Scott Morris, Warren Mosler, Carlos Mucha, Alexandria Ocasio-Cortez and Team, Erik Olin Wright, Saule Omarova, Martin O'Neil, Mike Otsuka, Katharina Pistor, Sanjay Reddy, John Roemer, Lawrence Rufrano, Julia Salazar, Bernie Sanders and Team, Sherle Schwenninger, Stefan Sciaraffa, Bob Shiller, Bill Simon, Alexandra Skaggs, Jeff Stein, Hillel Steiner, Lynn Stout, Jill Sung, Vera Sung, Dan Tarullo, Pavlina Tcherneva, Alan Thomas, Corbin Trent, Paul Tucker, Philippe van Parijs, Laura Underkuffler, Roberto Mangabeira Unger, Michael Warner, Elizabeth Warren and Team, and Randy Wray. He's also grateful to the many participants, including students, in talks, seminars, and symposia at Athens University, the Bank for International Settlements, the Century Foundation, Columbia

University, Cornell University, the Federal Reserve Bank of Chicago, the Federal Reserve Bank of Minneapolis, the Federal Reserve Bank of New York, the Federal Reserve Bank of St. Louis, Goethe-Universität, Harvard University, the International Monetary Fund, Lund University, McMaster University, the New School, the Office of Financial Research at the U.S. Department of Treasury, Oxford University, the Roosevelt Institute, the September Group, the Sorbonne Faculty of Law, Turin University, Vanderbilt University, the University of Verona, the Wharton School, the University of Wisconsin, the World Economic Roundtable, and Yale University.

Aaron would like to thank Ray Assar, Sven Berneker, Mathew Braham, Anna Boncompagni, Simona Capisani, Stuart Chapin, Michael Cholbi, Marshall Cohen, Annalisa Coliva, Carl Cranor, Ben Genta, Matthew Coates, David Theo Goldberg, Stephen Darwall, Peter Dietsch, Mark Fiocco, Frank Garcia, I. Aurora Garcia, Margaret Gilbert, Erin Glass, Kendra Gratteri, Jacob Heim, Jeff Helmreich, Pam Hieronymi, Louis-Philippe Hodgson, Mia Hosaka, Gerry Howard, Alin James, Elizabeth James, Wendy James, Mark Johnson, Frances Kamm, Niko Kolodny, Christine Korsgaard, Ari Koslow, Sharon Lloyd, Penn Maddy, Pietro Maffettone, Ben McKean, Marco Meyer, Sophia Moreau, Stephen Munzer, Jack Murphy, Chris Naticchia, Thi Nguyen, Martin O'Neil, Tom Parr, Casey Perin, Duncan Pritchard, Hami Ramani, Sanjay Reddy, Brett Riggle, Nick Riggle, Arthur Ripstein, Kate Ritchie, Lauren Ross, T.M. Scanlon, Karl Schafer, Gina Shouten, Martin Schwab, Greg Shaffer, Seana Shiffrin, Ken Simons, David W. Smith, Nick Smith, Cristiana Sogno, Jiewuh Song, Lucas Stanczyk, Alan Thomas, Clinton Tolley, Gary Watson, Leif Wenar, Andrew Williams, and Joost Ziff. He's also grateful to the many participants in colloquia at Yale University, the University of Durham, Bayreuth University, the Centre de Recherche en Éthique de l'Université de Montréal (CRÉUM), the Mershon Center at Ohio State University, UC Irvine Law School, and UC Irvine Department of Philosophy; in discussions held by the Southern California Law and Philosophy Group; and in two UC Irvine courses on the topic of money, a Fall 2019 graduate seminar and a Winter 2020 course for undergraduates.

NOTES

NOTES TO THE PREFACE

1 Baum was a feminist and suffragist who was influenced by his wife's politics and sensibility. He portrayed Dorothy, the heroine, as a plucky young woman who took charge of her hapless male companions. But if his message was one of female empowerment, his larger tale is still ultimately also a parable about money and "populist" politics. That suggestion was originally made by Henry M. Littlefield, "The Wizard of Oz: A Parable on Populism," *American Quarterly* 16, no. 1 (Spring 1964): 47–58, and then revived by Gore Vidal, "On Rereading the Oz Books," *New York Review of Books*, October 13, 1977. Other readings, with different emphases, include: Robert A. Divine et al., *America: Past and Present* (Glenview, IL: Scott, Foresman, 1984), 594–95; Hugh Rockoff, "The 'Wizard of Oz' as a Monetary Allegory," *Journal of Political Economy* 98 (1990): 739–51; William R. Leach, "The Clown from Syracuse: The Life and Times of L. Frank Baum" and "A Trickster's Tale: L. Frank Baum's *The Wonderful Wizard of Oz*," in L. Frank Baum, *The Wonderful Wizard of Oz*, ed. Leach (Belmont, CA: Wadsworth, 1991); David Graeber, *Debt: The First 5,000 Years* (New York: Melville House, 2011).

2 Richard Hofstadter, "The Paranoid Style in American Politics," *Harper's Magazine*, November 1964. Hofstadter is especially tough on populist conspiracism in his Pulitzer Prize-winning *The Age of Reform* (New York: Vintage, 1955), 70–93. He's more sympathetic to the substance of populist and progressive proposals in "Free Silver and the Mind of 'Coin' Harvey," in *The Paranoid Style in American Politics* (New York: Vintage, 1965), 279–92.

3 One of us—Bob—was there at Zuccotti Park for the duration of the "Occupation" from September through November 2011, while he worked at the nearby New York Federal Reserve. He gently explained to his fellow Occupiers that this is a big mistake, offering friendly tutorials on central banking. His colleagues at the Fed were curious and even sympathetic to some of the protesters' other demands. As we note later in the book, Bob was hired at the Fed in part because the bank was admirably worried about groupthink during the run-up to the 2008 crisis and wanted fresh eyes.

NOTES TO THE INTRODUCTION

1   See Bankrate, "63% of Americans Can't Afford $500 Car Repair or $1,000 Emergency Room Visit," January 6, 2016, https://www.bankrate.com/pdfs/pr/20160106-Money-Pulse.pdf.

2   Ben Berkowitz, "Bernanke Cracks Wise: The Best QE Joke Ever!," *CNBC*, January 16, 2014, https://www.cnbc.com/2014/01/16/bernanke-cracks-wise-the-best-qe-joke-ever.html.

3   MMT is hardly alone in observing this truism of accounting and working out consequences; most schools of heterodox and post-Keynesian economics proceed on this same basis. But youthful enthusiasts of MMT have done much to draw together and develop the key insights as well as get the word out in recent years. For a definitive textbook elaboration of the MMT approach to macroeconomics, see William Mitchell, L. Randall Wray, and Martin Watts, *Macroeconomics* (London: Red Globe Press, 2019). See also L. Randall Wray, *Modern Money Theory: A Primer on Macroeconomics for Sovereign Monetary Systems*, 2nd ed. (London: Palgrave Macmillan, 2015) and Stephanie Kelton's bestselling *The Deficit Myth: Modern Monetary Theory and the Birth of the People's Economy* (New York: Public Affairs, 2020).

4   The idea of giving purchasing power straight to people, bypassing the private banking system, isn't new. The Greenbackers proposed a paper version of it after the Civil War. It was championed in the 1930s by Major Douglas in the United Kingdom and Jacques Duboin in France. The economist Milton Friedman famously noted the possibility of "helicopter money" (without noting that the "helicopter drops" could be aimed in a good direction, instead of sprayed indiscriminately). Joseph Huber defended the idea in 1998, suggesting a 500 euro per month payment to Germans that would phase out quickly as income rose. The 2008 crisis prompted calls for short-term "helicopter drops" (Bernanke was even called "Helicopter Ben"), or "quantitative easing for the people," as a temporary stimulus. Oxford economist John Muellbauer proposed in 2014 that the European Central Bank pay 500 euros to every eurozone resident, and, post-Brexit, thirty-five economists signed off on a similar proposal in August 2016.

    This book is proposing "helicopter drops" on a regular basis, carefully managed with the new tools for inflation management we lay out in Chapter 12. The real obstacle is not technical feasibility, but the public perception of what is possible, rooted in bad theory and bad philosophy, just as Bernanke says. So aside from digging through the central-bank toolbox, this book starts from scratch, allowing us all to get our heads straight about what money is and what we can do with it. To know money, in short, is to know central banking and its potential.

NOTES TO CHAPTER 1

1   Immanuel Kant, *The Metaphysics of Morals* (orig. 1797), sec. 6:288, pp. 76–7,
     under the heading "What is money?" Edited by Lara Denis, translation by
     Mary Gregor (Cambridge: Cambridge University Press, 2017). Italics in
     original. Kant adds that taxes are not only sufficient but also necessary: "In
     this way only (so it seems to me) could a certain merchandise have become
     a lawful means of exchange of the industry of subjects with one another,
     and thereby also become the wealth of the nation, that is, money." That
     may go too far. As we explain later, "basic money" can be established infor-
     mally in a community. The need for formal law comes in when an economy
     is larger (though Kant may mean just that by "the wealth of the nation").
     University of California, Irvine philosophy graduate student Stuart Chapin
     dug up this passage.

2   Georg Friedrich Knapp, *The State Theory of Money* (Clifton, NY: Augustus
     M. Kelley, [1924] 1973), ch. 1, sec. 1, p. 1. First German publication 1905.

3   John Maynard Keynes, *A Treatise on Money*, vol. 1 (London: Macmillan,
     1930), Keynes called this "modern money," from which "modern monetary
     theory" originally derived its name.

4   Ludwig von Mises, *The Theory of Money and Credit*, trans. H. E. Batson
     (New York: Skyhorse Publishing, 2013), 78. First German publication 1912.

5   Mises falls into almost comic exaggeration when he says the state's position
     in the market "differs in no way from that of any other parties to commer-
     cial transactions" (Ibid., 68). No way at all? He himself notes the "legal con-
     cept of money" operating in debt settlement, along with legal tender law,
     minting money, arranging substitutes for money, and even "the provision
     that taxes are in the future to be paid in the new kind of money" (ibid., ch.
     VI). He merely minimizes their influence, and on flimsy grounds at best.
     This sort of fudging seems to have been popular at the time. Abba Lerner,
     in "Money is a Creature of the State," *American Economic Review*, 37, no. 2
     (1947), p. 312, notes that his London School of Economics colleagues used
     to trash Knapp for sport. They'd dismiss state power, but then "later in the
     course the state managed to creep back in . . . through its power, via the
     banking system which it could control . . . by the substitution of bank credit
     for gold." The state turned out to have a rather long list of "devices," includ-
     ing, finally, the issuance of "fiat money."

6   Mises, *Theory of Money*, ch. 4, sec. 3, p. 78.

7   Voltaire, *Candide*. All quotations in the text are taken from ch. 17. Available
     at http://www.esp.org/books/voltaire/candide.pdf.

8   Adam Smith, *An Inquiry into the Nature and Causes of the Wealth of Nations*, bk. 1, ch. 4. Available at https://www.gutenberg.org/files/3300/3300-h/3300-h.htm

9   A. Mitchell Innes, "What is Money?," *Banking Law Journal* 30 (1913): 391. See also his follow-up article, "The Credit Theory of Money," *Banking Law Journal* 31 (1914): 151–68. For a full discussion of Innes's theory, see Aaron James, "Money as Promise: Innes and the 'Fundamental Nature of a Financial Transaction'" (available on his UC Irvine Philosophy Department webpage, https://www.faculty.uci.edu/profile.cfm?faculty_id=4884).

10 This doesn't mean everything should have a price and be for sale—including people, babies, and organs, for example. A society can easily limit the scope of commercial transaction. Then there are neither market obligations nor market permissions in those transactions, and no way to "settle accounts." The US bans the sale of people, babies, organs, and sex, as well as murder services, as do most countries.

11 The most important exception is today's intergovernmental money: the International Monetary Fund's Special Drawing Right, or "SDR." It is genuine money among a relatively small group of parties—less than two hundred of them. But, formally, it's adopted only voluntarily, by signing on to the IMF treaty. The terms of the cooperative are enforced by informal sanction and threats of exclusion. We come back to the SDR in Chapter 6 and the Appendix "Making Global Finance Safe for Domestic Autonomy."

12 When lawyers and philosophers argue about such things, they'll say the noted "claims" and "obligations" travel together like an inseparable married couple ("correlatively," as the jargon goes). They are two sides of the same IOU.

13 Contracts often specify certain money payments. Even when they don't, a breach of contract often entitles aggrieved parties to money damages in cases of breach. Courts seldom require one literally to do exactly what was originally contracted—what lawyers call "specific performance"—since that can look like slavery. To meet your obligation, you can thus equally just pay money.

14 An item such as bitcoin can be more or less *money-like*, however, depending on how widely it's accepted among people (its "domain") and what range of obligations it is accepted for (its degree of "fungibility"). As dusk fades gradually into evening, so also being money-like is a matter of degree.

15 See "Covid-19 Relief Could be Catalist for a Digital Dollar," *Law360*, at https://www.law360.com/articles/1257079covid-19-relief-could-be-catalyst-for-a-digital-dollar.

16 See Robert Hockett, "Facebook's Proposed Crypto-Currency: More Pisces

Than Libra For Now," *Forbes*, Jun 20, 2019, https://www.forbes.com/sites/
rhockett/2019/06/20/facebooks-proposed-crypto-currency-more-pisces-
than-libra-for-now/#787134c02be2.

NOTES TO CHAPTER 2

1   The Fed isn't legally obliged to serve private bank interests, though it does
    coordinate with commercial banks in a hybrid public-private arrangement.
    The central bank is a public institution with a legal responsibly to serve the
    national interest. That's true despite the fact that privately owned banks
    have ownership stakes in the Fed's regional banks, seats on those regional
    banks' boards, and claims on income generated in a self-financing system.
    Even those "private" banks must be chartered, as part of the "finance fran-
    chise" we describe in Chapters 8 and 9.

2   Economist Abba Lerner described the new principles of what he called
    "functional finance" for public spending in the early 1940s. He went so far
    as to urge that "taxing is *never* to be undertaken merely because the gov-
    ernment needs to make money payments." That's by contrast with "sound
    finance," which does require taxes or borrowing to "pay for" spending, but
    amounts to outmoded gold standard logic. "Functional Finance and the
    Federal Debt," *Social Research* 10, no. 1 (1943): 40–41. New York Fed Chair-
    man Beardsley Ruml amplified key points in a 1946 article entitled "Taxes
    for Revenue Are Obsolete," *American Affairs* 13, no. 1 (1946). Even today,
    the Bank of England lays it all out on its website ("What is Money?," https://
    www.bankofengland.co.uk/knowledgebank/what-is-money), and former
    Fed chairs Alan Greenspan and Ben Bernanke have told Congress and tele-
    vision audiences much the same. See Agustino Fontevecchia, "Bernanke
    Fights Ron Paul in Congress: Gold Isn't Money," *Forbes*, July 13, 2011,
    https://www.forbes.com/sites/afontevecchia/2011/07/13/bernanke-fights-
    ron-paul-in-congress-golds-not-money/. For Greenspan's 2005 testimony
    before the Committee on the Budget of the House of Representatives, about
    fiat money and why we can always pay Social Security, see https://www.
    youtube.com/watch?v=DNCZHAQnfGU.

3   A dollar unit might still "exist" on a spreadsheet because one part of the
    government is marked up as having an asset. But the unit will still count as a
    liability of the Fed, which is also part of the government. For the *whole gov-
    ernment's* spreadsheet, the asset and liability cancel each other out to zero.

4   One could still say that spending is "paid for" or "funded" ultimately by
    inflation management, or even by the *real resources* whose use prevents
    inflation. Taxes will help there, and it would be misleading to say that no

taxes are ever necessary. But that does *not* mean "taxes pay for spending" in the sense usually meant when "pay for" questions come up. It is more accurate to say that *inflation management* or *real resources* "pay for" or "fund" spending, and that taxes may help there. Even then, *total* tax revenue, tallied up in a budget, is what is usually meant. And that aggregated figure wouldn't itself tell you whether prices or sectors are being targeted by taxes in the ways that would ideally help with inflation management.

5   The Fed also offers "term deposits," much like a certificate of deposit at a private bank. These are functionally similar to Treasurys, and it might clarify things to just use them instead of Treasurys. They look less like "loans" to the government and more like what Treasurys are: a way the government is pulling money out of the money supply, swapping liquid for less liquid assets, with a specified time to "maturity." You'd park your money at the central bank for an agreed-upon time period, after which it would reissue the dollars to you. You'd do that for security and a bit of interest, much as with a private bank.

6   Treasurys do have other functions as well—though these could be served by the "term deposits" mentioned in an earlier note. For one, the global financial system now depends on Treasurys as a safe asset. Issuing them may come along with the dollar's role as the world's reserve currency. They also provide a service to financiers. Wall Street's speculators are surely very grateful for the opportunity to park money in a safe, government asset—or at least they should be. How do the big financial firms decide what risks to take? By comparison with the sure money they could get from the government. (The two main formal models used by big financial firms rely on government bonds as a benchmark in this way.) The paragons of financial capitalism are happy to receive government assistance with their gambling habits. And, rest assured, they welcome that much "socialism."

7   The Fed balance sheet did once run with a certain efficient beauty for fluctuating up or down by trillions of dollars throughout the day, but always zeroing out by the close of business. But those glory days are over—and the Fed's ad hoc "facilities," often created as needed, resemble a Rube Goldberg device anyway. And why should Granny have to scrape by just for the sake of an aesthetic bookkeeping preference for one government balance sheet over another? Peter Stella, a former IMF official who led the central banking division, voices this aesthetic preference while nicely explaining the Fed's plumbing; see "Peter Stella on Debt, Safe Assets, and Central Bank Operations: A Macro Musings Transcript," interview by David Beckworth, *The Bridge*, Mercatus Center at George Mason University, February 18, 2019, https://www.mercatus.org/bridge/podcasts/02182019/

peter-stella-debt-safe-assets-and-central-bank-operations.

8   Frank N. Newman, former deputy secretary of the US Treasury, put the Treasury's perspective this way: "I recall from my time at the Treasury Department that the assumption was always that there was money in the fed account to start with. Nobody seemed to know where it came from originally or when; perhaps it was established in biblical times. But as a matter of practice, if the treasury wanted to disburse $20bn a given day, it started with at least that much in its fed account. Then later [it] would issue new treasuries and rebuild its account at the fed. (I don't not recall ever using an overdraft.) . . . Every cycle is: spend first, then issue treasuries to replenish the fed account. The fact that Treasury started the period with some legacy funds in Fed account is not really relevant to understanding the current flow of funds in any year." Stephanie Kelton, "Former Dept. Secretary of the U.S. Treasury Says MMT Critics Are 'Reaching,'" *New Economic Perspectives*, October 30, 2013, https://neweconomicperspectives.org/2013/10/former-dept-secretary-u-s-treasury-says-critics-mmt-reaching.html.

9   Working carefully through the accounting, Stephanie Kelton (formerly Bell) explains how this helps the Fed set interest rates. She also argues that taxes *cannot* pay for anything. Outstanding liabilities are merely cancelled, much as when a promise is made and then fulfilled. You don't "get your promise back" and somehow "save it" for future promising. In legal speak, a promise or contract is said to be "discharged" or "extinguished"; the debt simply disappears from existence. Stephanie Bell, "Do Taxes and Bonds Finance Government Spending?," *Journal of Economic Issues* 34, no. 3 (Sept. 2000): 603–20.

10   See Greenspan's comments to the Committee on the Budget, House of Representatives, March 2, 2005 https://www.youtube.com/watch?v=DNCZHAQnfGU.

11   Assuming, that is, that the international consequences are being managed. The international monetary system is essential for smoothing dangerous "imbalances." We explain how international money—the Special Drawing Right—helps in Chapter 6 and the Appendix "Making Global Finance Safe for Domestic Autonomy."

12   See Greenspan's 1997 speech at https://www.federalreserve.gov/boarddocs/speeches/1997/19970114.htm

13   But note the craven lunacy of Senator Ted Cruz, who for purposes of self-aggrandizement exploited a peculiarity of the US system, which requires the "debt limit" to be officially raised each year. That rule does nothing but encourage such treachery; the US should anyway honor its promises and scrap this legislative formality.

14   What if the sorts of people who buy government bonds started hav-
      ing major jitters about what seemed like *really* high public debt levels?
      The Fed would have to use its tools to bring interest rates down to a pre-
      ferred level. It might have to be on the lookout ahead of time, and react
      quickly, using tools we describe in Chapter 12. Economist Brad deLong,
      who seems amenable to the present "functional finance" perspective,
      notes some related ways things can go wrong on his blog, *Brad deLong's
      Grasping Reality*, "By Popular Demand: What Is 'Modern Monetary
      Theory'?," January 21, 2019, https://www.bradford-delong.com/2019/01/
      what-is-modern-monetary-theory.html. Economist Paul Krugman
      worries about an unlikely debt "snowball" scenario, in which the aver-
      age rate of interest exceeds the rate of overall growth in "What's Wrong
      with Functional Finance? (Wonkish)," *New York Times*, February 12,
      2019, https://www.nytimes.com/2019/02/12/opinion/whats-wrong-with-
      functional-finance-wonkish.html. But central banks have many tools
      for anticipating and preventing adverse outcomes, aside from interest-
      -rate targeting. The Fed can stop issuing Treasurys all together, as sug-
      gested earlier, or it can raise the safety margins for private bank lending,
      for example. Again, Chapter 12 lays out the Fed toolkit. Stephanie Kel-
      ton replies to Krugman along similar lines in "Modern Monetary The-
      ory Is Not a Recipe for Doom," *Bloomberg Opinion*, February 21, 2019,
      https://www.bloomberg.com/opinion/articles/2019-02-21/modern-mo
      netary-theory-is-not-a-recipe-for-doom.

15   People working in the financial system make similar claims. There's Frank
      Newman, for example, who draws upon his experience as deputy secretary
      of the US Treasury, and as a chairman and CEO of commercial banks in
      both the US and China. See his *Freedom from National Debt* (Minneapolis,
      MN: Two Harbors Press, 2013). There's Peter Stella, who nicely explains the
      Fed's machinery (see n. 7 above). And there is Warren Mosler, the finan-
      cier who helped heterodox economists develop MMT, offering an insider
      perspective. *The 7 Deadly Innocent Frauds in Economic Policy* (Valance Co.
      Inc., 2010), available at moslereconomics.com.

16   Interview with Paul Samuelson, *The Life, Ideas and Legacy of John May-
      nard Keynes*, directed by Mark Blaug (1988), at https://www.youtube.com/
      watch?v=4_pasHodJ-8.

17   Another of *Strangelove's* generals, Buck Turgidson, laid out the cost-ben-
      efit calculus in the War Room. America would suffer the lower death toll
      and emerge with significant deterrence capacity left over. And since the
      bombing is already in process, you know, better to go all-in now, seizing
      the moment of surprise, to minimize causalities. To President Muffley's

objection that this is "mass murder," not war, he replies "Mr. President, I'm not saying we wouldn't get our hair mussed." Like Ripper, and not unlike Samuelson, Turgidson minimizes the downside. He ignores options that are still open (i.e., recalling or shooting down the bombers), presuming that long-run civilization would simply require awful things.

18   As noted in the Introduction, this is a key way we differ from some MMT economists, who ask the legislature to manage inflation with fiscal policy. Some argue that this is more "democratic." We're skeptical a legislature will be consistently reliable enough about such delicate matters. And "independent" central banking can be consistent with "democratic accountability," as we explain in Chapter 14.

NOTES TO CHAPTER 3

1   J. L. Austin, "Performative Utterances," in *Philosophical Papers* (Oxford: Oxford University Press, 1961), 235. See also Austin, *How to Do Things with Words*, 2nd ed., eds. J. O. Urmson and Marina Sbisà (Cambridge, MA: Harvard University Press, 1975).

2   John Searle, *Making the Social World: The Structure of Human Civilization* (Oxford: Oxford University Press, 2010), 12.

3   Aesop's *Complete Fables,* trans. Olivia and Robert Temple (Penguin Classics, 2003), fable 46.

4   "What Are the Federal Reserve's Objectives in Conducting Monetary Policy?," FAQs, Board of Governors of the Federal Reserve System, last updated December 11, 2019, https://www.federalreserve.gov/faqs/money_12848.htm (italics added).

5   This will probably require an expanded legal mandate. One of us—Bob—will happily draft new legislation upon request.

NOTES TO CHAPTER 4

1   Hobbes did advise sovereigns to uphold civility and equity, which were good for stability. So a wise dictator would surely use money and the bankers for general benefit, from self-interest. General prosperity can pacify the masses and cultivate a perception of his benevolence, which will also flatter his vanity. Even so, the sovereign ruler is under no obligation to us, and may be too stupid or careless to govern wisely. When he does good things, it may be out of fear of rebellion—and perhaps his beheading.

2   Rousseau, *The Social Contract*, in *The Social Contract and Other Later Political Writings*, ed. and trans. Victor Gourevitch (Cambridge: Cambridge Press, 1997).

3   See Aaron James, *Assholes: A Theory* (New York: Doubleday, 2012), 4n.

4   We suspect that Rousseau himself would agree, had he thought more about money. See, e.g., Robert Hockett, "Rousseauvian Money" (Cornell Legal Studies Research Paper Series No. 18–48, Cornell Law School, Ithaca, NY, last revised May 28, 2019), https://papers.ssrn.com/sol3/papers.cfm?abstract_id=3278408.

5   Facundo Alvaredo, Bertrand Garbinti, and Thomas Piketty, "On the Share of Inheritance in Aggregate Wealth: Europe and the USA, 1900–2010," *Economica* 84 (2017): 239–60. See also Christopher Ingraham, "People Like the Estate Tax a Whole Lot More When They Learn How Wealth is Distributed," *Washington Post*, February 6, 2019, https://www.washingtonpost.com/us-policy/2019/02/06/people-like-estate-tax-whole-lot-more-when-they-learn-how-wealth-is-distributed/.

6   Steven Levitsky and Daniel Ziblatt, *How Democracies Die* (New York: Crown, 2018).

7   It is a problem that Rousseau spoke so vaguely of the "general will," roughly meaning "the will of the people." The Jacobins used Rousseau's words to rationalize guillotine bloodbaths. But the idea of the "general will" was always supposed to be given meaning within democratic institutions—the very ones now being subverted. In essence it was the will of the people as aggregated by just institutions. See Frederick Neuhouser, *Foundations of Hegel's Social Theory: Actualizing Freedom* (Cambridge, MA: Harvard University Press, 2000), chapter 2 in particular.

8   The trick is to co-opt new rivals before they co-opt your essential supporters—at least long enough to pass rule on to the tribe or the family (so that today's supporters are assured of staying on the gravy train). Democracies are different because you need the support of more people, a larger "selectorate." For this analysis, see Bruce Bueno de Mesquita and Alastair Smith, *The Dictator's Handbook* (New York: Public Affairs, 2011) and Bruce Bueno de Mesquita et al., *The Logic of Political Survival* (Cambridge, MA: MIT Press, 2005).

9   The international system even encourages the struggle for resource control. As long as a dictator effectively holds power, he's treated in international commerce as though he has every right to sell his country's resources and borrow in its name. That's a legal decision on our part, and we could decide differently. An international agreement could ban all such business. Or a few key trade partner countries could simply change their domestic property rules, so that title in goods or funds from autocratic countries doesn't transfer over. As we now allow things to be, our oil and gadget purchases in the democracies keep dictators in power—and in turn degrade our eco-

nomic and political systems. This is all laid out in Leif Wenar, *Blood Oil* (Oxford: Oxford University Press, 2015). See also Aaron James, "Why We Must Lift the Resource Curse," in Wenar et al., *Beyond Blood Oil: Philosophy, Policy, and the Future* (Lanham, MD: Rowman and Littlefield, 2018).

10   People also tend to reelect incumbents if things are going well right before the election and throw the bums out if not. They mainly vote the party line, not because the party represents independent policy preferences, but because they decide what to prefer based on party affiliation, which is decided based on racial, gender, ethnic, religious, regional, or class groups. And those trends get *worse* when people pay close attention. Christopher H. Achen and Larry M. Bartels, *Democracy for Realists* (Princeton: Princeton University Press, 2016).

11   John Dewey, *The Political Writings*, eds. Debra Morris and Ian Shapiro (Indianapolis: Hackett, 1993), 122.

12   This is the thought in part three of John Rawls's landmark work *A Theory of Justice* (Cambridge, MA: Harvard University Press, 1971), which followed Rousseau's rationalist theory of moral education.

13   Jean-Jacques Rousseau, "Discourse on the Sciences and Arts *or* First Discourse," in *The Discourses and Other Early Political Writings*, ed. Victor Gourevitch (Cambridge: Cambridge University Press, 1997).

14   Rousseau, "Discourse on the Origins and Foundations of Inequality Among Men *or* Second Discourse," in *The Discourses*. A perceptive discussion of the "Second Discourse" is Frederick Neuhouser, *Rousseau's Critique of Inequality* (Cambridge: Cambridge University Press, 2014).

15   Rousseau ignores money in his later positive vision of democracy, *The Social Contract*. Rawls saw the general point but his *A Theory of Justice* never brought out the special role of monetary policy—which he simply rolled into the economic branch of a society's "basic structure" of institutions.

16   Rousseau, "Second Discourse."

17   For a similar, overlapping list of reasons to worry about inequality, see T. M. Scanlon, *Why Does Inequality Matter?* (Oxford: Oxford University Press, 2018).

18   John Bargh, "At Yale We Conducted a Study to Turn Conservatives into Liberals. The Results Say a Lot About Our Political Divisions," *Washington Post*, November 22, 2017, https://www.washingtonpost.com/news/inspired-life/wp/2017/11/22/at-yale-we-conducted-an-experiment-to-turn-conservatives-into-liberals-the-results-say-a-lot-about-our-political-divisions.

19   Cailin O'Connor and James Owen Weatherall, *The Misinformation Age: How False Beliefs Spread* (New Haven: Yale University Press, 2019).

NOTES TO CHAPTER 5

1   A. Mitchell Innes, "What is Money?," *Banking Law Journal* 30 (1913): 392. See also his follow-up article, "The Credit Theory of Money," *Banking Law Journal* 31 (1914): 151–68.

2   Nietzsche, *On the Genealogy of Morals and Ecce Homo*, trans. and ed. Walter Kaufmann (New York: Vintage, 1967), 64–65.

3   To give credit where credit is due, there were earlier pioneers of a "credit theory" of money, such as John Law, in his 1705 *Money and Trade Considered*, and Sir James Steuart, in his 1767 *An Inquiry into the Principles of Political Economy*. Henry Dunning Macleod, who was criticized by Karl Marx, had similar thoughts in *The Theory and Practice of Banking*, vols. I and II, published, respectively, in 1855 and 1856. Also noteworthy are Henry Thornton, 1845; James Ferguson, *Treatise on Civil Society*; and Montesquieu, *The Spirit of the Laws* (1748).

4   Henry Thornton was a British banker who developed an intimate knowledge of the London financial markets of the late eighteenth century. His *Enquiry into the Nature and Effects of the Paper Credit of Great Britain* (1802) is chock full of insights into the endogenous credit nature of money that even contemporary economic orthodoxy would do well to learn. Marx, for his part, is often mistaken for a backward "metallist" where money is concerned, owing to his use of the word 'money' primarily in connection with so-called "commodity money." Once we observe that he simply uses a different term—"fictitious capital"—for what people today mean by "money," however, we see at once that he has a rich, Thorntonian understanding of the role played by credit-money in fueling boom-and-bust cycles. This is evident not only in volume 1 (1867) of *Capital*, but also in the posthumously published volumes 2 (1885) and 3 (1894), not to mention *Theories of Surplus Value* (1905-1910). Similar remarks hold of Walter Bagehot, founder of *The Economist* magazine, whose *Lombard Street* (1873) remains to this day the canonical statement of the need for a central bank "lender of last resort" thanks to the mood-swinging character of endogenously generated credit-money. As for Steuart and Montesquieu, who were roughly contemporaneous with Adam Smith, it is regrettable that more who read the latter did not also read the former. For while Smith is insightful on many matters—money and the vulnerabilities of exchange economies to collective action challenges that require government solutions—are not among them. It was for Keynes to rediscover this of Montesquieu. Steuart, sadly, still awaits rediscovery—till now, anyway.

NOTES TO CHAPTER 6

1   Aristotle, *Politics* 1.9.1257a-b; Adam Smith, *Wealth of Nations*, bk. 1, ch. 5.

2   Paul A. Samuelson, *Economics*, 9th ed. (New York: McGraw Hill, 1973), 55.

3   Irving Fisher, *The Money Illusion* (New York: Adelphi, 1929).

4   Here is Alfred Marshall in his 1890 *Principles of Economics*, a high point of classical theory, on why he ignores money in favor of intellectual squinting: "We may throughout this volume neglect possible changes in the general purchasing power of money. Thus the price of anything will be taken as representative of its exchange value relatively to things in general." (New York, Cosimo Classics, 2009), 62.

5   Here's how another big classical theorist, A. C. Pigou, put the idea: "Monetary facts . . . have no direct significance for economic welfare. In this sense money clearly is a veil. It does not comprise any of the essentials of economic life." *The Veil of Money* (London: Macmillan, 1949), 14.

6   The anthropologist Caroline Humphrey, who details this case, explains: "No example of a barter economy, pure and simple, has ever been described, let alone the emergence from it of money; all available ethnography suggests that there never has been such a thing." "Barter and Economic Disintegration," *Man* 20, vol. 1 (March 1985): 48.

7   The anthropologist David Graeber, in *Debt: The First 5,000 Years* (New York: Melville House, 2011), helpfully introduces Nietzsche along with historical examples of debt relationships to expose the "myth of barter." We're suggesting Nietzsche is useful as "conjectural history."

8   In the language of contemporary moral philosophy, a good part of morality can be about "what we owe to each other." In philosopher T. M. Scanlon's influential book, *What We Owe to Each Other*—once featured on the TV show *The Good Place*—right and wrong are just a matter of what we can or cannot justify to others. If someone asks, "How could you?" maybe you have a reasonable answer; you could indeed justify your actions to her. But if you tried to explain and really couldn't, not on terms the person asking couldn't reasonably complain of, then what you've done would not be justifiable to her. You honestly explain your motivations: "Well, since you ask, yes, I actually did roll through that stop sign, cutting you off; not exactly because I drive a BMW, but because, you see, my time is really valuable. Yours, less so, right? (Plus, you know, God does not exist.)" But that "justification" plainly wouldn't be sufficient. If you said *that*, she'd give you an incredulous stare, a stink-eyed look, and rightly so. See Scanlon's *What We Owe to Each Other* (Cambridge, MA: Harvard University Press, 1998). Here's a December 2019

Vox podcast, *The Ezra Klein Show*, with *Good Place* creator Michael Schur and his philosopher consultant (UCLA professor and Scanlon student) Pamela Hieronymi: https://www.vox.com/podcasts/2019/12/10/21002589/the-ezra-klein-show-mike-schur-the-good-place-moral-philosophy.

9   Indeed, rooted in promise and mutual obligation as it is, money is one of the most morally rich institutions there is—a remarkable thing in what we are told is "the root of all evil." See Robert Hockett, "Rousseauvian Money" (Cornell Legal Studies Research Paper Series No. 18–48, Cornell Law School, Ithaca, NY, last revised May 28, 2019), https://papers.ssrn.com/sol3/papers.cfm?abstract_id=3278408.

10   For the classic treatment, see Irving Fisher, *Booms and Depressions: Some First Principles* (New York: Adelphi, 1932). On the Great Recession, see Atif Mian and Amir Sufi, "Consumers and the Economy, Part II: Household Debt and the Weak US Recovery," *FRBSF Economic Letter*, January 18, 2011, https://www.frbsf.org/economic-research/files/el2011-02.pdf.

11   If you took economics in college, you may recall the celebrated Arrow-Debreu general equilibrium models—a prime example. The basic framework goes back to the nineteenth-century French economist Léon Walras, and still dominates macroeconomic modelling. The canonical systematization of this approach to the economy remains Gérard Debreu's elegant *Theory of Value* (1954)—a spectacularly beautiful, and equally useless, little monograph whose author forewarns the reader in its very first chapter that money is assumed away as inessential. Not surprisingly, in view of Keynes's observation that life within time and without certainty is what necessitates money, Debreu also assumes away uncertainty (as distinguished from actuarial risk) and reduces time itself to no more than two periods—"before" and "after"—in a "two-period model."

12   Here's a nice example of such a model, which expressly includes "no money": John B. Long, Jr., and Charles I. Plosser, "Real Business Cycles," *Journal of Political Economy* 91, no. 1 (February. 1983): 39–69. Money wonks might recognize the name of Charlie Plosser, a monetary "hawk" who served as president of the Philadelphia Fed from late 2006 to early 2015.

13   The heterodox economist Steve Keen did predict the 2008 crisis using models. His models track flows between different sectors, public and private, at home and abroad, and allow one to identify unsustainable "imbalances," in that case on private-bank and household balance sheets, as he explains in *Can We Avoid Another Financial Crisis?* (Cambridge, UK: Polity, 2017). He draws on important work in "sectoral balance accounting" by Wynne Godley, e.g., in Wynne Godley and Marc Lavoie, *Monetary Economics: An Integrated Approach to Credit, Money, Income, Production and Wealth* (New

York: Palgrave Macmillan, 2006).

14 J. M. Keynes, "A Monetary Theory of Production," a short 1933 essay that originally appeared in German, available in English at https://www.hetwebsite.net/het/texts/keynes/keynes1933mtp.htm

15 Milton Friedman, "The Role of Monetary Policy," *American Economic Review* 58, no. 1 (March 1968): 3.

16 *Onion*, February 16, 2010, https://www.theonion.com/u-s-economy-grinds-to-halt-as-nation-realizes-money-ju-1819571322.

17 As for what to make of this weirdly "intersubjective" sort of reality, it can be a matter of how we think about what other people are thinking. For the whole story, see Aaron James, "Money, Recognition, and the Outer Limit of Obliviousness" (available on his UC Irvine Philosophy Department webpage, at https://www.faculty.uci.edu/profile.cfm?faculty_id=4884).

18 A. Mitchell Innes, "The Credit Theory of Money," *Banking Law Journal* 31 (1914): 155.

19 For a sketch of what an updated IMF truer to Keynes's vision and adequate to the needs of the contemporary world economy might look like, see Robert Hockett, "Bretton Woods 1.0: A Constructive Retrieval for Sustainable Finance," *New York University Journal of Legislation & Public Policy* 16, no. 1 (2013), https://scholarship.law.cornell.edu/facpub/921/. On why expanded use of the SDR is required by fairness, see Aaron James, "The Fairness Argument for International Money" (available at his UC Irvine Philosophy Department webpage, at https://www.faculty.uci.edu/profile.cfm?faculty_id=4884).

NOTES TO CHAPTER 7

1 This view doesn't square even with Milton Friedman's "monetarism," at least on one reading of its essentials. But the classical image of a "neutral veil" persists, encouraging economists to largely segregate monetary policy from the rest of economics.

2 Again, the standard equilibrium models don't occur in continuous time. The influential Arrow-Debreu model of efficient markets under perfect competition is a good example, as we noted in Chapter 6.

3 For some of the many ramifications, relevant to contemporary financial systems, that flow from this truth, see Robert Hockett, "The Capital Commons: Digital Money and Citizens' Finance in a Productive 'Commercial Republic'" (manuscript, 2018).

NOTES TO CHAPTER 8

1   Some who cry "End the Fed!" don't really mean it, or don't quite know what they are imagining. Those who do mean it should offer a credible plan to manage not only the immediate crisis but also the heightened risks of a more volatile cycle of booms and busts, decades of lost growth, protracted harm to millions of people, and the consequent cultural and political upheavals, including new threats to democracy. And, no, it won't do to name-drop Fed skeptics such as F. A. Hayek, Ludwig von Mises, and Milton Friedman; something intelligent must be said about the truly grave crisis risks for real people in vast numbers and the future of society. Some will want to keep a nationalized money and merely limit the Fed's role in managing its overall supply, say, by returning to a national gold standard, or a functional equivalent under fiat money (e.g., by setting money issuance by some arbitrary, fixed limit). But that also brings enormous crisis risks in a growing economy, as we'll see.

2   See Robert Hockett, "Money's Past Is Fintech's Future: Wildcat Crypto, the Digital Dollar, and Citizen Central Banking," *Stanford Journal of Blockchain Law & Policy*, June 28, 2019, https://stanford-jblp.pubpub.org/pub/wildcat-crypto-fintech-future.

NOTES TO CHAPTER 9

1   For more on this model and what's wrong with it, see Robert C. Hockett and Saule T. Omarova, "The Finance Franchise," *Cornell Law Review* 102:1143 (2017) and Robert Hockett, "Finance without Financiers," in Erik Olin Wright, ed., *Democratizing Finance* (New York: Verso, forthcoming 2020), also available at https://ssc.wisc.edu/~wright/929-utopias-2018/wp-content/uploads/2018/01/Hockett-Finance-without-Financiers-17-June-2017.pdf. In its original formulation as developed by Knut Wicksell, the "loanable funds" story included bank-generated credit-money, which Wicksell called "bank money," *in addition* to preaccumulated money. The more modern rendition, which figures into Greg Mankiw's widely used economics textbook and much op-ed commentary, treats loanable funds as *preaccumulated*. When you encounter the phrase "loanable funds" nowadays, then, you are probably reading or hearing from someone with little if any idea of how banks and the banking system actually function. Krugman's columns seem at best unclear on this point.

NOTES TO CHAPTER 10

1   A fully developed, detailed proposal of the form described below is elab-
    orated in Robert Hockett, "The Capital Commons: Digital Money and
    Citizens' Finance in a Productive 'Commercial Republic'" (manuscript,
    2018). See also Robert Hockett and Saule Omarova, "The People's Led-
    ger" (in progress). A version of the plan that is as well suited to state and
    local governments and the US Treasury as it is to the Fed is elaborated
    in Robert Hockett, "The Democratic Digital Dollar," *Harvard Business
    Law Review* 10, no. 1 (2020), https://www.hblr.org/wp-content/uploads/
    sites/18/2020/02/The-Democratic-Digital-Dollar_HBLR_FINAL.pdf Leg-
    islation drafted by Bob to put such a plan in place for the State of New York
    was introduced in the New York State Assembly and the New York State
    Senate in October of 2019. A white paper explains the New York proposal
    in greater detail. See Robert Hockett, "The New York State Inclusive Value
    Ledger: A Peer-to-Peer Savings & Payments Platform for an All-Embracing
    and Dynamic State Economy" (manuscript, 2019), available at the website
    of New York Assemblymember Ron Kim, https://ronkimnewyork.com/
    downloads/The-New-York-Inclusive-Value-Ledger-Sept-2019.pdf.   This
    white paper has since been refined, generalized, and published in the Har-
    vard Business Law Review as: https://www.hblr.org/wp-content/uploads/
    sites/18/2020/02/The-Democratic-Digital-Dollar_HBLR_FINAL.pdf The
    US House Financial Services Committee is also now considering Bob's
    "Treasury Dollar" plan, a quickly implementable means by which the Trea-
    sury Department can make digital payments and saving available to all cit-
    izens, businesses, and legal residents of the country. See, e.g., https://papers
    ssrn.com/sol3/papers.cfm?abstract_id=3563007;   https://www.forbes.
    com/sites/rhockett/2020/03/29/why-now-for-a-digital-treasury-dollar-
    because-coronavirus/#2e6191151305;   and   https://www.forbes.com/sites
    /rhockett/2020/03/24/how-to-keep-the-digital-dollar-democratic-a-trea-
    sury-dollar-bill—treasury-direct-plan/#5a6200f837c8.

2   See, e.g., Daniel Alpert, Robert Hockett, and Nouriel Roubini, "The Way
    Forward," Policy Paper, New America Foundation, October 10, 2011,
    https://www.newamerica.org/economic-growth/policy-papers/the-
    way-forward/.

3   For these last two points, see Robert Hockett and Richard Vague, *Debt,
    Deflation, and Debacle: Of Private Debt Write-Down and Public Recovery*,
    Global Society of Fellows, the Global Interdependence Center at the Federal

Reserve Bank of Philadelphia, April 9, 2013, https://www.interdependence. org/wp-content/uploads/2013/04/Debt-Deflation-and-Debacle-RV-and-RH1.pdf.

4   There is overlap between this proposal and others. See Nick Gruen, *Central Banking for All: A Modest Proposal for Radical Change*, Nesta, March 2014, https://media.nesta.org.uk/documents/central_banking_for_all. pdf; Dirk Niepelt, "Reserves for Everyone—Towards a New Monetary Regime?," VOXEU Center for Economic Policy Research Policy Portal, Jan. 21, 2015, https://voxeu.org/article/keep-cash-let-public-hold-central-bank-reserves; "Central Banks Should Consider Offering Accounts to Everyone," *Economist*, May 26, 2018, https://www.economist.com/finance-and-economics/2018/05/26/central-banks-should-consider-offering-accounts-to-everyone; and, with fuller elaboration, Jonathan McMillan, *The End of Banking: Money, Credit, and the Digital Revolution* (Zurich: Zero/One Economics, 2014); and Morgan Ricks, John Crawford, and Lev Menand, "Digital Dollars," *George Washington Law Review* (forthcoming), https:// papers.ssrn.com/sol3/papers.cfm?abstract_id=3192162. See also the 2014 and 2015 "Fedcoin" proposals made by JP Koning, David Andolfatto, and Robert Sams. One of us—Bob—has also been working with New York state legislators and the US House Financial Services Committee over the past year to put a state-level version of this plan into place. See Hockett, sources cited in ch. 10, n. 1 above.

5   Many critics argued that monetary policy alone doesn't suffice to address the 2008 crisis, particularly in a "liquidity trap." Fiscal measures also were needed. We agree with that criticism. But the weaknesses of monetary policy observed during 2009–2012 are more rooted in franchised monetary policy than in monetary policy as such. Our "insourcing" proposal shows why.

6   For more on "QE for the people" and "helicopter money" proposals, see, e.g., Anatole Kaletsky, "How About Quantitative Easing for the People?," *Reuters*, August 1, 2012, http://blogs.reuters.com/anatole-kaletsky/2012/08/01/how-about-quantitative-easing-for-the-people/; Martin Wolf, "Central Banks Need a Helicopter," *Financial Times*, December 4, 2008, https://www. ft.com/content/c9b60ecf-2b41-329d-8aad-a94daf7af45f. The "helicopter" colloquialism originates with Milton Friedman, "The Role of Monetary Policy," *American Economic Review* 58, no. 1 (March 1968): 1–17. Keynes used the metaphor of burying money in bottles a bit over thirty years earlier. J. M. Keynes, *The General Theory of Employment, Interest, and Money* (London, Macmillan: 1936).

7See Hockett and Omarova, "The Finance Franchise," *Cornell Law Review*

102:1143 (2017).

8   On some of those public secondary and tertiary market-making activities, see, e.g., Robert Hockett, "Republican Home-Owning," White Paper, Federal Reserve Bank of St. Louis, December 2018, https://www.stlouisfed.org/~/media/files/pdfs/hfs/assets/2018/tipping-points/hockett_tipping_points_paper_2018_12.pdf?la=en; Robert C. Hockett and Saule T. Omarova, "'Private' Means to 'Public' Ends: Governments as Market Actors," *Theoretical Inquiries in Law* 15, no. 1 (January 2014): 53–76; Robert Hockett, "How to Make QE More Helpful: By Fed Shorting of Commodities, *Benzinga*, October 11, 2011, https://www.benzinga.com/news/11/10/1988109/how-to-make-qe-more-helpful-by-fed-shorting-of-commodities; and Robert Hockett, "A Jeffersonian Republic Through Hamiltonian Means: Values, Constraints, and Finance in an American 'Ownership Society,'" *Southern California Law Review* 79, no. 1 (2005–2006): 45–164.

9   We could have done it over a century ago, and certainly by the time of Fedwire's introduction in 1918 or of the banking reforms of the New Deal era. On the history of Fedwire, see, e.g., Adam Gilbert, Dara Hunt, and Kenneth C. Winch, "Creating an Integrated Payment System: The Evolution of Fedwire," *FRBNY Economic Policy Review* 3, vol 2 (July 1997): 1–7.

10 Those advantages include: (1) transactions can be recorded and tracked in an indelible and replicable way; (2) they can be highly private and secure; (3) they can be settled and "cleared" almost simultaneously; and (4) they can readily link up with multiple national, subnational, or transnational payments infrastructures.

For further detail, see Robert Hockett, "Money's Past Is Fintech's Future: Wildcat Crypto, The Digital Dollar, and Citizen Central Banking," *Stanford Journal of Blockchain Law & Policy*, June 28, 2019, https://stanford-jblp.pubpub.org/pub/wildcat-crypto-fintech-future.

NOTES TO CHAPTER 11

1   Harry Cockburn, "China Blacklists Billions of People from Booking Flights as 'Social Credit' System Introduced," *Independent*, Nov. 22, 2018, https://www.independent.co.uk/news/world/asia/china-social-credit-system-flight-booking-blacklisted-beijing-points-a8646316.html. The scheme is dramatized in "Nosedive," an episode of the Netflix series *Black Mirror*.

2   Even limited government can be difficult to justify if natural rights are as forceful as some libertarians claim. In his famous book *Anarchy, State, Utopia* (New York: Basic Books, 1974), the Lockean libertarian philosopher Robert Nozick assumed natural rights as nearly absolute "side constraints."

He thought he could justify a "minimal state," but his argument on that score, though brilliant and influential, is arguably incoherent: it either requires anarchy, or permits a more robust social welfare state; it doesn't justify something in between—a minimal state. This is the book where Nozick had a famous dustup with John Rawls's *A Theory of Justice*, which revived the political philosophy of Rousseau.

3   In Rawls's version, we'd choose principles from self-interest, without knowing our actual social position (from behind a "veil of ignorance"). We'd insist upon the protection of our basic liberties, but then require principles for access to opportunities and the general distribution of economic goods. We then work in stages from moral foundations in liberty, opportunity, and equality toward more concrete applications—to constitutions, systems, laws, and policies, which might include our systems of social accounting.

4   Money arguably runs even deeper, structuring our very agency. On how scorekeeping in games "captures" and potentially corrupts our agency, autonomy, and values, see C. Thi Nguyen, "Gamification and Value Capture," ch. 9 in *Games: Agency as Art* (Oxford: Oxford University Press, forthcoming 2020). Nguyen's analysis can be extended to money as a kind of scorekeeping and helps explain its corrupting influence.

NOTES TO CHAPTER 12

1   On the shadow banks, see Hockett, "Finance without Financiers," in Erik Olin Wright, ed., *Democratizing Finance* (New York: Verso, forthcoming 2020), also available at https://ssc.wisc.edu/~wright/929-utopias-2018/wp-content/uploads/2018/01/Hockett-Finance-without-Financiers-17-June-2017.pdf.

2   See Robert Hockett, "A Fixer-Upper for Finance," *Washington University Law Review* 87, no. 6 (2010): 1213-91, https://papers.ssrn.com/sol3/papers.cfm?abstract_id=1367278.

3   See Robert Hockett, "The Macroprudential Turn: From Institutional 'Safety and Soundness' to Systemic 'Financial Stability' in Financial Supervision," *Virginia Law and Business Review* 9, no. 2 (2014): 201-56, https://papers.ssrn.com/sol3/papers.cfm?abstract_id=2206189.

4   See Robert Hockett, "How to Make QE More Helpful: By Fed Shorting of Commodities," *Benzinga*, October 11, 2011, https://www.benzinga.com/news/11/10/1988109/how-to-make-qe-more-helpful-by-fed-shorting-of-commodities.

5   See Robert Hockett, "Open Labor Market Operations," *Challenge* 62, no. 2 (2019): 113-27, https://papers.ssrn.com/sol3/papers.cfm?abstract_

id=3298823.

6   Daniel Tarullo, drawing from his experience as a former Governor on the
    Federal Reserve Board, explains how limited existing theories of inflation
    dynamics are. He concludes that "there is no well-elaborated and empiri-
    cally grounded theory that explains contemporary inflation dynamics in
    a way useful to real-time policy-making." Here he means well-worn con-
    cepts that rely on "unobservable variables," including those of "inflation
    expectations" and the "Philips curve" trade-off between unemployment
    and inflation. He recommends focusing far more on "observables" while
    letting go of standard theory. "Monetary Policy without a Working Theory
    of Inflation" (Hutchins Center Working Paper no. 33, Hutchins Center on
    Fiscal and Monetary Policy, Washington, DC), https://www.brookings.
    edu/research/monetary-policy-without-a-working-theory-of-inflation/.

NOTES TO CHAPTER 13

1   In order to be *really* bulletproof, a government should attain *monetary sov-
    ereignty*, defined as follows. It (1) issues its own money, in a chosen unit
    of account; (2) imposes a tax liability in that unit, which ensures its "cur-
    rency" (by the fear of prison); (3) borrows only or mainly in its own money;
    (4) has a "floating" rather than a fixed exchange rate (or a "dirty float," with
    occasional intervention that limits an upper or lower bound on rates of
    exchange with other moneys); (5) has limited trade dependence in essential
    goods such as food or energy sources, in order to mitigate foreign exchange
    and inflation risk; (6) has reasonably effective, noncorrupt institutions
    for inflation management, via an "independent" central bank, or, where
    politically feasible, appropriate legislative planning. See also the Appendix
    "Making Global Finance Safe for Domestic Autonomy."

2   This is proposed in Robert Hockett, "Save Europe's Marriage with
    a Trial Separation," *Bloomberg*, June 12, 2012, https://www.bloom-
    berg.com/opinion/articles/2012-06-12/save-europe-s-marriage-
    with-a-trial-separation. Also see Robert Hockett, "What the Euro's
    Current Difficulties Really Mean," *The Hill*, July 4, 2015, https://thehill.com/
    blogs/pundits-blog/international/246834-what-the-euros-current-difficul-
    ties-really-mean.

3   This point was once controversial. Dani Rodrik, more than any economist,
    set things straight in his influential papers and his book, *One Economics,
    Many Recipes* (Princeton: Princeton University Press, 2007).

4   Joseph Stiglitz, *Making Globalization Work* (New York: W. W. Norton,
    2006).

5 Tunisia, for example, might move form "import substitution" to an employer of last resort, as suggested by Fadhel Kaboub, "ELR-Led Economic Development: A Plan for Tunisia" (Working Paper no. 499, The Levy Economics Institute of Bard College, Annandale-on-Hudson, NY, May 2007, http://www.levyinstitute.org/pubs/wp_499.pdf). Some countries might minimize "trade dependence" in essential basic goods where feasible, or otherwise prearrange commodity "swap lines" in case of emergency. Germany wisely arranged for a commodity swap during postwar reconstruction, for example. See Robert Hockett, "Bretton Woods 1.0: A Constructive Retrieval for Sustainable Finance," *New York University Journal of Legislation and Public Policy* 16, no. 2 (2013): 401-83, https://scholarship. law.cornell.edu/facpub/921. An "oil swap" (of crude for refined oil, without dollar payments) could help with Venezuela's current inflation crisis.

NOTES TO CHAPTER 14

1 See Aaron James, *Assholes: A Theory* (New York: Doubleday, 2012); Aaron James, *Assholes: A Theory of Donald Trump* (New York: Doubleday, 2016).

2 Proponents of modern monetary theory or MMT tend to take this view, often while proposing a federal "job guarantee" that, once enacted, automatically gives everyone a chance to work, with no new inflationary pressures. The public wage is simply kept low enough not to pull people out of private employment, so that wages aren't generally bid up. This particular policy (which we return to in Chapter 15) acts as an "automatic stabilizer" and so doesn't require constant legislative adjustment.

3 Abba P. Lerner, "The Economic Steering Wheel or The Story of the People's New Clothes," ch. 1 in *Economics of Employment* (New York: McGraw-Hill, 1951) (based on a 1941 essay).

4 See Francesco Bianchi, Thilo Kind, and Howard Kung, "Threats to Central Bank Independence: High-Frequency Identification with Twitter" (NBER Working Paper No. 26308, National Bureau of Economic Research, Cambridge, MA, issued September 2019, last revised January 2020), https://www. nber.org/papers/w26308. In defense of Trump's position, if not his reasons, we note that the low unemployment numbers are not yet translating into rising wages or salaries, which are still at historic lows. Trump will not tell you that, as he wants to boast about "low unemployment," but we tell you now so you'll know why we, too, believe Powell should keep interest rates low.

5 See Joshua Cohen and Charles Sable, "Directly Deliberative Polyarchy," among other essays in Joshua Cohen's *Philosophy, Politics, Democracy: Selected Essays* (Cambridge, MA: Harvard University Press, 2009). See

also Cohen and Sabel's "Global Democracy," *New York University Journal of International Law and Policy* 37 (2005): 763–97, https://scholarship.law.columbia.edu/faculty_scholarship/513.

6   Quoted in Peter Deitsch, François Claveau, and Clément Fontan, *Do Central Banks Serve the People?* (Cambridge, UK: Polity Press, 2018), 82–6.

7   One of us—Bob—actually was hired by the New York Fed specifically to form a "contrarian thinking department." That's a remarkable case of a central bank's actually attempting to institutionalize, internally, a "cross-check" accountability mechanism.

8   The Fed constantly makes "political" decisions, in a perfectly good sense of the term: they're major decisions that affect everyone, and they bear on the most basic values at issue in retail politics. Economists often contrast "monetary" and "fiscal" policy, the latter being said to be "distributive" and "political," while the former not. But there isn't really a clean difference. Both are "allocative" or "distributive," by different methods. Take "QE for the people," via a "helicopter drop." There's less collateral damage in regard to inequality than the initial rounds of QE after the 2008 crisis. Or take corporate bond buying, which is basically "hidden industrial policy." Why not use bond buying schemes to reduce carbon emissions? Why not exclude arms producers? The decision not to is a "political" one. On all of these points, see Deitsch, Claveau, and Fontan, *Central Banks*.

9   See Robert Hockett, "Bringing It All Back Home: How to Save Main Street, Ignore K Street, and Thereby Save Wall Street," *Fordham Urban Law Journal* 36, no. 3 (2009): 421–45, https://scholarship.law.cornell.edu/cgi/viewcontent.cgi?article=1043&context=facpub.

10   "A Professor and a Banker Bury Old Dogma on Markets," *The New York Times,* Sept. 20, 2008, at https://www.nytimes.com/2008/09/21/business/21paulson.html

11   Along with the above point about admitting mistakes, Deitsch, Claveau, and Fontan note that diversity of methods, opinions, and people improves the capacity for "error correction."

12   Robert Hockett and Daniel Dillon, "Income Inequality and Market Fragility: Some Empirics in the Political Economy of Finance, Part I," *Challenge* 62, no. 5 (2019): 354–74, https://www.tandfonline.com/doi/abs/10.1080/05775132.2019.1638026, and "Income Inequality and Market Fragility: Some Empirics in the Political Economy of Finance, Part II," *Challenge* 62, no. 6 (2019): 427–52, https://www.tandfonline.com/doi/abs/10.1080/05775132.2019.1656894. See also former Fed governor Sarah Bloom Raskin's 2013 speech, "Aspects of Inequality in the Recent Business Cycle," Speeches, Board of Governors of the Federal Reserve System, https://www.federalre-

serve.gov/newsevents/speech/raskin20130418a.htm.

13 On "asshole capitalism" and asshole bankers, see Aaron James, "Asshole Capitalism," ch. 6 in *Assholes: A Theory*.

14 Robert Hockett, "Wells Fargo, Glass-Steagall and 'Do You Want Fries with That?' Banking," *The Hill*, September 22, 2016, https://thehill.com/blogs/pundits-blog/finance/297256-wells-fargo-glass-steagall-and-do-you-want-fries-with-that-banking.

15 Robert Hockett, "Warren, Yellen, and Bank Regulation's Forgotten Toolkit," *Forbes*, June 21, 2017 https://www.forbes.com/sites/rhockett/2017/06/21/warren-yellen-and-bank-regulations-forgotten-toolkit/#48bf68f23367.

16 See, e.g., Robert Hockett, "The Macroprudential Turn: From Institutional 'Safety and Soundness' to Systemic 'Financial Stability' in Financial Supervision," *Virginia Law and Business Review* 9, no. 2 (2014): 201–56, https://papers.ssrn.com/sol3/papers.cfm?abstract_id=2206189, and Robert Hockett, "Practical Guidance on Macroprudential Finance-Regulatory Reform," Harvard Law School Forum on Corporate Governance and Financial Regulation, November 22, 2013, https://corpgov.law.harvard.edu/2013/11/22/practical-guidance-on-macroprudential-finance-regulatory-reform/.

17 See Aaron James, "Preparing for Mass Unemployment: Precautionary Basic Income" in *The Ethics of Artificial Intelligence*, ed. Matthew Liao (Oxford: Oxford University Press, forthcoming). Also available under "Academic Publications" at James's UC Irvine website, https://www.faculty.uci.edu/profile.cfm?faculty_id=4884.

18 See David Graeber, *Bullshit Jobs: A Theory* (New York: Simon and Schuster, 2018).

19 See Nina Banks, "The Black Woman Economist Who Pioneered a Federal Jobs Guarantee," Institute for New Economic Thinking, February 22, 2019, https://www.ineteconomics.org/perspectives/blog/the-black-woman-economist-who-pioneered-a-federal-jobs-guarantee.

20 One recent philosophical treatment of surfing—as an attuned, embodied exercise of skill—draws lessons for why we should continue the leisure revolution in capitalism that began in the 1940s introduction of the forty-hour workweek. Working less *contributes* to society and the world-historical attunement of capitalism to our changing planet as much as conventional work. Aaron James, *Surfing with Sartre: An Aquatic Inquiry into a Life of Meaning* (New York: Doubleday, 2017).

NOTES TO CHAPTER 16

1   The Green New Deal Resolution, which one of us—Bob—helped draft, is here: Recognizing the Duty of the Federal Government to Create a Green New Deal, H.R. 109, 116th Cong. (2019), https://www.congress.gov/bill/116th-congress/house-resolution/109/text. The animating vision was Robert C. Hockett and Rhiana Gunn-Wright, "The Green New Deal: Mobilizing for a Just, Prosperous, and Sustainable Economy" (Cornell Legal Studies Research Paper no. 19–09, Cornell Law School, Ithaca, NY, last revised March 19, 2019), https://papers.ssrn.com/sol3/papers.cfm?abstract_id=3342494. See also Robert Hockett, *Financing the Green New Deal: A Plan of Action and Renewal* (forthcoming 2020).

2   Ibid.

3   Ibid.

4   Ibid.

NOTES TO CHAPTER 17

1   See Robert Hockett, *A Republic of Owners* (New Haven: Yale University Press, forthcoming 2020).

2   Ibid.

NOTES TO EPILOGUE

1   Wynne Godley and Marc Lavoie, *Monetary Economics: An Integrated Approach to Credit, Money, Income, Production and Wealth* (New York: Palgrave Macmillan, 2006).

2   Robert Hockett, "Bretton Woods 1.0: A Constructive Retrieval for Sustainable Finance," *New York University Journal of Legislation and Public Policy* 16, no. 2 (2013): 401–83, https://scholarship.law.cornell.edu/facpub/921.

3   International Monetary Fund, *Reserve Accumulation and International Monetary Stability,* April 13, 2010, https://www.imf.org/external/np/pp/eng/2010/041310.pdf, and International Monetary Fund, *Enhancing International Monetary Stability—A Role for the SDR?,* January 7, 2011, https://www.imf.org/external/np/pp/eng/2011/010711.pdf. See also Michael Pettis, "An Exorbitant Burden," *Foreign Policy,* September 7, 2011, http://www.foreignpolicy.com/articles/2011/09/07/an_exorbitant_burden; Michael Pettis, *The Great Rebalancing: Trade, Conflict and the Perilous Road Ahead for the World Economy* (Princeton: Princeton University Press, 2013); Joseph Stiglitz, *Making Globalization Work* (New York: W. W. Norton.,

2006); Jared Bernstein, "Dethrone 'King Dollar," *New York Times*, August 28, 2014, https://www.nytimes.com/2014/08/28/opinion/dethrone-king-dollar.html; C. Fred Bergsten, "The Dollar and the Deficits," *Foreign Affairs*, November/December 2009, https://www.foreignaffairs.com/articles/united-states/2009-10-15/dollar-and-deficits; and Aaron James, "The Fairness Argument for International Money" (available on his UC Irvine Philosophy Department website, at https://www.faculty.uci.edu/profile.cfm?faculty_id=4884).

NOTES TO APPENDIX II

1   See https://www.treasurydirect.gov/

2   See Robert Hockett & Lawrence Rufrano, "Digital Dollars for All," *Wall Street Journal*, April 6, 2020, available at https://www.wsj.com/articles/digital-dollars-for-all-11586215100.

3   See Robert Hockett, *Digital Greenbacks: A Sequenced 'TreasuryDirect' and 'FedWallet' Plan for the Democratic Digital Dollar,* 72 ADMINISTRATIVE LAW REVIEW __ (2020) (forthcoming), available at https://papers.ssrn.com/sol3/papers.cfm?abstract_id=3599419.

4   See Federal Deposit Insurance Corporation, 2017 FDIC Survey of Unbanked and Underbanked Households, available at https://www.fdic.gov/householdsurvey/.

5   See *Digital Greenbacks*, op. cit., note 4; also Robert Hockett, The Treasury Dollar Act of 2020, available at https://papers.ssrn.com/sol3/papers.cfm?abstract_id=3563007#:~:text=In%20addition%20to%20all%20citizens,transacting%20in%20Treasury%20Dollars%20as.

6   See "Digital Dollars for All," op. cit., note 2.

7   Digital Greenbacks, op. cit., note 4.

8   See, e.g., Robert Hockett, "Our Corona Response's Missing Ingredient— Mobilize the Supply Side!," *Forbes*, March 18, 2020, available at https://www.forbes.com/sites/rhockett/2020/03/18/our-corona-responses-missing-ingredient--mobilize-the-supply-side/#396b41ab3252.

9   See, e.g., Robert Hockett, "The US Must Take Equity Stakes in the Companies It Rescues," *Financial Times*, March 28, 2020, available at https://www.ft.com/content/86a333d0-6dc3-11ea-89df-41bea055720b; Robert Hockett, "The US Must Tackle the Coronavirus Pandemic with a Playbook out of the Great Depression and World War II, not the Financial Crisis," *Business Insider*, March 29, 2020, available at https://www.businessinsider.com/coronavirus-pandemic-us-should-ramp-up-ventilator-mask-manufacturing-2020-3; Robert Hockett, "We're at War

and Need Wartime Institutions to Keep the Economy Producing What's Necessary," *The Hill*, April 4, 2020, available at https://thehill.com/opinion/white-house/491166-were-at-war-and-need-wartime-institutions-to-keep-our-economy-producing.

10 Ibid.

11 Ibid.

12 See Robert Hockett, *Spread the Fed: Distributed Central Banking in Pandemic and Beyond*, 14 Virginia Law & Business Review __ (2020) (forthcoming), available at https://papers.ssrn.com/sol3/papers.cfm?abstract_id=3597724.

13 Ibid.

14 See Robert Hockett, "Community QE: Newly Eased Terms and a New 'Game Plan' for Use," *Forbes*, May 2, 2020, available at https://www.forbes.com/sites/rhockett/2020/05/02/community-qe2-newly-eased-terms-and-a-new-game-plan-for-use/#7427f80622fc.

15 Ibid.

16 See again Spread the Fed, op. cit., note 12.

17 See, e.g., Robert Hockett, *Paying Paul and Robbing No One: An Eminent Domain Solution for Underwater Mortgage Debt*, 19 (5) *Current Issues in Economics & Finance 1* (2013), available at https://www.newyorkfed.org/research/current_issues/ci19-5.html.

18 See Robert Hockett, "Optimize Community QE: An Open Letter to Fed Chair Powell," *Forbes*, June 14, 2020, available at https://www.forbes.com/sites/rhockett/2020/06/14/optimize-community-qean-open-letter-to-fed-chairman-powell/#73eef42a24d2.

19 See again *Spread the Fed*, op. cit., note 12.

ABOUT

THE AUTHORS

Robert Hockett, who holds advanced degrees in law, philosophy, and finance from Oxford and Yale Universities, has worked at the International Monetary Fund and the Federal Reserve Bank of New York, and continues to consult for many US federal, state, and local legislators and regulators. He helped draft Rep. Alexandria Ocasio-Cortez's "Green New Deal" resolution for the House of Representatives and has frequently assisted her, Senator Bernie Sanders, and Senator Elizabeth Warren with legislation. He is the Edward Cornell Professor of Law and a Professor of Public Policy at Cornell University and a regular contributor to Forbes magazine, where he covers finance, economics, law, and justice. He lives in New York City and Ithaca, NY.

Aaron James holds a PhD from Harvard and is professor of philosophy at the University of California, Irvine. He is the author of *Fairness in Practice: A Social Contract for a Global Economy*, the bestselling *Assholes: A Theory, Assholes: A Theory of Donald Trump, Surfing with Sartre* and numerous academic articles. He was awarded the Burkhardt Fellowship from the American Council of Learned Societies, spending the 2009–10 academic year at the Center for Advanced Study in the Behavioral Sciences at Stanford University, and was Visiting Professor at New York University. He lives in Irvine, CA.